Lecture Notes in Computer Sc

T0237754

Commenced Publication in 1973
Founding and Former Series Editors:
Gerhard Goos, Juris Hartmanis, and Jan van Leeuwen

Editorial Board

David Hutchison
Lancaster University, UK

Takeo Kanade
Carnegie Mellon University, Pittsburgh, PA, USA

Josef Kittler
University of Surrey, Guildford, UK

Jon M. Kleinberg
Cornell University, Ithaca, NY, USA

Friedemann Mattern
ETH Zurich, Switzerland

John C. Mitchell
Stanford University, CA, USA

Moni Naor
Weizmann Institute of Science, Rehovot, Israel

Oscar Nierstrasz
University of Bern, Switzerland

C. Pandu Rangan
Indian Institute of Technology, Madras, India

Bernhard Steffen
University of Dortmund, Germany

Madhu Sudan
Massachusetts Institute of Technology, MA, USA

Demetri Terzopoulos
University of California, Los Angeles, CA, USA

Doug Tygar
University of California, Berkeley, CA, USA

Moshe Y. Vardi
Rice University, Houston, TX, USA

Gerhard Weikum
Max-Planck Institute of Computer Science, Saarbruecken, Germany

Christine Hofmeister Ivica Crnkovic
Ralf Reussner (Eds.)

Quality of Software Architectures

Second International Conference
on Quality of Software Architectures, QoSA 2006
Västerås, Sweden, June 27-29, 2006
Revised Papers

 Springer

Volume Editors

Christine Hofmeister
Computer Science and Engineering Department
Lehigh University
Bethlehem, Pennsylvania 18015, USA
E-mail: crh@cse.lehigh.edu

Ivica Crnkovic
Software Engineering Lab
Mälardalen University
SE-721 23 Västerås, Sweden
E-mail: ivica.crnkovic@mdh.se

Ralf Reussner
Institute for Program Structures and Data Organization
University of Karlsruhe (TH)
Karlsruhe, Germany
E-mail: reussner@ipd.uka.de

Library of Congress Control Number: 2006937334

CR Subject Classification (1998): D.2.4, F.3, D.4, C.4, K.4.4, C.2

LNCS Sublibrary: SL 2 – Programming and Software Engineering

ISSN   0302-9743
ISBN-10   3-540-48819-7 Springer Berlin Heidelberg New York
ISBN-13   978-3-540-48819-4 Springer Berlin Heidelberg New York

This work is subject to copyright. All rights are reserved, whether the whole or part of the material is
concerned, specifically the rights of translation, reprinting, re-use of illustrations, recitation, broadcasting,
reproduction on microfilms or in any other way, and storage in data banks. Duplication of this publication
or parts thereof is permitted only under the provisions of the German Copyright Law of September 9, 1965,
in its current version, and permission for use must always be obtained from Springer. Violations are liable
to prosecution under the German Copyright Law.

Springer is a part of Springer Science+Business Media

springer.com

© Springer-Verlag Berlin Heidelberg 2006
Printed in Germany

Typesetting: Camera-ready by author, data conversion by Scientific Publishing Services, Chennai, India
Printed on acid-free paper   SPIN: 11921998   06/3142   5 4 3 2 1 0

Preface

Although the quality of a system's software architecture is one of the critical factors in its overall quality, the architecture is simply a means to an end, the end being the implemented system. Thus the ultimate measure of the quality of the software architecture lies in the implemented system, in how well it satisfies the system and project requirements and constraints and whether it can be maintained and evolved successfully. In order to treat design as a science rather than an art, we need to be able to address the quality of the software architecture directly, not simply as it is reflected in the implemented system.

Therefore, QoSA is concerned with software architecture quality directly by addressing the problems of:

- Designing software architectures of good quality
- Defining, measuring, evaluating architecture quality
- Managing architecture quality, tying it upstream to requirements and downstream to implementation, and preserving architecture quality throughout the lifetime of the system

Cross-cutting these problems is the question of the nature of software architecture. Software architecture organizes a system, partitioning it into elements and defining relationships among the elements. For this we often use multiple views, each with a different organizing principle.

But software architecture must also support properties that are emergent, that cannot be ascribed to particular elements. For this we often use the language of quality attributes. Quality attributes cover both internal properties, exhibited only in the development process (e.g., maintainability, portability, testability, etc.), and external properties, exhibited in the executing system (e.g., performance, resource consumption, availability, etc.). Quality attributes cover properties that are emergent, that have a pervasive impact, that are difficult to reverse, and that interact, thereby precluding or constraining other properties.

Thus in addition to examining software architecture quality, QoSA also aims to investigate quality attributes in the context of the problems of the design, evaluation, and management of software architecture. The papers selected for QoSA 2006 describe research and experience on these topics. Architecture evaluation is the most prevalent theme of the papers. The approaches vary from formal models to support evaluation to experience with process-centered approaches. The focus of the evaluation varies from evaluation of a particular quality attribute, such as performance or safety, to approaches where the evaluation covers a number of quality attributes, determined by the evaluator. Other themes for QoSA 2006 were processes for achieving, supporting and ensuring architecture quality. These papers go beyond the problem of evaluation to address software architecture quality at the process level. A final significant theme is the problem of managing and applying architectural knowledge.

Of the 30 papers submitted, 12 were selected as papers for this post-conference proceedings volume. A number of shorter papers describing emerging results or case studies were also presented at QoSA; these papers are published as technical report No 2006/10, of the University of Karlsruhe, on Perspectives in Software Architecture Quality.

As a part of the QoSA conference, a special "Industrial Day" event was organized. This included two inspiring keynote presentations by Jan Bosch and Clemens Szyperski, three tutorials, and a panel in which representatives from several international software-intensive companies participated. The abstracts of the keynotes and tutorials are available in this proceedings volume.

We thank the members of the Program Committee and additional reviewers for their thorough, thoughtful, and timely reviews of the submitted papers. We thank Steffen Becker, Sven Overhage, and Judith Stafford for their work in supporting QoSA and Klaus Krogmann for preparing this LNCS proceedings volume. Finally, we thank the generous sponsors of QoSA 2006: University of Karlsruhe (TH), Mälardalen University, and Västerås City. This conference would not be possible without the support of all the above people and sponsors.

September 2006   Ivica Crnkovic
                                                    Christine Hofmeister
                                                         Ralf Reussner

Organization

General Chair

Ivica Crnkovic, Mälardalen University, Sweden

Program Committee Chair

Christine Hofmeister, Lehigh University, USA

Steering Committee

Ralf Reussner, University of Karlsruhe (TH), Germany
Judith Stafford, Tufts University, USA
Sven Overhage, Augsburg University, Germany
Steffen Becker, University of Karlsruhe (TH), Germany

Program Committee

Colin Atkinson, University of Mannheim, Germany
Len Bass, Software Engineering Institute, USA
Don Batory, University of Texas at Austin, USA
PerOlof Bengtsson, University of Karlskrona/Ronneby, Sweden
Jan Bosch, Nokia Research Center, Netherlands
Alexander Brandle, Microsoft Research, UK
Michel Chaudron, Technische Universiteit Eindhoven, Netherlands
Viktoria Firus, University of Oldenburg, Germany
Hassan Gomaa, George Mason University, USA
Ian Gorton, National ICT, Australia
Volker Gruhn, University of Leipzig, Germany
Wilhelm Hasselbring, University of Oldenburg / OFFIS, Germany
Jean-Marc Jezequel, University of Rennes / INRIA, France
Philippe Kruchten, University of British Columbia, Canada
Patricia Lago, Vrije Universiteit, Netherlands
Nicole Levy, University of Versailles, France
Tomi Mannisto, Helsinki University of Technology, Finland
Raffaela Mirandola, Politecnico di Milano, Italy
Robert Nord, Software Engineering Institute, USA
Frantisek Plasil, Charles University, Czech Republic
Iman Poernomo, King's College, UK
Sasikumar Punnekkat, Mälardalen University, Sweden
Andreas Rausch, University of Kaiserslautern, Germany

Matthias Riebisch, Technical University of Ilmenau, Germany
Bernhard Rumpe, University of Technology Braunschweig, Germany
Chris Salzmann, BMW Car-IT
Jean-Guy Schneider, Swinburne University, Australia
Michael Stal, Siemens, Germany
Clemens Szyperski, Microsoft, USA
Hans van Vliet, Vrije Universiteit, Netherlands
Wolfgang Weck, Independent Software Architect, Switzerland

Additional Reviewers

Sven Apel, University of Magdeburg, Germany
Roberto Lopez-Herrejon, University of Oxford, UK
Moreno Marzolla, INFN, Italy

Sponsoring Institutions

University of Karlsruhe (TH)
Mälardalen University
Västerås City

Table of Contents

Abstracts of the Keynotes

Abstracts of the Tutorials

Architecture Evaluation: Selecting Alternatives

Managing and Applying Architectural Knowledge

Architectural Evaluation: Performance Prediction

Processes for Supporting Architecture Quality

Models for Architecture Evaluation

Architectural Evaluation

Expanding the Scope of Software Product Families: Problems and Alternative Approaches

Jan Bosch

Software and Application Technologies Laboratory
Nokia Research Center, Helsinki, Finland

Abstract. Software product families have found broad adoption in the embedded systems industry. Product family thinking has been prevalent in this context for mechanics and hardware and adopting the same for software has been viewed as a logical approach. During recent years, however, the trends of convergence, end-to-end solutions, shortened innovation and R&D cycles and differentiaton through software engineering capabilities have lead to a development where organizations are stretching the scope of their product families far beyond the initial design. Failing to adjust the product family approach, including the architectural and process dimensions when the business strategy is changing is leading to several challenging problems that can be viewed as symptons of this approach. The keynote discusses the key symptoms, the underlying causes for these symptons as well as solutions for realigning the product family approach with the business strategy.

About

Prof. dr. ir. **Jan Bosch** is a Vice President and head of the Software and Application Technologies Laboratory at Nokia Research Center, Finland. Earlier, he headed the software engineering research group at the University of Groningen, The Netherlands, where he holds a professorship in software engineering. He received a MSc degree from the University of Twente, The Netherlands, and a PhD degree from Lund University, Sweden. His research activities include software architecture design, software product families, software variability management and component-oriented programming. He is the author of a book "Design and Use of Software Architectures: Adopting and Evolving a Product Line Approach" published by Pearson Education (Addison-Wesley & ACM Press), (co-)editor of several books and volumes in, among others, the Springer LNCS series and (co-) author of a significant number of research articles. He has been guest editor for journal issues, chaired several conferences as general and program chair, served on many program committees and organized numerous workshops. Finally, he is and has been a member of the steering groups of the GCSE and WICSA conferences.

C. Hofmeister et al. (Eds.): QoSA 2006, LNCS 4214, p. 1, 2006.
© Springer-Verlag Berlin Heidelberg 2006

Composing with Style – Components Meet Architecture
(Invited Talk)

Clemens Szyperski

Microsoft Research
One Microsoft Way, Redmond WA 98052, USA

Abstract. Composability itself is probably the least composable term in the theory of computer science. In this talk, I'll explore some of the troubling reasons why we have succeeded only so-so when it comes to the creation of composable software - and thus software components. Architecture can often come to the rescue, but only when applied with great style.

About

Clemens Szyperski joined Microsoft Research as a Software Architect in 1999. His team moved into a product incubation phase in 2001 and began production development in early 2003. A first product developed in an entirely new way will be released together with the upcoming Office System 2007. Since late 2005 he is now working on driving novel platform technology in Microsoft's new Connected Systems Division. His focus is on the end-to-end issues of leveraging component software to effectively build new kinds of software. He maintains an affiliation with Microsoft Research and continues his general activities in the wider research arena. His Jolt-award-winning book Component Software (Addison Wesley) appeared in a fully revised and extended second edition in late 2002. Software Ecosystem (MIT Press), co-authored with Dave Messerschmitt of UC Berkeley, was published in mid 2003. Clemens serves on numerous program committees, including ECOOP, ESEC/FSE, ICSE, and OOPSLA. He served as assessor and panelist for national funding bodies in Australia, Canada, Ireland, the Netherlands, and USA. He is a cofounder of Oberon microsystems, Zurich, Switzerland, and its now-public spin-off esmertec.

From 1994 to 1999, he was an associate professor at the School of Computer Science, Queensland University of Technology, Australia, where he retains an adjunct professorship. He held a postdoc scholarship at ICSI, affiliated with UC Berkeley in 1992/93. In 1992, he received his PhD in computer science from the Swiss Federal Institute of Technology (ETH) in Zurich under Prof. Niklaus Wirth and in 1987 his Masters in electrical engineering/ computer engineering from Aachen University of Technology (RWTH).

C. Hofmeister et al. (Eds.): QoSA 2006, LNCS 4214, p. 2, 2006.
© Springer-Verlag Berlin Heidelberg 2006

Documentation Principles and Practices That You Can Live with

Judith Stafford

Tufts University, Boston, USA

Abstract. Software architecture has become a widely-accepted conceptual basis for the development of non-trivial software in all application areas and by organizations of all sizes. Effectively documenting an architecture is as important as crafting it; if the architecture is not understood, or worse, misunderstood, it cannot meet its goals as the unifying vision for software development. Development-based architecture strategies, such as Rational's Unified Process, stop short of prescribing documentation standards. The Views and Beyond approach to software architecture provides practical guidance on the what, why, and how of creating IEEE 1471-2000 compliant documentation for your software architecture that will be used for years to come. The approach is based on the well-known concept of views and is presented in the context of prevailing prescriptive models for architecture, including the Unified Process and UML 2.0, which has improved support for representing key architectural elements over its predecessors.

Attendee Background

Participants should have experience with creating or using descriptions of large software systems and some knowledge of the Unified Modeling Language.

Tutorial Objectives

The primary aim of this tutorial is to teach developers what constitutes good documentation of a software architecture, why it is worth the effort to create and maintain a documentation package, and how to write it down. A secondary aim is to teach other stakeholders why they should care about architectural documentation and how they can use it to make their life easier, increase productivity, and decrease overall system development and maintenance costs.

About

Judith Stafford is a Senior Lecturer in the Department of Computer Science at Tufts University, and is also a visiting scientist at the Software Engineering Institute, Carnegie Mellon University. Dr. Stafford has worked for several years

C. Hofmeister et al. (Eds.): QoSA 2006, LNCS 4214, pp. 3–4, 2006.
© Springer-Verlag Berlin Heidelberg 2006

in the area of compositional reasoning and its application to software architectures and component-based systems. She has organized workshops, given invited talks, taught tutorials, and written widely in these areas including co-authoring the book that inspired this tutorial, Documenting Software Architectures: Views and Beyond, Addison Wesley, 2002 and several book chapters on software architecture and component-based software engineering.

Model-Based Software Development with Eclipse

Ralf Reussner and Steffen Becker

University of Karlsruhe (TH), Germany

Abstract. The tutorial consists of two parts. In the first part (45 min), Ralf Reussner focuses on the importance of an explicitly modelled software architecture. Besides an introduction into common architectural views, the role of the software architect is compared to "classical building" architects. As part of this, the often used comparison between building architecture and software architecture is critically reviewed. In particular, the role of an architect is discussed in model-driven software projects.

During the second part of the tutorial (135 min), Steffen Becker demonstrates online model driven development tools based on Eclipse. First, an introduction is given on the metamodelling tools of the Eclipse Modelling Framework (EMF) and on the Graphical Modelling Framework (GMF) used to generate a domain specific editors for user defined (meta-)models. Additionally, the MDA framework of the OMG is presented and the concepts are applied to the introduced tools.

A live demonstration of the capabilities of the introduced tools for model transformations shows finally how a domain specific modelling tool can be generated to a large extend automatically using an EMF-model instance and the generator of GMF. As a result, an editor based on the Eclipse Graphical Editing Framework (GEF) can be deployed and run using Eclipse.

About

Professor **Ralf Reussner** holds the Chair for Software-Design and -Quality at the University of Karlsruhe since 2006. His research group is well established in the area of component based software design, software architecture and predictable software quality. Professor Reussner shaped this field not only by over 60 peer-reviewed publications in Journals and Conferences, but also by establishing various conferences and workshops. In addition, he acts as a PC member or reviewer of several conferences and journals. As Director of Software Engineering at the Informatics Research Centre in Karlsruhe (FZI) he consults various industrial partners in the areas of component based software, architectures and software quality. He is principal investigator or chief coodinator in several grants from industrial and governmental funding agencies. He graduated from University of Karlsruhe with a PhD in 2001. After this, Ralf was a Senior Research Scientist and project-leader at the Distributed Systems Technology Centre (DSTC Pty Ltd), Melbourne, Australia. From March 2003 till January

C. Hofmeister et al. (Eds.): QoSA 2006, LNCS 4214, pp. 5–6, 2006.
© Springer-Verlag Berlin Heidelberg 2006

held the Juniorprofessorship for Software Engineering at the University of Old-
enburg, Germany, and was awarded with a 1 Mio EUR grant of the prestigious
Emmy-Noether young researchers excellence programme of the National German
Science Foundation.

Steffen Becker is a member of the research staff at the Chair for Software-
Design and -Quality at the University of Karlsruhe since 2006. In his PhD thesis
he concerned with combining model driven software development and prediction of the resulting Quality of Service properties of component based software
systems. As part of his work he is working on a component model enabling the
prediction of component based software systems. He is known in his field of research by several scientific publications and also as a member of the steering
committee of the QoSA conference and the WCAT workshop series at ECOOP.
He gained practical experiences during his internship as software engineer in
Johannesburg, ZA in 2000 as well as during consulting activities at the OFFIS
in Oldenburg, Germany. He holds a diploma in business administration and
computer science combined (Dipl.- Wirschaftsinformatik) from the Darmstadt
University of Technology.

Software Architecture Analysis and Evaluation

Heinz Züllighoven[1], Carola Lilienthal[1], and Marcel Bennicke[2]

[1] University of Hamburg, Germany
[2] Brandenburg University of Technology Cottbus, Germany

Abstract. A software architecture describes the structure of a software system on an abstract implementation independent level. In forward engineering it serves as a blueprint to prescribe the intended software structure (so-called architecture model). In reverse engineering it can provide an abstract view of the actual code structure of the existing software system (so-called code architecture). Architecture models and actual code architectures play a vital role for all comprehension and communication tasks during the development and evolution of large software systems. Therefore, architecture models and code architectures have to be explicitly represented and consistently maintained during the development, maintenance, and reengineering processes.

The need to insure compliance of the architecture model and the actual code architecture has drawn considerable attention in recent years. In order to facilitate maintainability and enhancement of a software system the compliance of the architecture model and the actual code architecture is essential. Various tools have been developed to analyse and evaluate the deviation of code architecture and architecture model. In this tutorial we present static analysis tools that may be used for architectural analyses. We demonstrate how these tools can create useful architectural views for different evaluation tasks such as identification of reconstruction scope, critical architectural elements and potential design irregularities. If possible we will analyse a software system provided by a participant of the workshop in a life demonstration.

About

Heinz Züllighoven, graduted in Mathematics and German Language and Literature, holds a PhD in Computer Science. Since October 1991 he is professor at the Computer Science Department of the University of Hamburg and head of the attached Software Technology Centre. He is one of the original designers of the Tools & Materials approach to object-oriented application software and the Java framework JWAM, supporting this approach. Since 2000, Heinz Züllighoven is also one of the managing directors of C1 Workplace Solutions Ltd. He is consulting industrial software development projects in the area of object-oriented design, among which are several major banks. Heinz Zllighoven has published a number of papers and books on various software engineering topics. An English construction handbook for the Tools & Materials approach has been published by Morgan Kaufmann in 2004. Among his current research

C. Hofmeister et al. (Eds.): QoSA 2006, LNCS 4214, pp. 7–8, 2006.
© Springer-Verlag Berlin Heidelberg 2006

interests are agile object-oriented development strategies, migration processes and the architecture of large industrial interactive software systems. In addition, he an his co-researchers are further developing a light-weight modeling concept for business processes which is tool-supported.

Carola Lilienthal holds a Diploma degree in computer science from University of Hamburg (1995). She is a research assistant at the University of Hamburg and is working in the Software Engineering Group of Christiane Floyd and Heinz Zllighoven. Since 1995 she is also working as a consultant for object oriented design, software architecture, software quality, agile software development and participatory design in several industrial projects. She has published a number of papers on various software engineering topics. Her research interests are the construction and analysis of large software systems, software architecture, software quality analysis and agile software development.

Marcel Bennicke holds a Diploma degree in computer science from Brandenburg University of Technology (2002). He is a research associate with the Software Systems Engineering Group at the same university. His research interests are software architecture, software quality and software quality analysis. Between 2004 and 2005 he has been working as a consultant in several industrial projects doing software quality analyses and introducing measurement programs in software development projects.

MEMS: A Method for Evaluating Middleware Architectures

Yan Liu[1], Ian Gorton[1], Len Bass[2], Cuong Hoang[3], and Suhail Abanmi[1]

[1] National ICT Australia (NICTA), Australia[1],
& School of Computer Science and Engineering, University of New South Wales, Australia
{jenny.liu, ian.gorton, suhail.abanmi}@nicta.com.au
[2] Software Engineering Institute, USA
ljb@sei.cmu.edu
[3] Engineering Faculty, University of Technology Sydney
vietcuong.hoang@student.uts.edu.au

Abstract. Middleware architectures play a crucial role in determining the overall quality of many distributed applications. Systematic evaluation methods for middleware architectures are therefore important to thoroughly assess the impact of design decisions on quality goals. This paper presents MEMS, a scenario-based evaluation approach. MEMS provides a principled way of evaluating middleware architectures by leveraging generic qualitative and quantitative evaluation techniques such as prototyping, testing, rating, and analysis. It measures middleware architectures by rating multiple quality attributes, and the outputs aid the determination of the suitability of alternative middleware architectures to meet an application's quality goals. MEMS also benefits middleware development by uncovering potential problems at early stage, making it cheaper and quicker to fix design problems. The paper describes a case study to evaluate the security architecture of grid middleware architectures for managing secure conversations and access control. The results demonstrate the practical utility of MEMS for evaluating middleware architectures for multiple quality attributes.

1 Introduction

Middleware refers to a broad class of software infrastructure technologies that use high-level abstractions to simplify construction of distributed systems. This infrastructure provides a distributed environment for deploying application-level components. These application components rely on the middleware to manage their life cycles and execution, and to provide off-the-shelf services such as transactions and security.

Consequently, the application component behavior and the middleware architecture are tightly coupled, and the middleware plays a critical role in achieving the

---

[1] National ICT Australia is funded through the Australian Government's Backing Australia's Ability initiative, in part through the Australian Research Council.

© Springer-Verlag Berlin Heidelberg 2006

quality attribute requirements of distributed applications. If the middleware architecture is poorly designed or implemented, contains subtle errors, or is inefficient or lacking in features, it may eventually lead to the failure of applications to meet their requirements.

It would therefore be valuable to have an evaluation method for designers of middleware-based applications to rigorously assess a technology and determine its fitness for purpose for an application. Such a method would also benefit the middleware developer community, who could use this approach to uncover potential design and implementation problems in their platforms.

Middleware creates new challenges and issues for software architecture evaluation methods. First, middleware technologies are *horizontal* in nature, providing mechanisms for a wide range of applications in many vertical application domains. The business goals for an application from the stakeholder's perspective are hence more likely to address the domain-specific application behavior rather than the specific requirements for the middleware itself. This indicates that evaluation methods for middleware should be driven by the concerns of individual quality attributes, instead of specific business goals.

Second, the ability of a middleware technology to support given quality attributes depends on the mechanisms and services provided by the infrastructure. Many competing middleware products exist, and they provide different mechanisms to address the same quality attribute. This indicates that evaluation methods require detailed technical inputs regarding the middleware infrastructure, including its programming model, APIs, configuration and deployment. This kind of knowledge helps to identify the effect of different middleware architectures on quality attributes.

Third, middleware technologies are becoming more and more complex. They typically have several thousand API calls and a collection of integrated services and tools of varying importance levels to different applications. This makes it difficult to evaluate the quality of a complete middleware technology. This requires evaluation methods to be flexible, and able to quickly provide feedback on alternative middleware architectures with respect to multiple quality attributes.

Finally, access to an adequate range of stakeholders for middleware systems is usually not possible. Stakeholders are used in many methods to prioritize requirements and to propose additional scenarios. When evaluating middleware, the developers of the middleware are usually not available. Also, the business goals for the middleware are not going to be represented by stakeholders associated with the application being constructed.

Software architecture evaluation methods exists in the literature and a comprehensive review can be found in [1] [8]. However, these methods are applied at the application level, where middleware is considered as features and constraints of the implementation of the applications. The strong relationship between a middleware technology and the quality of the overall system, and the issues of evaluating middleware architectures discussed above are not explicitly addressed. To the best of our knowledge, there has been little work on devising a systematic approach to evaluate the quality of middleware technologies.

In this paper, we present a structured approach to address the evaluation of middleware architectures, called MEMS. MEMS is a scenario-based evaluation approach with a clearly defined set of steps that helps evaluators determine the suitability of alternative middleware architectures for an application's quality goals. MEMS leverages generic qualitative and quantitative evaluation techniques by means of prototyping, testing, rating and analysis. The output of MEMS represents the ratings of each architecture against the quality attributes of interest.

This paper is organized as follows. Section 2 reviews related work in literature from two streams, software architecture evaluation methods and middleware evaluation approaches. Section 3 presents MEMS, its seven steps and the artifacts produced in detail. Section 4 demonstrates MEMS using a case study to evaluate the architectures of grid security infrastructure in the GT4 platform. The paper concludes in section 5.

2   Related Work

We consider related work from two streams, namely software architecture evaluation methods, and middleware evaluation.

2.1   Architecture Evaluation Methods

Software architecture evaluation methods and techniques have been widely studied. These methods and techniques have focused on understanding the relationship between software architecture and one or more quality attributes to ensure that the system ultimately achieves its quality goals while still supporting its functional requirements. A review of these techniques can be found in [1] and Chapter 6 of [3].

MEMS falls into the category of scenario-based software architecture evaluation methods. Scenarios are defined to understand how a software architecture responds with respect to attributes such as maintainability, reliability, usability, performance, flexibility and so on. Examples of scenario based methods are: Software Architecture Analysis Method (SAAM), Architecture Trade-off Analysis Method® (ATAM®) and Architecture Level Modifiability Analysis (ALMA). We consider related work in terms of their inputs, the roles involved and the output of the methods.

SAAM deals mainly with maintainability. Its inputs are software architecture descriptions and quality requirements from stakeholders. SAAM normally investigates and collects the stakeholder's requirements using interviews.

ATAM is a two-phase method. The first phase's inputs include general scenarios (or requirements from stakeholders), software architecture design documentation and the formation of the evaluation team. The tasks in the first phase are to transform general scenarios into specific scenarios and evaluate the software architecture against specific scenarios. The second stage of ATAM presents the results to stakeholders, who provide the business goals, and matches the software architecture with the business goals to analyze the impact of architecture changes based on each scenario. ATAM also deals with multiple quality attributes. ATAM collects

---

® Architecture Trade-off Analysis Method and ATAM are registered marks of Carnegie Mellon University.

stakeholder's requirements in brainstorming sessions on the scenarios related to the business goals.

PASA [23] is similar to ATAM's first stage, and is dedicated to the evaluation of performance of software architectures. PASA applies software performance engineering to the analysis step of the first phase of ATAM. PASA focuses on performance evaluation and its inputs include use cases, the software architecture to be assessed and the performance related scenarios are derived from use cases.

Mature approaches such as ATAM and SAAM have both technical and social aspects. The technical aspects deal with the collection of data and analysis techniques, while the social aspects deal with the interactions among stakeholders, software architects and evaluators. Technically, MEMS targets middleware, which is a component of the overall software architecture to be evaluated. Therefore it demands more inputs to support the techniques, tools and mechanisms to evaluate the middleware architectures and technologies. This also means the roles involved in MEMS are more technical, requiring architects and designers who have considerable knowledge and experience with the use of the middleware [11].

The relationship between architecture evaluation methods and software development processes is explored in [17]. According to [17], architecture-centric approaches, such as ATAM can be applied to analysis and testing activates of extreme programming activities. Design analysis using ATAM provides early feedback for understanding architectural trade-offs, decisions and risks. MEMS helps to enhance the development process by emphasizing quality attributes and focusing on architectural design decisions in projects where middleware is evolving rapidly to support emerging technologies, and agile development methods are applied,

2.2 Evaluation of Middleware

The i-Mate process [18] has been applied to evaluate COTS middleware technologies, especially for acquisition of middleware for enterprise applications [17]. i-Mate is similar to the first phase of ATAM, and requires stakeholders to input the business requirements for the middleware to be acquired. The evaluation of performance and scalability is conducted in a lab environment by running a predefined benchmark application on all the candidate middleware with the rest of the evaluation test environment remaining identical.

Both i-Mate and MEMS require middleware infrastructure specific techniques, because prototyping with the middleware is essential to conducting the assessment. MEMS is different from i-Mate in that MEMS is concerned with evaluating alternative solutions using a single middleware infrastructure. The business goals are imposed on the output of MEMS and are not a portion of the method. The evaluation is driven by concerns about the quality attributes for specific designs using middleware. In this sense, MEMS is more lightweight and agile than i-Mate.

Methods and techniques are also available to evaluate specific quality attributes of middleware systems [6][11][21]. Quantitative quality attributes, such as performance and availability can be accessed through measurement, analytical modeling and simulation. For example, [26] presented an availability model and analysis method for Sun's Java Application Server, Enterprise Edition 7. The study applied Markov reward modeling techniques on the target software system, and estimated the model parameters from lab or field measurements. Other practices include feature evaluation of middleware [14].

3 Overview of MEMS

MEMS is a scenario-based method for evaluating multiple quality attributes of middleware architectures. Similar to other scenario-based evaluation approaches such as SAAM and ATAM, MEMS is founded on key scenarios that describe the behavior of a middleware architecture with respect to particular quality attributes and in particular contexts. The quality goals and their expression in the form of key scenarios drive the evaluation process. MEMS defines the evaluation process in seven steps, which are described in the next section. MEMS' outputs the ratings of each architecture against the quality attributes of interest.

3.1 The Steps of MEMS

The seven steps of MEMS along with the artifacts produced at each step of the middleware evaluation are depicted in Figure 1.

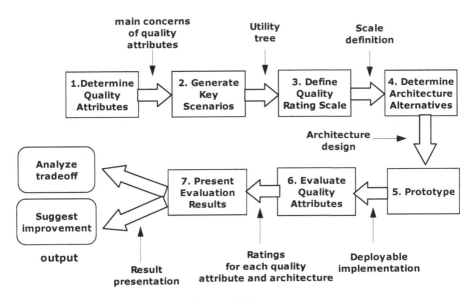

Fig. 1. MEMS Steps

Step 1. Determine Quality Attributes
The first step is for the evaluator to determine the quality attributes of interest. As discussed in section 1, one aspect that differentiates MEMS from SAAM, ATAM, and

i-Mate is that MEMS is not driven by quality requirements derived from the business goals. Instead, it addresses general quality attributes, such as performance and availability, scalability and security. The main concerns for a quality attribute must be specified within this step. One quality attribute may embody many specific concerns. For example, secure communication can be considered from four different views, namely privacy, integrity, authentication and authorization. The purpose of defining the general quality attribute concerns is to set the context for the next step which generates key scenarios for the quality attribute.

Step 2. Generate Key Scenarios
Similar to other scenario-based evaluation methods, scenarios are adopted as the descriptive means to capture concrete quality attributes requirements, as quality attributes by themselves are too abstract for analysis. For each identified attribute or its associated sub-concern, real scenarios are identified. This step also involves organizing scenarios and quality attributes. A practical approach for this is the ATAM's utility tree (see chapter 11 in [3]), which uses quality attribute names as an organizing vehicle.

Step 3. Define Quality Attribute Scale
Quantitative attributes can be evaluated using measurement, analytical modeling and simulation techniques. For qualitative attributes, one common approach to consolidating evaluation results is the weighted scoring method (WSM) [22]. The WSM method requires a clear and unambiguous definition of a rating scale, so that evaluators can give weights or scores to qualitative attributes with respect to the middleware architecture. This step is important for evaluators to have consistent rating criteria.

Step 4.Determine Architecture Alternatives
This step lists the alternative middleware architectures possible for the implementation being considered. Middleware provides multiple mechanisms and services to support the same functionality. Different mechanisms and services can be combined with patterns and frameworks to form middleware architectures. Hence one scenario usually has several alternative architecture solutions.

Step 5. Prototype
A prototype implementation is produced, one for each of the alternative architectures. This step requires skills in programming with the middleware infrastructure as well as knowledge of the techniques used in the middleware. A prototype is executed and measurements are taken for quantitative attributes of interest. Prototyping is also useful to obtain feedback on the architecture design and understand how it may impact other qualitative attributes.

Step 6. Evaluate Quality Attributes
Evaluation techniques from the literature are applied for evaluating individual quality attributes. For quantitative attributes, the evaluation focuses on producing the metric values for a quality attribute, such as transaction response time for

performance. Various techniques are available based on analytical modeling, simulation or prototype measurement. For qualitative attributes evaluators give ratings for each architecture against the rating scales defined for each quality attributes.

Step 7. Present Evaluation Results
The output of MEMS represents the ratings of each potential solution architecture against the quality attributes of interest. The results can be utilized from several different perspectives. They can be further input to other scenario-based architecture evaluation methods, such as ATAM for the trade-off analysis of quality attributes, or be used to provide feedback to developers of the middleware infrastructure to further improve the middleware, or be used to evaluate whether the middleware architecture can fulfil the quality requirements of the application to be built. The evaluation results are visually presented in a way that clearly identifies the ratings of each middleware architecture with regard to individual quality attributes.

3.2 Interaction and Iterations Within MEMS

MEMS is a lightweight approach as it only concerns interactions between two roles, namely software architect and developer. The role of software architect deals with the activities from step 1 to 4. The developer provides the expertise and the programming skills for developing the prototype in step 5. The developer has the experience to know the mechanisms and services from the middleware infrastructure that can support the quality goals defined for each architecture alternative. The software architect and the developer then work together on step 6 to evaluate quality attributes. The developer provides feedback on the definition of the rating categories and helps ensure it is clear and unambiguous. The software architect may go back to step 2 to refine the category definitions based on comments from the developer.

The architect then produces an evaluation form with the quality rating left blank for each architecture. The form includes the required quality goals, scenario and architecture descriptions, and the definition of the quality rating category. The developer will fill in the evaluation form with ratings for each quality attribute and architecture against the criteria defined in step 3.

The architect can further present the evaluation form to others who have equivalent knowledge, skills and experience as the developer participant in the evaluation team, and get them to fill in the form. Hence the role of developer may be filled by more than one person. With different developers assessing the architecture alternatives, a wider range of opinions can be canvassed. If the opinions are inconsistent, then the architect needs to further check the rating category definitions, that the architecture alternatives are described clearly, and the developers have a clear understanding of the middleware infrastructure being used.

4   Case Study: Evaluating Middleware for a Grid Security Infrastructure

Grid computing is a new paradigm for wide area distributed computing that is based on services to access and publish useful data and programs [9][10]. In a grid system, entities such as individual users and resources (including hardware resources such as CPUs, disks and computers, and software resources such as services), and data are loosely connected and managed in a dynamic virtual organization (VO). One paramount concern for a grid environment is secure communication and access control between grid entities which can be geographically and organizationally diverse.

The Globus Toolkit version 4 (GT4) [12] is an open source grid middleware technology that implements the Grid Security Infrastructure (GSI) to support security management of users, applications and resources in a grid. GSI is the GT4 component that supports privacy, integrity, as well as single sign-on and delegation of credentials for grid users. It also includes facilities for verifying the identity of a grid entity (authentication) and, based on that, determining the actions the entity is allowed to perform (authorization) [22].

Introducing security control to grid entities affects other quality attributes, such as performance and scalability. The GT4 security architecture alternatives also have different levels of impact on security, usability, the programming effort required and the resulting system's extensibility. Hence, in this section we follow MEMS to evaluate possible GSI architectures in GT4 for multiple quality attributes, namely performance, scalability, availability, security, usability, programmability and extensibility.

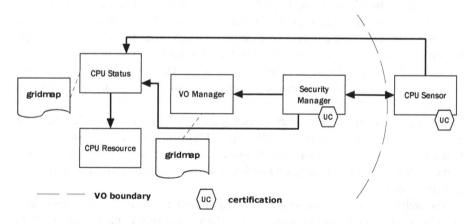

Fig. 2. Secure access control to Web service resources in GT4

4.1   Secure Access Control of Web Services Resources

We consider a typical scenario using GT4 to implement secure conversations and access control for Web services. An illustrating example is shown in Figure 2. A VO includes one manager application and some resources. A resource is wrapped by a Web service which provides the interfaces defined in WSDL for access to the state of the resource. For example, the *CPU Status* Web service in Figure 2 provides an interface to poll the CPU usage of the machine it serves.

For security purposes, if a service outside the VO, such as the *CPU Sensor* service in Figure 2, wants access to the CPU usage, it must be authenticated and authorized to do so. A service outside the VO must perform mutual authentication with the *Security Manager* and the *Security Manager* will authorize the service based on its security policy. The authorization is achieved by using a grid map file associated with each resource, which specifies the accounts that can access the resource. If the user account for the *CPU Sensor* service is within the grid map file then the *CPU Sensor* Web service will be authorized so it can invoke the interface to get CPU usage; otherwise its request is denied.

This simple scenario covers the basic concerns of using GSI to support Web services in a grid environment with secure conversation and access control to resources. Alternative architectures to implement this general scenario are evaluated below using MEMS.

4.2 Step One: Determine Quality Attributes

In this example, the quality attributes concerns are motivated by the general scenario described in section 4.1. The following quality attributes are deemed of interest from the evaluator's perspective; performance, scalability, availability, usability, programmability and extensibility. Comprehensive definitions of quality attributes are provided in [1]. The specific concerns of each quality attribute and relevant evaluation techniques must be first determined. This is essential to set the context for considering the key scenarios that express the quality attributes.

Performance concerns the responsiveness of the middleware in terms of the round trip time for a request through the middleware infrastructure. Transaction response time can be estimated by measuring it at runtime, developing an analytical model to represent the overall behavior or by simulation. In this evaluation we measure the round trip time directly from the system at runtime.

Scalability concerns the ability of a system to handle an increased volume of requests. Scalability is the function of system's performance and the scaling factor. In this paper the scale factor is considered as the load imposed on the middleware and scalability represents how throughput changes as the load scales. Metrics for scalability are provided in [9] for different types of distributed applications.

Availability describes any part of the system that can, if it fails, cause an interruption of service. This can be as simple as a process failure or as catastrophic as a computer system crash. Availability depends on the rate or possibility of failure and the time required for recovery. In this evaluation, availability is assessed in a coarse grained manner by counting the number of single failure points in a design alternative.

Usability concerns the goals of ease of use. It has many aspects, as summarized in [4]. In this evaluation, we consider single sign-on (SSO) as one of the primary usability features for a system with secure communication. This capability allows an authenticated user access to all permitted assets and resources without re-authentication.

Security is a system property, reflecting the ability of the system to protect itself from accidental or deliberate attack. In this evaluation, we consider the security attribute of GSI based on its support for secure communication to achieve integrity, privacy, authentication and authorization.

Programmability in this evaluation means the customizability of an off-the-shelf application with the use of the GT4 API. Current middleware systems provide many services to support alternative architecture designs, and middleware significantly reduces the programming effort by hiding the complex implementation of the services from the developers who build applications on top of the middleware. Many uses of these services can be done by simply configuring a descriptor file. However some architecture designs require customized implementation in code. This is a tradeoff between the flexibility of the programming model and the simplicity of the descriptor approach.

Extensibility is a system property, which measures the ability to extend a system. In this evaluation we are concerned with the level of effort, such as implementing configuration or deployment tasks, required to implement likely extensions. Extensions can be through the addition of new functionality, new resources, new type of users, or through modifications to current functionality.

In this evaluation, availability, usability, security, programmability and extensibility are considered as qualitative attributes, and therefore their evaluation techniques reply on expert opinion. The experts can be the developers or architects, who have a deep understanding of the middleware infrastructure and are familiar with the mechanisms and APIs. These experts rate each architecture alternative against the definition of the rating category, which are explained in detail in section 4.3.3.

4.3   Step Two: Generate Key Scenarios for Each Quality Attribute

The purpose of generating scenarios is to refine the context under which the related quality attributes are assessed. Given the general scenario of providing secure conversations and access control for the resource management of Web services based application in a VO, the following key scenarios were derived and organized using the utility tree in Table 1.

4.4   Step Three: Define Rating Scale

We use a coarse grained scale, defined as high (H), middle (M) and low (L). The rating scale is defined in Table 2. We didn't adopt an ordinal scale, for example from 1 to 5, because the values do not truly represent the differences between scales in ratio or distance. In fact, the differences in their values only give indications of their relative rankings. As discussed in section 3, if needed, the scaling definition can be refined later to be more fine grained definition or use ordinal scales.

Note that security has four sub-categories, and the rating scale definition is applicable to each of them. In order to aggregate the overall rating of security from the ratings given to individual sub categories, each sub-category has to be weighted. The value of the weight represents how much the sub category contributes to the overall security quality attribute assessment. The scale definition as High, Middle and Low must be assigned some value and then the overall rating can be calculated. Finally the rating in the form of number is converted back into the descriptive form as High, Middle or Low. The value assigned can be arbitrary as it is just used as a means for calculation. A simple algorithm in is used for calculation as shown in Table 3.

Table 1. Tabular form for a utility tree for organizing key scenarios

Quality Attribute	Attribute Refinement	Scenario
Performance	Request response time	A CPU Sensor sends a request to the *CPU Status* Web service to get the CPU usage of the node the service is running on. This includes the overhead of initializing secure conversation. The request completes within 30 seconds with a peak load of 20 concurrent requests.
Scalability	Throughput under the scale of number of requests	As the request load scales from 1 to 20, the throughput is maintained and all requests complete within 30 seconds
Availability	Single point of failure	No scenario is generated
Usability		Single sign-on. By using a proxy certificate, the *CPU Sensor* only has to sign in once to create the proxy certificate. The proxy certificate is then used for all subsequent authentications.
Security	Integrity, privacy, authentication and authorization	Secure access control to the CPU usage state is supported with regards to the four security attributes.
Programmability		No scenario is defined
Extensibility		When a new resource is available in the VO, changes are required either for configuration or implementation.

4.5 Step Four: Determine Architecture Alternatives

GSI includes mechanisms for both resource- and client-side grid security. On the resource side, GSI mechanisms include X.509 credentials for identifying the resource. On the client side, mechanisms include facilities to create temporary credentials, called a proxy, used to perform SSO and delegation. The client performs mutual authentication with the target resource using the certificates and establishes a secure, encrypted communication channel after this initial handshake.

Table 2. Rating scale definition

Quality Attribute		Scale Definition		
		High	**Middle**	**Low**
Availability (only consider the security architecture)		No single point failure	only one single point of failure	The number of single points of failures > 1
Usability (SSO)		Fully supported	Supported but with limitations	Not supported
Security	Integrity			
	Privacy			
	Authentication			
	Authorization	Support for identity-based authorization	Only support for identity-based authorization	Not supported
Programmability		Support for customized implementation with templates, patterns or frameworks	Support for out-of-the-box implementations by using APIs	Support for annotations, configurations and APIs for setting properties
Extensibility		Only changes in configuration or implementation for setting properties are required	Changes for configuration and out-of-box implementation are required	Customized implementations are required using middleware templates, patterns or frameworks

Table 3. Rating calculation with sub-categories

1. Assign values to High, Middle and Low to convert the rating of each sub-category into values correspondingly.

$$H \leftarrow 1, M \leftarrow 2/3, L \leftarrow 1/3$$

2. Calculate the overall rating based on weight and the converted rating of each sub-category

$$Rate = \sum_{i=1}^{n} Weight_n \times Rate_n \qquad (\sum_{i=1}^{n} Weight_n = 1)$$

where n is the number of sub-categories

3. Convert back the value of the overall rating into the descriptive form.

$$Rate \leftarrow \begin{cases} H & (2/3 < Rate \leq 1) \\ M & (1/3 < Rate \leq 2/3) \\ L & (0 < Rate \leq 1/3) \end{cases}$$

The client can also delegate its credentials to the resource to enable subsequent resource access without further intervention. The resource makes use of the grid map file to associate the presented credentials with a local user account. It can then spawn processes with the local user account's privileges. Optionally, it can make use of tools such as the Community Authorization Service (CAS) for fine-grained authorization.

GSI supports both transport-level security and message-level security. Transport-level security achieves authentication between grid entities using TLS and X509 certificates. Message-level security implements support for *WS-Security* and *WS-SecureConversation* specifications. Details of above mechanisms can be found in Chapters 15 and 16 in [25].

Based on this understanding of GSI in GT4, a Web service client is connected to the Web service by mutual authentication using an X.509 credential. Since GT4 messages are Simple Object Access Protocol (SOAP)-based, message-level security is turned on to provide protection for and to ensure integrity of these messages. By using these mechanisms, security protection is achieved at a per-message level for SOAP messages. The major difference relies on the architecture for authorization.

The following candidate architectures are identified for the general scenario described in section 4.1 to achieve secure conversation and resource access control.

Architecture 1: Only the grid map file is used to check the privilege of the *CPU Status* Web service client, which is the *CPU Sensor* outside the VO. The grid map file is a simple text-based file stored in local disk storage. It is a single point of failure if the grid map file is compromised. SSO is not supported as each SOAP request has to be authorized. The implementation uses the GT4 programming model and GSI APIs, so the out-of-the-box solution can be applied. As regard to the extensibility, no change is required for adding a new client or a new resource.

Architecture 2: This architecture utilizes delegation over secure conversation. After mutual authentication, the *Security Manager* delegates its credential to the *CPU Sensor*, so that it can access the *CPU Status* Web service on behalf of the *Security Manager*. Again the grid map file is single point of failure, along with the credential delegation of GSI. The delegation is per method based, which means SSO support is limited to the duration of the method invocation. Delegation and secure conversation are configured in a security descriptor. However, to properly use delegated credentials, programming is required to implement the *Security Manager*. No change is required for adding a new client or a new resource.

Architecture 3: The GT4 Delegation Service (DS) is used to delegate credentials between services in this architecture. Besides the grid map file, a black list file is attached with the resources. A request is denied if its account is within the black list even if the request from a user account may be permitted according to the grid map file. The grid map file and DS are two single points of failures. There is a significant amount of coding required to implement this architecture apart from modifying the configuration file. This architecture doesn't require changes to configuration or implementation when a new client or resource is added.

Architecture 4: This architecture uses CAS for role-based authorization. It requires a custom authorization plug-in to collect information about the caller at a *Policy Information Point* (PIP) and implement authorization at *Policy Decision Point* (PDP). Previous architectures all use default implementation of PIP and PDP, while this architecture has to provide customized implementation to enforce the assertion embedded in the CAS credential, which specifies the privilege to access a resource.. Considerable work is required to configure roles, permissions and services on CAS as well as programming custom PIP and PDP implementations at services. CAS is now the single point of failure. Adding a new resource or a new client requires the configuration of roles in CAS.

Due to space limitations, we omit the details of each architecture. They can be found in [19].

4.6 Step Five: Prototype

The four architectures were implemented in this step. When deployed, the Web service is wrapped as in Fig. 3. First, the components such as *Security Manager* are compiled into an archive. Then a Web service wraps each component. The security codes are embedded within the component's implementation and the generated Web service stubs. This generates a .gar file which can be deployed to a GT4 container. Finally, this GT4 WS-core container can be deployed to a Tomcat 5.0 container resulting in a Web service implementation using GSI.

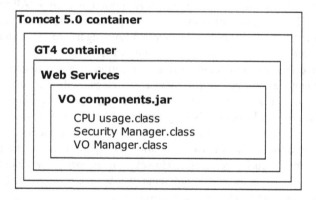

Fig. 3. The deployment of the prototype implementation

In order to measure performance and scalability, a request workload is emulated by a multi-threaded Java client, which generates concurrent requests to CPU Status Web service. A test bed is setup in a lab environment. The machine hosting the server is a Dell workstation, with 3GHz dual processors and 2GB RAM. The sever runs GT4 on Fedora core 3 and a Tomcat v5.0 server.

4.7 Step Six: Evaluate Quality Attributes

Response time and throughput are measured under a workload that scales from 1 to 20 concurrent clients. The results are shown in Fig. 4. The first diagram shows the round trip time of a request going through the security architecture. When the number of clients increases, the round trip time rises exponentially. Below 10 clients, the performance of the four architectures produces comparable performance and the difference is exacerbated when the number of clients exceeds 10. This illustrates the different scalability of each solution. The second diagram further demonstrates that the throughput degrades beyond a certain workload. This indicates that a bottleneck exists and it can not scale, which in turn limits and degrades the overall throughput. We apply the metrics in [20] to assess the scalability for the case of a system with a single non-scalable bottleneck and increasing users.

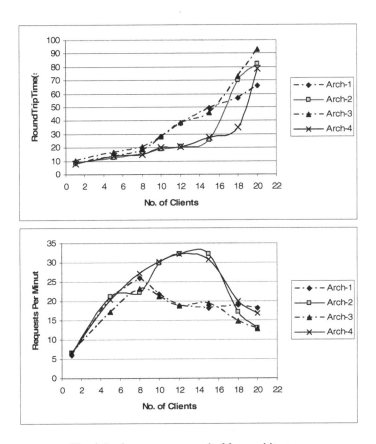

Fig. 4. Performance measured of four architectures

For the rest of the qualitative attributes, the development team gave ratings for each quality attribute based on the detailed architecture descriptions, the rating scale definition and the prototype implementation. In this case study, two developers who participated in the architecture design and prototype implementation provided ratings. The correlation of scores between/among two or more evaluators who rate the same scale is then estimated to measure the *homogeneity* of their ratings using inter-rate reliability analysis method [7].

4.8 Step Seven: Presenting the Results

The overall results are presented in a radar diagram in Fig. 5 with each axis representing an individual quality attribute. It clearly demonstrates how each architecture alternative performs with respect to a specific quality attribute. We also assessed the inter-rater reliability using Cohen's Kappa (chapter 2 in [13]) and the computed Kappa is 0.85^2.

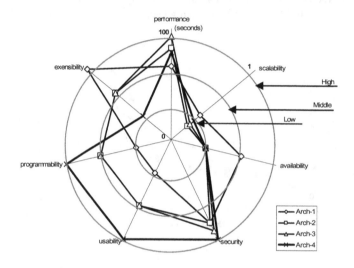

Fig. 5. Overall evaluation results of GSI architectures

5   Conclusion and Future Work

This paper present MEMS, a method dedicated to evaluating alternative middleware architectures. It takes into account the tight coupling among quality attributes and mechanisms, tools and services utilized to implement a middleware architecture.

MEMS is more lightweight and agile than existing approaches in term of the roles involved and the artifacts required for input. We demonstrated the method by evaluating the grid security infrastructure of GT4. We plan to obtain a response on this work from the GT4 community about our evaluation and the overall method. In the future, we plan to perform more case studies in applying MEMS to evaluate other middleware, enhancing its method with tradeoff analysis and verifying MEMS is a repeatable approach.

---

[2] If Kappa is greater than 0.70, it can be concluded that the inter-rater reliability is satisfactory.

References

1. Ali Babar, M., and Gorton, I.: Comparison of Scenario-Based Software Architecture Evaluation Methods, 11th Asia-Pacific Software Engineering Conference, p600 – 607, (2004).
2. Barbacci, M., Klein, M. H., Longstaff, T.A., Weinstock, C. B.: Quality Attributes, Technical report, CMU/SEI-95-TR-021, (1995).
   http://www.sei.cmu.edu/publications/documents/95.reports/95.tr.021.html
3. Bass, L., Clements, P., and Kazman, R.: Software Architecture in Practice, 2nd Edition, Published by Addison-Wesley in the SEI Series, 2003.
4. Bass, L., John, B. E., Kates, J.: Achieving usability through software architecture, Technical Report, CMU/SEI-2001-TR-005,
   http://www.sei.cmu.edu/publications/documents/01.reports/01tr005.html
5. Boehm, B., In., H.: Identifying Quality-Requirement Conflicts, *IEEE Software*, vol. 13, no.2, IEEE computer society, p25-35, (1996).
6. Cecchet, E., Marguerite, J., Zwaenepoel, W.: Performance and scalability of EJB applications ACM Conference on Object-Oriented Programming, Systems, Languages and Applications (Oopsla'02) (2002).
7. Cronbach, L. J. Coefficient alpha and the internal structure of tests. *Psychometrika, 16,* 297-333, (1951).
8. Dobrica, L., E. Niemela: A Survey on Software Architecture Analysis Methods, IEEE Transactions on Software Engineering, 28(7), (2002).
9. Foster, I., Service-oriented science, Science: vol. 308. no. 5723, p814 – 817, (2005)
10. Foster, I., Kesselman, C. and Tuecke, S. The Anatomy of the Grid: Enabling Scalable Virtual Organizations, Lecture Notes in Computer Science, vol. 2150, 2001.
11. Gorton, I., Liu, A., Brebner, P.: Rigorous Evaluation of COTS Middleware Technology, IEEE Computer, vol. 36, no. 3, p50-55, (2003).
12. Globus Toolkit, http://www.globus.org/
13. Gwet, K., Handbook of Inter-Rater Reliability, STATAXIS Publishing Company, ISBN, 0970806205.
14. Harmer, T., Stell, A., McBride, D.: UK Engineering Task Force Globus Toolkit Version 4 Middleware Evaluation, UK Technical Report UKeS-2005-03, (2005).
15. http://www.nesc.ac.uk/technical_papers/UKeS-2005-03.pdf
16. Lawlor, B. and Vu, L.: A Survey of Techniques for Security Architecture Analysis, Science and Technical Report, DSTO-TR-1438, (2003).
17. Nord, R. L Tomayko, J.E., Software Architecture-Centric Methods and Agile Development, *IEEE Software*, vol. 23, no. 2, pp. 47-53, Mar/Apr, 2006.
18. Liu, A., Gorton, I.: Accelerating COTS Middleware Acquisition: The i-Mate Process. IEEE Software 20(2): 72-79 (2003)
19. Liu, Y., Gorton, I., Abanmi, S., Hoang, C., A secure configuration manager for adaptive server framework, NICTA Summer Scholarship Project Proposal, Nov, (2005).
20. Jogalekar, P., Woodside, M.: Evaluating the Scalability of Distributed Systems, IEEE Transactions on Parallel and Distributed Systems, vol. 11, no.6, p 589-603, (2000).
21. Kanoun, K., Kaaniche, M., Laprie, J. C.: Qualitative and Quantitative Reliability Assessment, IEEE Software, p 77-87, (1997).
22. Kontio, J.: A Case Study in Applying a Systematic Method for COTS Selection, Proc. 18th Int'l Conf. Software Eng., IEEE CS Press, Los Alamitos, Calif.,p. 201–209, (1996).
23. Robert L. Nord, James E. Tomayko, "Software Architecture-Centric Methods and Agile Development," *IEEE Software*, vol. 23, no. 2, pp. 47-53, Mar/Apr, 2006.

24. Smith, C. U., Willams, L. G. : Performance Engineering of CORBA-based Distributed Systems with *SPE·ED*, *Lecture Notes in Computer Science: Computer Performance Evaluation Modelling Techniques and Tools,* Springer, (1998)
25. Sotomayor, B., Childers, L., Globus Toolkit 4: Programming Java Services, written by Borja Sotomayor and Lisa Childers, and published by Elsevier.
26. Tang, D., Kumar, D.; Duvur, S.; Torbjornsen, O.: Availability measurement and modeling for an application server, International Conference on Dependable Systems and Networks, p669 – 678, (2004).

Evaluating Alternative COTS Assemblies from Imperfect Component Information

Hernán Astudillo[1], Javier Pereira[2], and Claudia López[1]

[1] Universidad Técnica Federico Santa María, Departamento de Informática,
Avenida España 1680, Valparaíso, Chile
{hernan, clopez}@inf.utfsm.cl
[2] Universidad Diego Portales, Escuela de Ingeniería Informática,
Av. Ejército 441, Santiago, Chile
javier.pereira@udp.cl

Abstract. Component-based approaches to elaborate software must deal with the fact that in practical settings, components information may be incomplete, imprecise and uncertain, and requirements may be likewise. Architects wanting to evaluate candidate architectures regarding requirements satisfaction need to use whatever information be available about components, however imperfect. Imperfect information can be dealt with using specialized analytical formalisms, such as fuzzy values for imprecision and rough sets for incompleteness; but if used, evaluations need to compare and rank using non-scalar, non-symbolic values. This article presents an approach to systematically describe components' imperfect information, and to evaluate and rank whole component assemblies, by using credibility values-based "support scores" that aggregate imperfect information about requirements, mechanisms and components. The approach builds on the Azimut framework, which offers progressive refinement of architectural entities via architectural policies, architectural mechanisms, components, and component assemblies. An example of the proposed approach and "what-if" analysis are illustrated.

1 Introduction

Component-based software development proposes building systems by using pre-existing components, to reduce development time, costs and risks and to improve product quality; achieving these goals requires an adequate selection of components to reuse. Most current methods of component evaluation and selection are not geared to support human specialists in the systematic exploration of design spaces because they require rather complete and/or consistent descriptions of components behavior, connections and prerequisites. Unfortunately, in practice architects have at hand incomplete, imprecise, and uncertain information about components, and perhaps even about requirements. Even more, mathematical formalisms that describe imperfect information are not directly amenable to comparing alternatives.

This article builds on the Azimut approach [12], which proposed progressive refinement of architectural abstractions and artifacts via architectural policies,

C. Hofmeister et al. (Eds.): QoSA 2006, LNCS 4214, pp. 27–42, 2006.
© Springer-Verlag Berlin Heidelberg 2006

mechanisms, components and assemblies. It presents an approach to evaluate and compare whole component assemblies, even if the available information is imperfect (possibly incomplete, imprecise and uncertain), by defining "support scores" that reflect the "strength" of architectural artifacts (mechanisms, components and assemblies) to satisfy specific sets of requirements (expressed as architectural policies). Support scores aggregate imperfect information about requirements and components, using as parameters the minimal credibility degree that architects are willing to accept, thus providing a means to explore design spaces using different risk preferences.

The reminder of this article is structured as follows: Section 2 characterizes the problem; Section 3 surveys some related work; Section 4 presents an intuitive formulation of the key Azimut concepts; Section 5 characterizes the architectural imperfect information we can handle; Section 6 reformulates the key Azimut concepts to deal rigorously with imperfect information; Section 7 introduces support scores; Section 8 illustrates the use of the support scores with a realistic example; and Section 9 discusses future work and conclusions.

2 Motivation

The construction of software systems using components offers great promise of reducing development times and costs while increasing quality, but its realization requires that architects be able to choose among alternative solutions composed from available components that best fit the requirements.

In practice architects have at hand incomplete, imprecise, and uncertain information about components, and perhaps even about requirements. Imperfect information can be dealt with using specific mathematical formalisms, such as fuzzy values for imprecision and rough sets for incompleteness. Since architects wanting to compare candidate architectures need to use whatever information is available, however imperfect it may be, they need to compare and rank the non-arithmetic values used to characterize their components.

Thus, a practical and scalable approach to component-sets comparison must have these properties:

1. **Relate component-sets to requirements (specially to NFRs).** It is sometimes quite complex to relate components (and sets thereof) to specific requirements, and specially to NFRs (non-functional requirements) due to their systemic nature.
2. **Record imperfect information.** In real situations, architects have at hand incomplete, imprecise and uncertain component information; indeed, even requirements may be likewise.
3. **Allow direct comparison of whole component sets.** Architects need to play what-if and sensitivity games, which rely on being able to compare alternative solutions, i.e. component sets as wholes agains each other.

This article presents a threefold technique that meets the above requirements:

Architectural abstractions. Using *policies, mechanisms, components* and *assemblies of components*, they connect solutions to requirements, and were introduced in the Azimut framework [12], as an aid to systematic derivation of component-sets from NFRs.

Layered catalogs. The above mentioned architectural abstractions are characterized using imperfect information by means of *catalogs* [13] that allow incomplete, imprecise and uncertain values (using appropriate mathematical formalisms).

Support scores. The degree in which a given component-set "seems to support" a given set of requirements is quantified with a set of scores, borrowed from decision-support techniques for establishing preference based on voting [20], that aggregate the available information, however imprecise it be, thus allowing direct comparison between component-sets.

3   Other Systematic Processes for Selecting Components

Several techniques have been proposed for component evaluation and selection [14,3,15,19,10,11,2,7] that identify reuse candidates using search criteria like functionality, non-functional requirements (NFRs) or architectural restrictions that each component and/or the whole system must satisfy. Some of these techniques [19,10,11,2] give semi-automated support to the selection process with multi-criteria decision support techniques, such as AHP (Analytic Hierarchy Process) [21] or WSM (Weighted Scoring Method) [26].

Most techniques require rather complete and consistent descriptions of component behavior, connections and prerequisites. But in practice, architects have at hand only imperfect information about available components, which is then a key requirement to supporting COTS selection processes in realistic settings. Shaw [22] originally proposed the notion of *credentials*, as incremental (partial) and evolving specifications in a context of symbolic manipulation (for example, credibility is an enumeration that indicates the source of a value, not a truth-value about it).

Some MDA (Model-Driven Architecture) [16] projects, such as CoSMIC [9] and UniFrame [5], generate component-based systems, but require the use of formal component specification languages to describe available components, and from these descriptions (consistent and precise) they automate the component selection and integration process.

Also, most approaches [14,3,15,19,10,11] explore the space of available components but do not allow exploring possible alternative designs using intermediate abstraction levels. Architects are thus forced to deal with a large conceptual gap between the spaces of components and requirements, and must describe exhaustively the relationships between them. Working with intermediate abstraction levels enables to reduce this gap and work with smaller design spaces. CRE [2] and CARE [7] use the NFR Framework [6] to derive more specific requirements or design solutions when considering quality attributes or NFRs, but the NFR Framework does not explicitly distinguish requirements more detailed than the design solutions that satisfy them, and the derivation process among them depends on the architect's knowledge of possible refinements, without recourse to a systematic and possible automated derivation support.

4   Intuitive Formulation of Key Concepts

The Azimut approach [13,12] supports architects in generating component assemblies for a given set of requirements relies on multi-dimensional catalogs of *architectural policies, mechanisms and components,* and derivation rules among constructs of these levels. The Azimut goal is enabling architects to gather component characterizations, however imprecise and incomplete, and derive component assemblies for the specific requirements at hand. This article explains how the Azimut approach deals with the imperfect information under which architects normally must generate, evaluate, compare and select architectural artifacts.

4.1   Architectural Policies and Mechanisms

Architects may reason about the overall solution properties using architectural policies, and later refine them (perhaps from existing policy catalogs) into artifacts and concepts that serve as inputs to software designers and developers, such as component models, detailed code design, standards, protocols, or even code itself. Thus, architects define policies for specific architectural concerns and identify alternative mechanisms to implement such policies. For example, an availability concern may be addressed by fault-tolerance policies (such as master-slave replication or active replication) and a security concern may be addressed by access control policies (such as identification-, authorization- or authentication-based) [8].

Each *reification* yields more concrete artifacts; thus, architectural decisions drive a process of successive reifications of NFRs that end with implementations of mechanisms that do satisfy these NFRs.

To characterize such reifications, we use a vocabulary taken from the distributed systems community [27], duly adapted to the software architecture context.

Architectural Policy: The first reification from NFRs to architectural concepts. Architectural policies can be characterized through specific concern dimensions that allow describing NFRs with more details.

Architectural Mechanism: The constructs that satisfy architectural policies. Different mechanisms can satisfy the same architectural policy, and the differences between mechanisms is the way in which they provide certain dimensions.

Component: A software artifact that is executable, multiple-use, non-context-specific, composable with other components, encapsulated (i.e., non-investigable through their interfaces), and a unit of independent deployment and versioning [23].

Assembly: A set of components; although in practice assemblies include components with some coherence or mutual fit, we do not require that *a priori* since such properties might not be directly derivable from the information available at a given point in time.

As a brief example (in Fig. 1, see [12] for details), consider communication among applications. One architectural concern is the communication type, which might have the dimensions of sessions, topology, sender, and integrity v/s timeliness [4]; to this we add synchrony. Then, the requirement *send a private report to subscribers by Internet* might be mapped in some project (in architectural terms) as requiring communication 'asynchronous, with sessions, with 1:M topology, with a push initiator mechanism, and priorizing integrity over timeliness'. Based on these architectural requirements, an architect (or automated tool!) could search among known mechanisms for a combination that provides this specified policy; lacking additional restrictions and using well-known standards and software, a good first fit for mechanism is SMTP (the standard e-mail protocol).

Finally, in absence of further restrictions, any available component that provides SMTP should be a good fit for the given requirement.

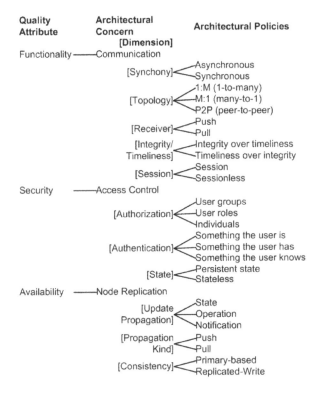

Fig. 1. Content from which policies may be extracted

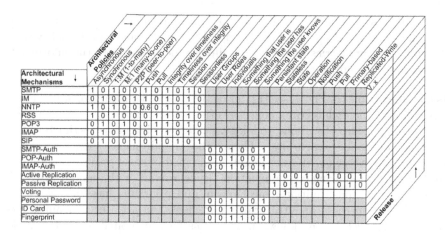

Fig. 2. Partial Content of Mechanisms Catalog

4.2 Multi-layered Catalogs

Azimut catalogs store architect's knowledge about architectural policies, mechanisms and components, as well as the satisfaction rules among them.

A **policies catalog** gathers platform-independent architectural policies, and incorporates knowledge for architectural concerns and dimension states collected from authoritative sources of the relevant discipline (e.g. Tannenbaum [24] for replication and Britton [4] for middleware communication).

A **mechanisms catalog** records well-known architectural mechanisms, which are design-level constructs, implementation-independent, that potentially satisfy architectural policies (e.g. SMTP). A given mechanism may satisfy several policies, and a given policy may be satisfied by several mechanisms. Figure 2 shows the partial content of a mechanisms catalog for an example later expanded.

Finally, an Azimut **components catalog** describes available components. Figure 3 shows the partial content of a components catalog.

5 Imperfect Information

In real-world deployment situations, catalog preparators might not know or not be certain whether a given component implements a certain mechanism (e.g. SendMail vis-a-vis SMTP). Likewise, system requirements themselves may be imprecise, incomplete or uncertain, and consequently it would be difficult to know which mechanisms do fit the requirements.

5.1 Modeling Imperfect Information

Azimut catalogs [13] characterize artifacts using dimensions, but in practice this information may be partial and/or incomplete: since each dimension has several

COTS	SMTP	IM	NNTP	RSS	POP3	IMAP	SIP	SMTP-Auth	POP-Auth	IMAP-Auth	Active Replication	Passive Replication	Voting	Personal Password	ID Card	Fingerprint
SendMail	1	0	0	0	0	0	0	1	0	0				1		
CourierMailServer	1	0	0	0	1	1	0	0.6	0.6	0.6				1	0	0
SurgeMail	1	0	0	0	1	1	0	0.6	0.6	0.6				1	0	0
DNews	0	0	1	0	0	0	0	0		0				0.6		
LeafNoad	0	0	1	0	0	0	0	0	0	0						
CyrusIMAPServer	0	0	0	0	1	1	0	0	0.6	0.6	0.6			1	0	0
LifeKeeper	0	0	0	0	0	0	0	0	0	0	0.6	0.6				
SurgeMail(Cluster)	1	0	0	0	0	0	0	0.4	0.4	0.4	0.6	0.6		0.4	0	0

Fig. 3. Partial Contents of Components Catalog

associated states, *indeterminacy, imprecision* or *uncertainty* may appear if some stakeholders have trouble establishing which dimension state(s) do hold in a specific situation.

Each kind of imperfect information demands a particular representation and analytic approach:

- *Incomplete information* (indeterminacy) has been successfully dealt with by rough sets [17]; for example, our catalog(s) might not say anything about SMTP's support for Node Replication Consistency.
- *Imprecision* (fuzziness) is usually modeled with fuzzy values [25]; for example, SMTP may be said by some catalog author to "largely support" active replication since it is stateless and is not really hard to enhance or embed to operate in a replicated fashion.[1]
- *Uncertainty* (changeability of information) can also be subject to formal treatment, but we limit ourselves to let architects enact change by updating catalogs and propagating changes to second-order measures as required (and perhaps changing their decisions as well).

Additionally, architectural information gathered in catalogs could in principle be elaborated by different stakeholders or even by third parties. This provides a way of sharing architectural information and of gathering complementary sources about any given artifact, but also introduces one more kind of information imperfection:

- *(Un)reliability* is usually modeled by probability statements; for example, the above information may be tagged with a 90% reliability because we trust this catalog.[2]

---

[1] An architectural judgement, of course!

[2] We may actually trust the catalog's author, but we sidestep complex trust issues in this article.

5.2   Causes of Imperfect Information

Three main issues hamper obtaining good information about policies, mechanisms and components: information retrieval methods; dimensions and states; and stakeholders [20].

1. **Information retrieval methods** The quality of information is largely determined by the quality of the procedures, tools and techniques used in data acquisition or appraisal [3]; criteria such as cost, scheduling or implementation complexity may condition the architect's confidence on the available information.
2. **Dimensions and states** Stakeholders must select dimensions and define states on them to best reflect the current situation of architectural choice. Three properties are required to guarantee an appropriate set of dimensions:
   - *exhaustivity*: there are no relevant dimensions outside the appraisal process;
   - *low redundancy*: there are no two dimensions that carry the same kind of information;
   - *cohesion*: each dimension allows a choice, everything else remaining equal, and its states are necessary and sufficient to the appraisal process.
3. **Stakeholders** Stakeholders should exhibit rationality and have a complete methodological toolbox to correctly appreciate which states hold on each dimension when a specific artifact is described.

Unfortunately, in normal cases most of previous conditions are not satisfied, and thus full knowledge is unrealistic. Even more so, in many practical situations these three issues combine to impede complete, unambiguous and certain information about mechanisms and components.

6   Revisiting Concepts to Deal with Imperfect Information

A proper analytic treatment of imperfect information is simplified with a more rigorous definition of the key concepts intuitively introduced in Section 4.

6.1   Key Concepts and Definitions

We introduce several definitions in order to model, and deal with, imperfect information. Notice that only imprecision, modeled by credibility statements will be considered in this article.

Definition 1. *A* **state indicator** *is any procedure, rule, technique or process that stakeholders can apply to know which state(s) do hold in a given dimension, for a specific artifact (mechanism or component). If a single state holds, the indicator is called "pointed", otherwise "non-pointed".*

---

[3] We use "appraisal" instead of "evaluation" to avoid assuming that dimensions encode measurable properties.

Definition 2. *A **credibility indicator** reflects how trustworthy are the state(s) returned by a state indicator. If the state indicator is pointed, credibility is allocated to the single state; otherwise, it is distributed among the different states returned by the state indicator.*

Credibility is *not* treated here as a probability (likelihood); it is a truth value of a statement, not a distribution function.

Definition 3. *A **software architectural dimension** has the following properties:*

- *It is accepted by a set of stakeholders as a model representing an attribute or effect of an architectural mechanism;*
- *it is defined in terms of states;*
- *in a specific decision situation, the stakeholders may accord the ordering of states in a scale of preferences.*

Once stakeholders compare any pair of states in a dimension and conclude that one state is more important than the other or that both states are equally important, they establish a preference scale, and enables decision-making processes. This leads to the following definitions:

Definition 4. *An **architectural policy** is the first reification from NFRs to architectural concepts. It establishes a constraint over an architectural dimension and reflects the states that the stakeholders expect to be held by a software artifact. An architectural policy must reference the dimension on which the constraint must be set, and the specific states to be satisfied in such dimension.*

Definition 5. *An **architectural mechanism** is an intermediate architectural abstraction that represents a standard or common specification of several software components (see below). Mechanisms are characterized by the architectural dimensions that they provide (satisfy); each mechanism may implement several policies, and each policy may be implemented by several mechanisms.*

Definition 6. *A **software component** must be [23] multiple-use, non-context-specific, composable with other components, encapsulated (i.e., non-investigable through its interfaces), and a unit of independent deployment and versioning. In Azimut, components are characterized according to the architectural mechanisms that they implement; each component may implement several mechanisms, and each mechanism may be implemented by several components.*

Architectural policies are characterized through specific states on concern dimensions, which in turn allow describing NFRs with more details. Accordingly, a mechanism may or may not satisfy a given architectural policy. In fact, states in a dimension are ordered in terms of preferences by policies; thus, mechanisms satisfying policies are preferred to those that don't satisfy them. In other words, the preferences between mechanisms are set by the way in which they provide certain policies through its dimensions.

7 Evaluation of Component Assemblies

Fuzzy statements are acceptable and adequate representations of imprecise knowledge concerning required policies and available mechanisms and components. Statements like "mechanism X supports policy Z with credibility 0.3" or "component Y implements mechanism X with credibility 0.75" will be used as basis for derivation of component assemblies from requirements.

Indeterminacy appears in catalogs when there is no credibility value assigned to a statement, either because no information is available or because the architects have not defined a credibility value yet. For example, in Figure 2, the entry SMTP does not provide any information concerning individual authorization in the security dimension; this does not mean that credibility is zero, but that there is no available information. Absence of knowledge is not knowledge of absence.

For the sake of focusing, the remainder of this article only deals with imprecision as fully modeled and illustrated, and indeterminacy is modeled as a case of null credibility.

7.1 Support Scores

Assume a specific situation where architectural mechanisms are described by dimensions and are implemented by components. Let D, M, C be the sets of dimensions, mechanisms and components, and n_d, n_m, n_c the respective set sizes. Similarly, let P be a set of architectural policies of size n_p. We say that *a policy $p \in P$ is represented by dimensions in D* if there exists a set $D_p \subset D$ helping to describe it.

The number $\mu(d, m) \in [0, 1]$ is defined as the *credibility level* that a mechanism $m \in M$ *supports* a policy p on the dimension $d \in D_p$. Consequently, $\forall d \in D - D_p$, $\mu(d, m) = 0$ holds.

Analogously, let a component $c_i \in C$ ($i = 1, \ldots, n_c$) be the set $c_i = \{m_{i,1}, m_{i,2}, \ldots, m_{i,n_m} \in M\}$ of mechanisms it implements; a mechanism $m \in M$ is implemented by a component c_i with credibility level $\mu(c_i, m_{i,j}) \in [0, 1]$.

We introduce abstraction-specific support scores, which count arguments in favor of a statement of valid refinement (notice that scores are not a probability but a credibility value). Score formula take as parameters the minimal credibility levels that its users (i.e. the architects) are willing to accept, denoted by α and β as defined below.

Definition 7. *The* **support score of a mechanism m for policy p**, *at minimum level* $\alpha \in (0, 1]$, *is*

$$S_{mech}(p, m, \alpha) = \frac{\mid C(m, D_p) \mid}{\mid D_p \mid} \tag{1}$$

where $C(m, D_p) = \{d \in D_p \mid \mu(d, m) \geq \alpha\}$.

In other words, the formula takes into account the **arguments in favor** of the statement "m satisfies policy p". Thus, if a mechanism has enough credibility on a dimension to support the policy, then it provides a favorable argument. The threshold α denotes the minimal credibility expected from considered mechanisms. This parameter has the same interpretation than the usual threshold proposed in the well-known decision aiding methods called ELECTRE [18]. Normally, $\alpha \geq 0.5$ suggests that the architects needs enough votes to accept a credibility level. At the contrary, $\alpha < 0.5$ is a very weak argument and any credibility level satisfying this inequality should not be accepted.

Definition 8. *The* **support score of a component** *c* **for policy** *p*, *at minimum levels* $\alpha, \beta \in (0, 1]$, *is*

$$S_{comp}(p, c, \alpha, \beta) = \frac{\mid C(c, D_p) \mid}{\mid D_p \mid} \tag{2}$$

where $C(c, D_p) = \{d \in D_p \mid \mu(d, m) \geq \alpha, \mu(c, m) \geq \beta, m \in M\}$.

This score counts the arguments in favor of c regarding the statement "c satisfies policy p". The thresholds α and β denote the minimal credibility expected from mechanisms and from components, respectively. They have the same interpretation given above.

Definition 9. *Given a n-item component assembly* $A = \{c_i \in C, i = 1 \ldots n\}$, *the* **support score of a component assembly** *A* **for policy** *p* *is*

$$S_{assem}(p, A, \alpha, \beta) = \frac{\mid C(A, D_p) \mid}{\mid D_p \mid} \tag{3}$$

where $C(A, D_p) = \{d \in D_p \mid \exists i, j : max_{c_i \in A}\mu(c_i, m_{i,j}) \geq \beta \wedge \mu(d, m_{i,j}) \geq \alpha, m_{i,j} \in M\}$.

Here, $max_{c_i \in A}\mu(c_i, m_{i,j})$ returns the credibility value of the component where a mechanism is implemented with the greatest credibility. Similarly, $\mu(d, m_{i,j}) \geq \alpha$ counts for the attribute where the mechanism j implemented by the component i provides dimension d with credibility superior or equal to α. This support score counts dimensions in favor of the statement "A satisfies the policy p". Again, α and β denote the minimal credibility expected from mechanisms and from components, respectively.

Intuitively, the support scores count the arguments for a given component or assembly as solution to a given policy, where "credible" means having an index value above the corresponding credibility threshold.

8   Example and Discussion

The measures introduced in Section 7.1 are now illustrated using the sample catalogs presented in Section 4.2. Let p be a policy for the following requirements:

- *communication*: asynchronous, 1:M topology, push receiver, integrity over timeliness
- *security*: individual authorization; authentication based on something the user knows
- *availability*: persistent state replication, and replicated-write consistency

A simple inspection of figure 2 allows to identify the mechanisms that might satisfy the required architectural policies.

Table 1. Support Score of Mechanisms

$S_{mech}(p, m, \alpha)$	$\alpha = 1$	$\alpha = 0,6$
$m = SMTP$	4/8	4/8
$m = IM$	2/8	2/8
$m = NNTP$	3/8	4/8
$m = RSS$	3/8	3/8
$m = POP3$	1/8	1/8
$m = IMAP$	1/8	1/8
$m = SIP$	0	0
$m = SMTP - Auth$	2/8	2/8
$m = POP3 - Auth$	2/8	2/8
$m = IMAP - Auth$	2/8	2/8
$m = Personal Password$	2/8	2/8
$m = IDCard$	1/8	1/8
$m = Fingerprint$	1/8	1/8
$m = Active Replication$	2/8	2/8
$m = Passive Replication$	1/8	1/8
$m = Voting$	0	0

Table 1 shows the support score of each mechanism for this policy. Those mechanisms with the highest support scores are most promising and will contribute more to the support scores of components and assemblies; hence they become the focus of the selection process.

The support score of each mechanism depends on the number of required architectural policies that are supported by it and on the required α threshold (which denotes willingness to use imprecise information). A given mechanism may get different support scores for different α values. If the credibility degree of the available information about an specific mechanism is low, then the support score increases if the required α threshold decreases. For instance, if we vary the credibility degree from 1 to 0.6, the NNTP's support score grows from 3/8 to 4/8; hence, we can maintain NNTP as an alternative mechanism for the required policy.

Also, considering set a α threshold, each mechanism may have several values for its support scores. This information can indicate a ranking of mechanisms regarding the number of supported policies. For example, when $\alpha = 1$, SMTP is the mechanism that provides a better solution, but for $\alpha = 0.6$, both SMTP and NNTP are good solutions. However, since none of the available mechanisms can provide support for all required policies (eg. support score equal to 1), we need to identify components that implement one or more mechanisms simultaneously.

Table 2 presents the support scores of the available components (see Figure 3). Again, the highest support scores will be the focus of our attention. This score varies depending on two thresholds, α y β, which indicate the minimal acceptable

Table 2. Support Score of Components

$S_{comp}(p,c,\alpha,\beta)$	$\alpha = 1$ $\beta = 1$	$\alpha = 1$ $\beta = 0.6$	$\alpha = 1$ $\beta = 0.3$	$\alpha = 0.6$ $\beta = 1$	$\alpha = 0.6$ $\beta = 0.6$	$\alpha = 0.6$ $\beta = 0.3$
$c = SendMailv.8.1$	6/8	6/8	6/8	6/8	6/8	6/8
$c = CourierMailServer$	4/8	6/8	6/8	6/8	6/8	6/8
$c = SurgeMail$	4/8	6/8	6/8	6/8	6/8	6/8
$c = DNews$	0	2/8	2/8	4/8	6/8	6/8
$c = LeafNode$	0	0	0	4/8	4/8	4/8
$c = CirusImapServer$	1/8	2/8	2/8	2/8	2/8	2/8
$c = LifeKeeper$	0	2/8	2/8	2/8	2/8	2/8
$c = SurgeMailCluster$	4/8	6/8	8/8	6/8	6/8	8/8

credibility about mechanism and component information, respectively. Thus, the support score of an specific component can be affected changing the value of α, β, or both.

Considering fixed values for α and β, we can rank the components regarding their support score for the policy. When $\alpha = \beta = 1$, SendMail becomes the component that can contribute most to an assembly's support score. If we accept the fuzzyness of available component information, we can decrease the required α and β thresholds. Other components implementing SMTP get a support score equal to 6/8 when we accept a β lower than 1.

The support score of components that implement NNTP is smaller because NNTP has a low certainty score on the *push* value of *receiver* dimension. Then, all components implementing this mechanism increase their score when α decreases. Also, DNews gets a higher score when β threshold is reduced. Architects might use this information to drive their selection process, and search information to add more precision about the support of *push* value, or about the access control mechanisms that are implemented by DNews. With such information architects might increase (or decrease) the support score for this component.

Cyrus IMAP Server and LifeKeeper have the smallest support scores. With this information, we can suspect that these components will not implement a good solution, or that they must be complemented with other component to satisfy all required policies.

SurgeMail(Cluster) looks like as the most promising option. Its support score grows when α and β become smaller. We can assume that this component might be a good solution, but it would be useful to collect more information to increase the credibility scores. If we reduce tolerance for arguments (β increases), SurgeMail(Cluster) drastically reduces its support score.

The number of possible component-sets for n components is $\sum_{i=1}^{n} \binom{n}{i}$. Architects need to reduce this number in order to diminish the complexity of their job. The Azimut framework uses several heuristics to work with a smaller number of component-sets: using only non-redundant components in each assembly, and avoiding mechanism and component combinations that are not feasible in the real world. The support score of some feasible component assemblies is shown in Table 3.

Table 3. Support Score of Assemblies

$S_{assem}(p, A, \alpha, \beta)$	$\alpha = 1$ $\beta = 1$	$\alpha = 1$ $\beta = 0.6$	$\alpha = 1$ $\beta = 0.3$
$A = SendMailv.8.1 + LifeKeeper$	6/8	8/8	8/8
$A = SurgeMail$	4/8	6/8	8/8

The component assemblies have support scores that depend on mechanism combinations. If an assembly has maximal support score, then the mechanisms implemented by its components cover all required policies (e.g. [SendMail, LifeKeeper]).

There are credibility thresholds conditions under which the architects decisions are optimal in the sense of policy coverage, even when information does not reach perfection. If the credibility of SurgeMail(Cluster) to implement SMTP-Auth goes from 0.4 to 0.9, we have that

$$S_{assem}(p, [\text{SurgeMail(Cluster)}], 1, 0.6) = 1.$$

Thus, the architects could be invited to increase the value of β in order to be more strict.

This model enables derivations rules among knowledge layers, and allows architects to know to which extent a mechanism, component or assembly does cover a given policy. For example, a comparison of assemblies [SurgeMail(Cluster)] and [SendMail,LifeKeeper] suggests quickly that support score of the latter is larger, and thus a "better" choice (similarly to decision rules used in ranking procedures by the PROMETHEE method [18]).

8.1   Supporting What-if Analysis

Dealing with fuzzyness and indeterminacy of available information implies expecting, and dealing with, changes in available information as well. The proposed process encourages architects to gather more information about mechanisms and components in order to increase their credibility factors; or to look for new mechanisms and components that could satisfy the required architectural policies.

To support these changes, the Azimut approach facilitates a what-if analysis allowing architects to consider several credibility factors to calculate the corresponding support score. For instance, if we simulate that [SurgeMail(Cluster)] has a credibility factor 0.6 in SMTP-Auth, then its score increases to 1 (with a α threshold remaining at 0.6). In such case, both assemblies [SurgeMail(Cluster)] and [SendMail,LifeKeeper] become alternative options with equal support score. And, if our selection criteria were minimal number of components, we would now select [SurgeMail(Cluster)] instead of [SendMail,LifeKeeper].

This kind of analysis enables architects to evaluate the robustness of the selection process as to how fragile is the selected assembly when available information changes.

9   Conclusions

This article has proposed a set of measures ("support scores") to aggregate imperfect information about architectural entities, allowing comparisons and ranking among candidate architectures, and thus enabling architects to explore a design space according to their preferred credibility thresholds.

The approach makes use of multi-dimensional Azimut catalogs [13], which hold information on architectural *policies*, *mechanisms* and *components*; catalogs may themselves be elaborated by third parties or by stakeholders, and can grow incrementally from new data. The key aspect of the Azimut [12] approach is the representation of quality attributes as architectural policies, their systematic reification into architectural mechanisms, and the latter's reification into components.

The described approach has three key advantages:

- it allows to evaluate components assemblies directly against NFRs satisfaction;
- it allows to record imperfect information (incomplete, imprecise and uncertain);
- it allows to evaluate and compare whole component assemblies at once.

Another characteristic is its reliance in quantitative manipulation rather than the symbolic approaches taken by most approaches; we believe that this will allow dealing with much larger design spaces, but this conjecture has not been empirically tested as yet. The simple framework here introduced is currently being expanded to fully account for indeterminacy and imprecision, and ongoing work is developing a technique to generate component assemblies by using the evaluation measures without having to explore by hand the whole design space.

References

1. Astudillo, H.; Pereira, J.; López, C.: Identifying "Interesting" Component Assemblies for NFRs Using Imperfect Information. Accepted in EWSA 2006.
2. Alves, C.; Castro, J.: "CRE: A Systematic Method for COTS Components Selection." 15th Brazilian Symposium on Software Engineering, 2001.
3. Alves, C.; Finkelstein, A.: "Challenges in COTS-Making: a Goal-Driven Requirements Engineering Perspective." Proc. 14th Intl. Conf. on SEKE 2002 (2002).
4. Britton, C.; Bye, P.: *IT Architectures and Middleware: Strategies for Building Large, Integrated Systems (2nd Ed)*. Addison-Wesley Professional, 2004.
5. Cao, F.; Bryant, B.; Raje, R.; Auguston, M.; Olson, A.; Burt, C.: "A Component Assembly Approach Based on Aspect-Oriented Generative Domain Modeling." ENTCS 2005, pp.119-136.
6. Chung, L.; Nixon, B.; Yu, E.; Mylopoulos, J.: *Non-Functional Requirements in Software Engineering*. Kluwer Academic Publisher, 2000.
7. Chung, L.; Cooper, K.: "COTS-Aware Requirements Engineering and Software Architecting." Procs. IWSSA 2004.

8. Firesmith, D.: "Specifying Reusable Security Requirements." Journal of Object Technology, 3(1), pp.61-75, 2004. http://www.jot.fm/issues/issue_2004_01/column6

9. Gokhale, A.; Balasubramanian, K.; Lu, T.: "CoSMIC: Addressing Crosscutting Deployment and Configuration Concerns of Distributed Real-Time and Embedded Systems." Procs. OOPSLA 2004, ACM Press, p. 218-219.

10. Kontio, J.: "A case study in applying a systematic method for COTS selection." Procs. ICSE 1996, p. 201-209.

11. Kunda, D.; Brooks, L.: "Applying Social-Technical Approach to COTS Selection." Procs. 4th UKAIS Conference, 1999.

12. López, C.; Astudillo, H.: "Explicit Architectural Policies to Satisfy NFRs using COTS." Workshop NfC 2005 in MoDELS'2005, Oct 2005. In: *Satellite Events at the MoDELS 2005 Conference*, J.-M. Bruel (Ed.), LNCS 3844, pp. 227-236, Springer, Jan 2006.

13. López, C.; Astudillo, H.: "Multidimensional Catalogs for Systematic Exploration of Component-Based Design Spaces". First International Workshop on Advanced Software Engineering (IWASE 2006).

14. Ncube, C.; Maiden, N.: "PORE: Procurement-Oriented Requirements Engineering Method for the CBSE Development Paradigm." International Workshop on CBSE, 1999.

15. Ochs, M.: "A COTS Acquisition Process: Definition and Application Experience." Procs. 11th ESCOM Conference, Shaker, Maastricht, 2000.

16. Object Management Group: *MDA Guide Version 1.0.1*, 2003. http://www.omg.org/cgi-bin/doc?omg/03-06-01

17. Pawlak, Z.: *Rough Sets*. Kluwer Academic Publishers, 1991.

18. Pomerol, J.C., Barba-Romero, S.: *Multicriterion Decision in Management - Principles and Practice*. Kluwer Academic Publishers, 2000.

19. Philips, B.; Polen, S.: "Add Decision Analysis to Your COTS Selection Process." *The Journal of Defense Software Engineering*, Software Technology Support Center Crosstalk, April 2002.

20. Roy, B.; McCord, M.: *Multicriteria Methodology for Decision Aiding*. Kluwer Academic Publishers, 1996.

21. Saaty, T.: *The Analytic Hierarchy Process*. New York: McGraw-Hill, 1990.

22. Shaw, M.: "Truth vs Knowledge: The Difference Between What a Component Does and What We Know It Does". Proceedings of the 8th International Workshop on Software Specification and Design (IWSSD'96), IEEE Computer Society, pp.181-185, 1996.

23. Szyperski, C.: *Component Software (2nd Ed.)*. Addison-Wesley Professional, 2002.

24. Tannenbaum, A.; van Steen, M.: *Distributed Systems Principles and Paradigms*. Prentice Hall, 2002.

25. Zadeh, L.A.: "*Fuzzy sets,*" Information & Control, Vol. 8, 1965, pp. 338-353.

26. Slack, N., Chambers, S. and Johnston, R.: *Operations Management*. Financial Times Prentice Hall, 4th edition, 2004.

27. Policy and Mechanism Definitions. http://wiki.cs.uiuc.edu/MFA/Policy+and+Mechanism

28. Authentication Mechanisms. http://sarwiki.informatik.hu-berlin.de/Authentication_Mechanisms

Building Up and Reasoning About Architectural Knowledge

Philippe Kruchten[1], Patricia Lago[2], and Hans van Vliet[2]

[1] University of British Columbia
Vancouver, Canada
pbk@ece.ubc.ca
[2] Vrije Universiteit
Amsterdam, the Netherlands
{patricia, hans}@few.vu.nl

Abstract. Architectural knowledge consists of architecture design as well as the design decisions, assumptions, context, and other factors that together determine why a particular solution is the way it is. Except for the architecture design part, most of the architectural knowledge usually remains hidden, tacit in the heads of the architects. We conjecture that an explicit representation of architectural knowledge is helpful for building and evolving quality systems. If we had a repository of architectural knowledge for a system, what would it ideally contain, how would we build it, and exploit it in practice? In this paper we describe a use-case model for an architectural knowledge base, together with its underlying ontology. We present a small case study in which we model available architectural knowledge in a commercial tool, the Aduna Cluster Map Viewer, which is aimed at ontology-based visualization. Putting together ontologies, use cases and tool support, we are able to reason about which types of architecting tasks can be supported, and how this can be done.

1 Introduction

Software that is being used, evolves. For that reason, quality issues like comprehensibility, integrity, and flexibility are important concerns. For that reason also, we not only bother about today's requirements during development but also, and maybe even more so, about the requirements of tomorrow.

This is one of the main reasons for the importance of software architecture, as for instance stated in Bass *et al.* [1]: a software architecture manifests the early design decisions. These early decisions determine the system's development, deployment, and evolution. It is the earliest point at which these decisions can be assessed.

There are many definitions of software architecture. Many talk about components and connectors, or the 'high-level conception of a system'. This high-level conception then is supposed to capture the 'major design decisions'. Whether a design decision is major or not really can only be ascertained with hindsight, when we try to change the system. Only then it will show which decisions were really important. A priori, it is

C. Hofmeister et al. (Eds.): QoSA 2006, LNCS 4214, pp. 43–58, 2006.
© Springer-Verlag Berlin Heidelberg 2006

often not at all clear if and why one design decision is more important than another one [9].

Architectural design, even well documented according to all the good recipes [5, 12, 14], is only one small part of the *Architectural Knowledge* that is required to design a system, or that is needed to guide a possibly multisite development team, or that can be exploited out of a system to build the next one, or that is required to successfully evolve a system. Van Vliet and Lago have pointed rightfully that all the assumptions that were made during the architectural design, all the linkage to the environment are a key component of architectural knowledge [16, 28]. Similarly, Bosch and others have pointed out that design decisions, the tight set of interdependencies between them, and their mapping to both the requirements, needs, constraints upstream, or the design and implementation downstream are also a key component of architectural knowledge [2, 15, 25].

We can usually get at the architectural *Design* part, ultimately by reverse engineering if there was no explicit documentation. This amounts to the *result* of the design decisions, the solutions chosen, not the reasoning behind them. The *Context* and some of the *Rationale* may be partially retrieved from management documents, vision documents, requirements specs, etc. Design *Decisions* and much of the *Rationale* are usually lost forever, or reside only in the head of the few people associated with them, if they are still around.

So the reasoning behind a design decision, and other forces that drive those decisions (such as: company policies, standards that have to be used, earlier experiences of the architect, etc.), are not explicitly captured. This is tacit knowledge, essential for the solution chosen, but not documented. At a later stage, it then becomes difficult to trace the reasons of certain design decisions. In particular, during the evolution one may stumble upon these design decisions, try to undo them or work around them, and get into trouble when this turns out to be very costly if not impossible. The future evolutionary capabilities of a system can be better assessed if this type of knowledge would be explicit. We use the term *assumptions* as a general denominator for the forces that drive architectural design decisions. Just like it is difficult to distinguish between the *what* and the *how* in software development, so that one person's requirements is another person's design, it is also difficult to distinguish between assumptions and decisions. Here too, from one perspective or stakeholder, we may denote something as an assumption, while that same thing may be seen as a design decision from another perspective. As a result, we are left with:

Architectural Knowledge = Design Decisions + Design   (1)

In this paper, we focus on the Design Decisions and their rationale. We distinguish four types of design decisions:

• **Implicit and undocumented:** the architect is unaware of the decision, or it concerns "of course" knowledge. Examples include earlier experience, implicit company policies to use certain approaches, standards, and the like.
• **Explicit but undocumented:** the architect takes a decision for a very specific reason (e.g., the decision to use a certain user-interface policy because of time constraints). The reasoning is not documented, and thus is likely to vaporize over time.

- **Explicit, and explicitly undocumented:** the reasoning is hidden. There may be tactical company reasons to do so, or the architect may have personal reasons (e.g., to protect his position).
- **Explicit and documented:** this is the preferred, but quite likely exceptional, situation.

1.1 The Role of Knowledge Management

The main value of a software company is its intellectual capital. As Rus and Lindvall [21] state: *The major problem with intellectual capital is that it has legs and walks home every day.* This is not only a problem when a key person, such as a software architect, goes on holiday, moves on to the next project, or even quits his job, but also when the company educates staff. It is in the interest of companies to transform architectural knowledge, such as design decisions, from the architects' minds to explicit knowledge on paper. Individual experts should share their knowledge amongst each other and with the rest of the company. The field of research that studies these topics is called *knowledge management.* A key motivation for our research is to support the sharing of architectural knowledge.

1.2 Dimensions of Architectural Knowledge

Nonaka and Takeuchi identify three levels of knowledge [20]:

- **Tacit:** mostly in the head of people
- **Documented:** there is some trace somewhere
- **Formalized:** not only documented, but organized in a systematic way.

The same categorization may be applied to architectural knowledge. The first three types of design decisions identified above then are examples of tacit knowledge. We aim to formalize part of this tacit knowledge. We readily recognize that only part of this knowledge can, and need, be formalized. We need only formalize what is subsequently useful to persons that exploit the architectural knowledge. To get insight into this need, we developed a use-case model for architectural knowledge.

As shown in figure 1, there is also a level of maturity of architectural knowledge: some design decisions, or elements of the design may be tentative, not fully integrated, whereas others are hard coded, immutable elements.

Finally, there is a time dimension to architectural knowledge. Certain architectural knowledge may be valid or relevant in some version of the architecture and/or system, but might be overridden, become invalid or irrelevant after a certain modification is made. Thus, we should not only retain the latest version of the architectural knowledge, but its version history as well.

1.3 Design Rationale

Capturing design rationale has been a key research topic for many years, leading to interesting models, tools and methods [4, 6, 13, 18, 19], but it has failed to transfer to practice [3, 17]. Why? This is mostly because the burden to capture assumptions and decisions outweighs largely the immediate benefits that the architect may draw. These benefits would be felt much later, or by others. If we are not careful to address the key problem: how to move this knowledge out of the tacit level into at least the documented level and then the formalized level, all what we may do with architectural knowledge could follow the same route as design rationale has done over the years: nice ideas, but not practical. One way is to automate the collection of rationale (or of decisions, or both). These observations are corroborated in a recent empirical study of architecture design rationale: documenting architecture design rationale is deemed important, but methodology and tool support is lacking [22].

1.4 Contribution of the Paper

The remainder of this paper is devoted to a discussion of what Architectural Knowledge entails, in terms of an ontology for design decisions, and typical usages thereof (with a focus on design decisions), followed by a sketch of the extent to which a commercial tool, the Aduna Cluster Map Viewer, supports the storage and use of Architectural Knowledge. This then leads to an agenda of research questions we think need answers for Architectural Knowledge modeling and usage to become a practical reality. These research questions mainly concern suitable visualization and task-specific support. As a running example, we use the set of design decisions of the SPAR Aerospace Robotic Arm. A companion paper [26] gives a more elaborate discussion of the use-case model, including a sample application of some of these use cases in an industrial application.

2   An Ontology of Design Decisions

In this section we describe an ontology of architectural design decisions, and their relationships. An earlier version hereof was published in [15]. This ontology will later be used to structure architectural knowledge of the SPAR Aerospace Robotic Arm. The use cases of section 3 refer to this structure, and tools like the Aduna Cluster Map Viewer operate on architectural knowledge structured this way.

2.1 Kinds of Architectural Design Decisions

2.1.1 Existence Decisions ("Ontocrises")
An existence decision states that some element/artifact will positively show up, i.e., will *exist* in the system's design or implementation.

There are *structural decisions* and *behavioral decisions*. Structural decisions lead to the creation of subsystems, layers, partitions, components in some view of the architecture. Behavioral decisions are more related to how the elements interact together to provide functionality or to satisfy some non functional requirement (quality attribute), or connectors. *Examples:*

− Dexterous Robot (DR) shall have a Laser Camera System.
− DR shall use the Electromagnetic (EM) communication system to communicate with GroundControl.

Existence decisions are not in themselves that important to capture, since they are the most visible element in the system's design or implementation, and the rationale can be easily captured in the documentation of the corresponding artifact or element. But we must capture them to be able to relate them to other, more subtle decisions, in particular alternatives (see section 2.3).

2.1.2 Bans or Non-existence Decisions ("Anticrises")

This is the opposite of an existence decision, stating that some element will *not* appear in the design or implementation. They are a subclass of existential decisions in a way.

This is important to document precisely because such decisions are lacking any "hooks" in traditional architecture documentation. They are not traceable to any artifact present. Ban decisions are often made as we gradually eliminate possible alternatives. *Examples:*

– DR shall not block HST solar arrays, or communications systems.

2.1.3 Property Decisions ("Diacrises")

A property decision states an enduring, overarching trait or quality of the system. Property decisions can be design rules or guidelines (when expressed positively) or design constraints (when expressed negatively), as some trait that the system will not exhibit. Properties are harder to trace to specific elements of the design or the implementation because they are often cross-cutting concerns, or they affect too many elements. Although they may be documented in some methodologies or process in Design guidelines (see RUP, for example), in many cases they are implicit and rapidly forgotten, and further design decisions are made that are not traced to properties. *Examples:*

– DR motion should be accurate to within +1 degree and +1 inch.
– DR shall withstand all loads due to launch.

2.1.4 Executive Decisions ("Pericrises")

These are the decisions that do not relate directly to the design elements or their qualities, but are driven more by the business environment (financial), and affect the development process (methodological), the people (education and training), the organization, and to a large extent the choices of technologies and tools. Executive decisions usually frame or constrain existence and property decisions. *Examples:*

- Process decisions:
– All changes in subsystem exported interfaces (APIs) must be approved by the CCB (Change Control Board) and the architecture team.
- Technology decisions:
– The system is developed using J2EE.
– The system is developed in Java.
- Tool decisions:
– The system is developed using the System Architect Workbench.

Software/system architecture encompasses far more than just views and quality attributes *à la* IEEE std 1471-2000 [13]. There are all the political, personal, cultural, financial, technological aspects that impose huge constraints, and all the associated decisions are often never captured or they only appear in documents not usually associated with software architecture.

2.2 Attributes of Architectural Design Decisions

This subsection contains a list of attributes we deem essential. It may be extended with other attributes, such as cost, or risks associated with the design decision.

2.2.1 Epitome (or the Decision Itself)
This is a short textual statement of the design decision, a few words or a one-liner. This text serves to summarize the decisions, to list them, to label them in diagrams.

2.2.2 Rationale
This is a textual explanation of the "why" of the decision, its justification. It should not simply paraphrase or repeat information captured in other attributes, but have some valued added. If the rationale is expressed in a complete external document, for example, a tradeoff analysis, then the rationale points to this document. Note that rationale has two facets: an intrinsic rationale as a property of the design decision, and an extrinsic one, represented by its relationships to other design decisions. The latter is contained in any of the relationships discussed in section 2.3.

2.2.3 Scope
Some decision may have limited scope, in time, in the organization or in the design and implementation (see the Overrides relationship below). By default (if not documented) the decision is universal. *Examples:*

- **System scope:** The Communication subsystem [is coded in C++ and not in Java]
- **Time scope:** Until the first customer release [testing is done with Glider].
- **Organization scope:** The Japanese team [uses a different bug tracking system]

2.2.4 Author, Time-Stamp, History
The person who made the decision, and when the decision was taken. Ideally we collect the history of changes to a design decision. Important are the changes of State, of course, but also changes in formulation, in scope, especially when we run incremental architectural reviews. *Example:*

- "Use the UNAS Middleware"—tentative (Ph. Kruchten, 1993-06-04); decided (Ph. Kruchten, 1993-08-05); approved, (CCB, 1994-01-16); Scope: not for test harnesses; (Jack Bell, 1994-02-01); approved (CCB, 1994-02-27).

2.2.5 State
Like problem reports or code, design decisions evolve in a manner that may be described by a state machine or a statechart. See fig.1. This scheme may be too simple for certain environments, or too complicated for others; it has to match a specific decision and approval process. The states can be used to make queries, and as a filter when visualizing a Decision Graph; for example, omit ideas, or display them in green.

You would not include the ideas, tentative, and obsolesced decisions in a formal review, for example.

There is an implied "promotion" policy, which is used to check consistency of decision graphs (models), with the level of state being successively: 0: idea and obsolesced; 1: rejected; 2: tentative and challenged; 3: decided; 4: approved.

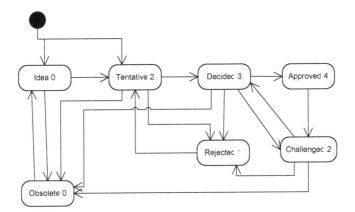

Fig. 1. State machine for a decision. **Idea**: Just an idea, captured not to be lost, when doing brainstorming, looking at other systems etc.; it cannot constrain other decisions other than ideas. **Tentative**: allows running "what if" scenarios, when playing with ideas. **Decided**: current position of the architect, or architecture team; must be consistent with other, related decisions. **Approved**: by a review, or a board (not significantly different from decided, though, in low ceremony organizations). **Challenged**: previously approved or decided decision that is now in jeopardy; it may go back to approved without ceremony, but can also be demoted to tentative or rejected. **Rejected**: decision that does not hold in the current system; but we keep them around as part of the system rationale. **Obsolesced**: Similar to rejected, but the decision was not explicitly rejected (in favor of another one for example), but simply became 'moot', irrelevant as a result of some higher level restructuring, for example.

2.2.6 Categories
A design decision may belong to one or more categories. The list of categories is open ended; you could use them as some kind of keywords.

Categories will complement the taxonomy expressed above, if this taxonomy is not sufficient for large projects. (There is a danger in pushing taxonomy too far, too deep too early; it stifles creativity.) Categories are useful for queries, and for creating and exploring sets of design decisions that are associated to a specific concern or quality attribute. *Examples:*

- Usability
- Security

But the architects may be more creative and document also Politics: tagging decisions that have been made only on a political basis; it maybe useful to revisit them once the politics change. *Example:*

- "Use GIS Mapinfo" in Categories: politics, usability, safety, COTS

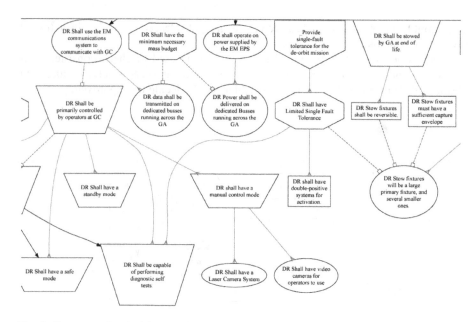

Fig. 2. Fragment of a decision graph for the SPAR Aerospace Dexterous Robotic Arm (DR). (Courtesy Nicolas Kruchten & Michael Trauttmansdorff)

2.3 Relationships Between Architectural Design Decisions

Decision A *"is Related to"* Decision B. This way, decisions form a graph-like structure. The use cases of section 3 refer to this structure, and the example in section 4 uses one. In the next subsections we discuss an initial set of relations between design decisions.

2.3.1 Constrains
Decision B is tied to Decision A. If decision A is dropped, then decision B is dropped. Decision B is contingent to decision A, and cannot be promoted higher than decision A. The pattern is often that a property decision (rule or constraint) constrains an existence decision, or that an executive decision (process or technology) constrains a property decision or an existence decision. *Examples:*

– "Must use J2EE" constrains "use JBoss"; taking the dotNet route instead of J2EE would make JBoss the wrong choice.

2.3.2 Forbids (Excludes)
A decision prevents another decision to be made. The target decision is therefore not possible. In other words, decision B can only be promoted to a state higher than 0 if decision A is demoted to a state of 0. (cf. section 2.2.5)

2.3.3 Enables
Decision A makes possible Decision B, but does not make B taken. Also B can be decided even if A is not taken. It is a weak form of Constrains. *Example:*

– "use Java" enables "use J2EE"

2.3.4 Subsumes

A is a design decision that is wider, more encompassing than B. *Example:*

– "All subsystems are coded in Java" subsumes "Subsystem XYZ is coded in Java"
Often a tactical decision B has been made, which is later on generalized to A. It is
often the case that the design decision could be reorganized to connect relatives of B
to A, and to obsolesce B (B can be removed from the graph).

2.3.5 Conflicts with

A symmetrical relationship indicating that the two decisions A and B are mutually
exclusive (though this can be sorted out by additional scoping decisions, cf. 0). *Example:*

– "Must use dotNet" conflicts with "Must use J2EE"

2.3.6 Overrides

A local decision A that indicates an exception to B, a special case or a scope where
the original B does not apply. *Example:*

– "The Communication subsystem will be coded in C++" overrides "The whole
system is developed in Java"

2.3.7 Comprises (Is Made of, Decomposes into)

A high level and somewhat complicated, wide-ranging decision A is made of or
decomposes into a series of narrower, more specific design decisions B1, B2, ... Bn.
This is the case in high-level existence decisions, where partitioning or decomposing
the system can be decomposed in one decision for each element of the decomposition.
Or the choice of a middleware system, which implies a choice of various mechanisms
for communication, error reporting, authentication, etc. This is stronger than
constrains, in the sense that if the state of A is demoted, all the Bi are demoted too.
But each B may be individually overridden.

Many of the rationale, alternatives etc. can be factored out and associated with the
enclosing decision to avoid duplication, while details on a particular topic are
documented where they belong. *Examples:*

– "Design will use UNAS as middleware" decomposes into
– "Rule: cannot use Ada tasking" and "Message passing must use UNAS messaging
services" and "Error Logging must use UNAS error logging services" and etc.

2.3.8 Is an Alternative to

A and B are similar design decisions, addressing the same issue, but proposing
different choices. This allows keeping around the discarded choices, or when
brainstorming to relate the various possible choices.

Note that not all alternatives are conflicts, and not all conflicts are alternatives. But
A conflicts with B is resolved by making A obsolete and an alternative to B.

2.3.9 Is Bound to (Strong)

This is a bidirectional relationship where A constrains B and B constrains A, which
means that the fate of the two decisions is tied, and they should be in the same state.

2.3.10 Is Related to (Weak)

There is a relation of some sort between the two design decisions, but it is not of any
kind listed above and is kept mostly for documentation and illustration reasons.

Examples are high level decisions that only provide the frame for other design decisions, while not being a true constraint (2.3.1) nor a decomposition (2.3.7).

2.3.11 Dependencies

We say that a decision A depends on B if B constrains A (2.3.1), if B decomposes in A (2.3.7), if A overrides B (2.3.6). See figure 2 for an example of decision graph that depicts a number of such dependencies.

2.4 Relationship with External Artifacts

Decisions are not only related to other decisions, but also to other artifacts, such as requirements or parts of the implemented system (i.e. the Architectural Design, the models, the code). Example relationships in this category are `traces from' and `does not comply with'.

3 A Use Case Model for Architectural Knowledge

Assuming for a while that we have defined a repository of architectural knowledge in the form of all design decisions, how would we use it? Who would use it, to do what? Ultimately, every bit of architectural knowledge stored should be used in at least one use case and, conversely, every use case should be answerable from the architectural knowledge captured. A use-case model has at minimal *actors* (what are the various roles involved) and *use cases* (what do these roles do).

3.1 Actors

Who would use, produce, and exploit Architectural Knowledge from our repository?

• *Architects*: the people designing the system (or a part of a large system). They need to document much of the design, they should bring the decisions and assumptions from tacit to documented or formalized
• *Other architects*: People who are designing parts that integrate with that system. They need to understand the parts not directly under their responsibility, to see what impact it has on their decisions.
• *Developers*: People involved in the implementation of the design and decisions.
• *Reviewers*: people involved in judging the quality or progress of a design
• *Analysts*: Mostly, people dealing with requirements they are interested in
• *Maintainers*: while evolving or correcting the system they need to understand the correlation between decisions they take and the current set of decisions.
• *Users*: Not the end-users of the system, but people who use Architectural Knowledge, for example to interface another system, to document the system etc.
• *Re-Users*: people who want to exploit all or some of the Architectural Knowledge to build a new system
• *Students*: people who want to study software architecture by looking at Architectural Knowledge from various angles

- *Researchers*: Researchers may want to look at Architectural Knowledge to find new patterns, new information, better mousetraps.
- *Software tools*: Tools may both add to the AK repository, or exploit automatically some of the contents (consistency checking, pattern recognition, report generation, etc.)

From this list we can identify roles of *passive users or consumers* of Architectural Knowledge: people who need to exploit Architectural Knowledge for their own understanding but who are not going to alter it or expand it. Examples are Developers, Reviewers, and Students.

Other roles are those of *active users or producers* of architectural knowledge: they add to the Architectural Knowledge repository, integrate it, mature the information in it. Examples include Architects and Software tools.

3.2 Use Cases

From interviews held with practicing architects, as well as our own experience, we identified the following initial set of use cases:

- *Incremental architectural review:* what pieces of Architectural Knowledge have been added or modified since the last review? Extract and visualize these elements; browse and explore dependencies or traces.
- *Review for a specific concern:* from a given perspective (such as security, safety, reuse, etc.) what are the knowledge elements involved? This consists in building in some sense a "view" of Architectural Knowledge restricted to that concern.
- *Evaluate impact:* if we want to do a change in an element, what are the elements impacted (decisions, and elements of design). This may branch out to various kinds of changes: change of an assumption, change of a design decision.
- *Get a rationale*: given an element in the design, trace back to the decisions it is related to.
- *Study the chronology:* over a time line, find what the sequence of design decisions has been.
- *Add a decision:* manually or via some tool; then integrate the decision to other elements of Architectural Knowledge. (Similarly for other AK elements).
- *Cleanup the system:* make sure that all consequences of a removed decision have been removed.
- *Spot the subversive stakeholder:* identify who are the stakeholders whose changes of mind are doing the most damage to the system.
- Similar but different, *Spot the critical stakeholder:* the stakeholder who seems to have the most "weight" on the decisions, and who therefore maybe the one that could be most affected by the future evolution of the system.
- *Clone Architectural Knowledge:* produce a consistent subset of Architectural Knowledge to prime the pump for a new system (reuse Architectural Knowledge).
- *Integration:* you want to integrate multiple systems and decide whether they fit. The tool would help answering questions about integration strategies.
- *Detection and interpretation of patterns:* are there patterns in the graphs that can be interpreted in a useful fashion, and lead to guidelines for the architects. For example: decisions being hubs ("God" decisions), circularity, decisions that gain weight over time and are more difficult to change or remove.

4 Ontology-Based Information Visualization: A Case Study

Aduna Cluster Map Viewer[1] [8] is a tool to visualize ontologies that describe a domain through a set of classes and their hierarchical relationships. In such ontologies, classes often share instances: a software architect can be both a security expert and involved in project X. The Aduna Cluster Map Viewer is especially well suited to graphically depict such relationships. Based on a user query, it selects and displays the set of objects that satisfy the query. Objects belonging to the same cluster are depicted in one bubble. Clusters can belong to one or more classes.

Figure 3 shows part of the XML representation of the set of design decisions for the SPAR Aerospace Robotic Arm that is used as input to the Aduna Cluster Map Viewer.

```
- <ObjectSet>
  - <Object ID="obj2">
      <Name>Motion should be accurate to
            within +1 degree and +1 inch</Name>
    </Object>
  - <Object ID="obj33">
      <Name>Shall withstand all loads due to launch</Name>
    </Object>
    <\ObjectSet>
- <ClassificationSet>
  - <Classification ID="onto">
      <Name>Ontocrises</Name>
      <Objects objectIDs="obj2 obj4 … obj33 …" />
      <SuperClass refs="kind" />
  - <Classification ID="system">
      <Name>System</Name>
      <Objects objectIDs="… obj32 obj33 …" />
      <SuperClass refs="scope" />
    </Classification>
  - </Classification>
      <Name>Approved</Name>
      <Objects objectIDs="obj1 obj2 …" />
      <SuperClass refs="state" />
    </Classification>
  <\ClassificationSet
```

Fig. 3. XML representation of design decisions. We have employed a taxonomy where the class DesignDecision has four subclassses: Kind (ontocrises, anticrises, etc; see section 2.1), Scope (System, Time, Organization; see section 2.2.3) and State (Idea, Tentative, etc; see section 2.2.5). We list here two design decisions, labeled obj1 and obj2. It further states that decisions labeled obj2, obj3 … are of type Ontocrises, while obj1, obj2 … have state Approved, Finally, decisions obj32, obj33 … have a System scope.

The same set of design decisions represented in XML in figure 3 is used to get the visualization of the example cluster map in Figure 4.

---

[1] http://aduna.biz/products/technology/clustermap

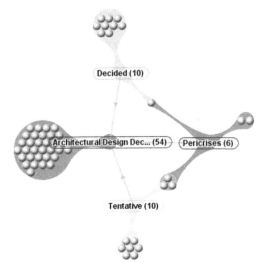

Fig. 4. The decisions are split into two types: pericrises and 'the rest'. For each of the decisions a state has been determined. State 'decided' contains the decisions that have been marked as decided. The figure shows the overlap between the clusters of all decisions, those that are pericrises, those that have been decided upon and those that are tentative. It shows that 10 decisions have been marked as decided, one of which falls in the class of pericrises. Of the remaining five pericrises, three are tentative.

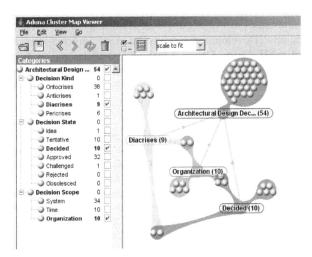

Fig. 5. Screenshot of Aduna Cluster Map Viewer. The left pane shows the various categories distinguished. It is generated from the XML file fed into the system. The user clicks the categories he is interested in. The right pane shows the results, including the intersections of the various sets. In this case, it shows the overlap between the clusters of all decisions, all diacrises, that are decided, and all organization-scoped decisions. A total of 10 decisions have been marked as decided, of which two fall in the class of diacrises, and three others are limited to organization scope. Of the remaining seven organization-scoped decisions, two are diacrises as well, but none of these are marked decided.

Figure 5 shows a screenshot of the Aduna Cluster Map Viewer. The selection panel on the left hand side is used to build a query whose result is depicted on the right hand side. Suppose we want to carry out some of the use cases in section 3.2. How would a tool like the Aduna Cluster Map Viewer aid the architecting process? For example, we can carry out 'clone AK' to create a new system by reusing all 'system' level decisions that are in state 'decided' (see Fig. 3). Use cases 'spot the critical stakeholder' and 'review for a specific concern' can be supported in a rather straightforward way by selecting all decisions that match a certain attribute value. 'Add a decision' or 'get a rationale' are realized by making selections or adding elements in the left pane (see Fig. 5).

This small case study shows that the Aduna Cluster Map Viewer can support many of our use cases in a rather straightforward way. A further discussion of tool support is given in section 5.

5   Conclusions

In this paper we discuss the notion of architectural knowledge, in particular the design decision part thereof. If we had a repository of architectural knowledge for a system, what would it ideally contain, how would we build it, and exploit it in practice? We describe a use case model for an architectural knowledge system, together with its underlying ontology. We present a small case study in which we model available architectural knowledge in a tool, the Aduna Cluster Map Viewer. Part of the use cases are handled by the tool, and part need further extension of the tool.

One of the most interesting unsolved issues is how to visualize architectural knowledge. The amount of information is overwhelming, so we have to abstract away from a lot of details. Developments in the area of information visualization are relevant here [7, 10, 27]. Most of these visualizations abstract away from details in the graph representation, and present the result in terms of tree maps, radial or conical representations, and the like. Fig. 2 gives an idea of a visualization of design decisions and constraints/requirements. In our opinion, though, this is not enough. The visualizations have to direct our attention to the very issue we want to convey, such as the subversive or critical stakeholder. For example, the Challenger accident in 1986 was ultimately due to low temperature. This problem had occurred before, but the link between low temperature and the rubber ring damage was not assessed and recognized until the right visualization was given [24].

If we can link our ontology of design decisions to the contents of actual design documents, we may exploit ontology-based browsers such as the Aduna Cluster Map Viewer [8] to explore these resources. This is a kind of data mining operation on documents containing architectural knowledge, with a targeted visualization. One such approach, using information retrieval techniques to obtain traceability information, is described in [11]. Assuming we have captured architectural knowledge as discussed above in some graph-like form, where the edges represent design decisions, and the vertices represent relationships between decisions, the different use cases correspond to certain operations on this graph. Some of these operations are relatively straightforward. They correspond to a subset operation (Clone AK, Review for a specific concern) or closure operation (Evaluate impact,

Cleanup the system).   An interesting variation of change impact analysis using Bayesian Belief Networks is discussed in [23]. A more interesting operation has to do with the detection or matching of patterns or, rather, antipatterns. Some of these can be cast as graph operations; for example the detection of a "God" decision boils down to selecting nodes with a high fan-in/fan-out. The identification and operationalization of time-related patterns still is an open issue.

We might think of a series of plug-ins/services that each supports a specific use case and an appropriate visualization for that use case. For instance, the use case examples used in section 4 are all based on the analysis of flat subsets, and show that a tool like the Aduna Cluster Map Viewer might prove useful for browsing the design decision space. Instead, we might need another tool (and another type of visualization) to carry out use cases needing to traverse a hierarchical structure of design decisions and other knowledge entities. For instance, a tool visualizing directed graphs in two- or three-dimensional space seems better suited for use cases like 'evaluate impact' or 'study the chronology', which require to visualize not only categories of entities but also how these entities are related.

From this exercise, as well as our earlier experiences, we corroborate that tool support for manipulating architectural knowledge should focus on two crucial issues: suitable visualization, and task-specific support.

The list of use cases and associated operations needs further underpinning. We are currently in the process of validating and prioritizing this list with architects and development groups in various commercial settings.

Acknowledgements

This research has partially been sponsored by the Dutch Joint Academic and Commercial Quality Research & Development (Jacquard) program on Software Engineering Research via contract 638.001.406 GRIFFIN: a GRId For inFormatIoN about architectural knowledge, and by an Eclipse Innovation grant from IBM.

References

1. Bass, L., et al.: Software Architecture in Practice. Addison-Wesley, Reading, MA (2003).
2. Bosch, J.: Software Architecture: the Next Step. In *First European Workshop on Software Architecture (EWSA 2004)*, (2004), Springer-Verlag, 194-199.
3. Buckingham Shum, S. Analyzing the usability of a Design Rational Notation. In Moran, T.P. and Carroll, J.M. eds. *Design Rationale Concepts, Techniques, and Use*, Lawrence Erlbaum Associates, Mahwah, NJ (1996) 185-215.
4. Burge, J.E. and Brown, D.C. Reasoning with design rationale. In Gero, J.S. ed. *Artificial Intelligence in Design '00*, Kluwer Academic Publishers, Netherlands (2000) 611-629.
5. Clements, P., Bachmann, F., Bass, L., et al.: Documenting Software Architectures: Views and Beyond. Addison-Wesley, Boston (2002).
6. Conklin, J. and Begeman, M.L.: gIBIS: A tool for all reasons. *Journal of the American Society for Information Science*, 40 (1989).
7. Fekete, J.-D.: The InfoVis Toolkit. In *IEEE Symposium on Information Visualization 2004 (INFOVIS'04)*, (2004), 167-174.

8. Fluit, C., Sabou, M. and van Harmelen, F. Ontology-based information visualisation. In Geroimenko, V. and Chen, C. eds. *Visualising the Semantic Web*, Springer-Verlag (2005).
9. Fowler, M.: Who Needs an Architect. *IEEE Software*, 20 (5) (2003) 11-13.
10. Granitzer, M., Kienreich, W., Sabol, V., et al.: Evaluating a System for Interactive Exploration of Large, Hierarchically Structured Document Repositories. In *IEEE Symposium on Information Visualization 2004 (INFOVIS'04)*, (2004), IEEE CS, 127-133.
11. Hayes, J.H., Dekhtyar, A. and Sundaram, S.K.: Improving After-the-Fact Tracing and Mapping: Supporting Software Quality Predictions. *IEEE Software*, 22 (2005) 30-37.
12. IEEE standard 1471:2000--Recommended practice for architectural description of software intensive systems. *IEEE*, Los Alamitos, CA (2000).
13. Klein, M. DRCS: An Integrated System for Capture of Designs and Their Rationale. In Gero, J.S. ed. *Artificial Intelligence in Design '92*, Kluwer AP (1993) 393-412.
14. Kruchten, P.: The 4+1 View Model of Architecture. *IEEE Software*, 12 (6) (1995) 45-50.
15. Kruchten, P.: An Ontology of Architectural Design Decisions. In 2nd *Groningen Workshop on Software Variability Management*, (2004), Rijksuniversiteit Groningen.
16. Lago, P. and van Vliet, H.: Explicit Assumptions Enrich Architectural Models. In *proceeding of ICSE 2005*, (2005), ACM Press, 206-214.
17. Lee, J.: Design Rationale: Understanding the Issues. *IEEE Expert 12* (1997) 78-85.
18. Lee, J.: SIBYL: a tool for managing group design rationale. In *ACM conference on Computer-supported cooperative work (CSCW90)*, (1990), 79 - 92.
19. Myers, K.L., Zumel, N.B. and Garcia, P.: Acquiring Design Rationale Automatically. *Artificial Intelligence for Engineering Design, Analysis and Manufacturing*, 14 (2000).
20. Nonaka, I., and Takeuchi, H.: The Knowledge-Creating Company: How Japanese Companies Create the Dynamics of Innovation, Oxford University Press (1995).
21. Rus, I. and Lindvall, M.: Knowledge Management in Software Engineering. *IEEE Software*, 19 (2002) 26-38.
22. Tang, A., Babar, M.A., Gorton, I., et al.: A Survey of Architecture Design Rationale. In *WICSA 5*, (2005), IEEE CS.
23. Tang, A., Nicholson, A., Jin, Y., et al.: Using Bayesian Belief Networks for Change Impact Analysis in Architecture Design. In WICSA 5, (2005), IEEE CS.
24. Tufte, E.R.: Visual explanations: images and quantities, evidence and narrative. *Graphics Press LLC*, Cheshire, CO (1997).
25. Tyree, J. and Akerman, A.: Architecture Decisions: Demystifying Architecture. *IEEE Software*, 22 (2005) 19-27.
26. van der Ven, J.S., et al. Using Architectural decisions. In Hofmeister, C., Crnkovic, I., Reussner, R. and Becker, S. eds. Perspectives in Software Architecture Quality, Universitaet Karlsruhe, Fakultaet fuer Informatik (2006).
27. van Ham, F.: Using Multilevel Call Matrices in Large Software Projects. In *IEEE Symposium on Information Visualization 2003 (INFOVIS'03)*, (2003), IEEE CS, 227-232.

Managing Architectural Design Decisions for Safety-Critical Software Systems

Weihang Wu and Tim Kelly

Department of Computer Science, University of York, York YO10 5DD
{Weihang.Wu, Tim.Kelly}@cs.york.ac.uk

Abstract. In this paper, we propose a negative scenario framework along with a mitigation action model as the linkage between safety quality attribute and architecture definition. The scenario framework provides an effective means of formulating safety concerns. The mitigation action model facilitates exploitation and codification of existing safety-critical system design knowledge. Finally, we present a series of steps that enable the justification of architectural design decisions that refine both requirements and architectures. We demonstrate and discuss the application of our framework by means of a case study.

1 Introduction

Over the last decade, the importance of quality requirements (characterised by quality attributes) has been well recognised in architectural design. Recently, the SEI[1] has established a design methodology termed *Attributed-Driven Design* (ADD) [6] to emphasise the active role of quality attributes (QAs) in architecture design. Quality attributes can be achieved by a set of design options ranging from coarse-grained design patterns to more finer-grained design techniques. The success of the design of an architecture thus lies with judicious decisions made when selecting the appropriate design options and composing the selected options into the architecture. Among quality attributes, a great significance has been given to software risks in the safety-critical system domain. Examples of the most serious computer-related accidents in the past 20 years such as Therac-25 [12] and Ariane 5 [13] can be attributed to flawed system and software architectures. However, existing practice fails to systematise architectural design approaches to addressing these safety concerns.

In this paper, we examine the factors involved in making the principled choices within a safety-related architectural design space and present an approach to rationalising the architectural decisions behind the selection and the impacts on both requirements specification and architectural modelling. The paper is organised in the following sections. Section 2 introduces the key concept of the "safety" quality attribute and existing practice in architectural design for safety. Section 3 presents our framework for decision making. Section 4 demonstrates this framework by means of a case study. Section 5 discusses preliminary findings and related work. Finally, section 6 presents concluding remarks.

---

[1] Software Engineering Institute at Carnegie Mellon University.

C. Hofmeister et al. (Eds.): QoSA 2006, LNCS 4214, pp. 59–77, 2006.
© Springer-Verlag Berlin Heidelberg 2006

2 Safety and Architecture

Safety is freedom from accidents or losses; software safety implies the contribution of software to safety in its system context [12]. The remainder of this section analyses the concept of safety as a quality attribute in terms of its underlying concerns and discusses existing solutions and their limitations.

2.1 Safety as a Quality Attribute

Like security, at the heart of defining the safety attribute is the identification and evaluation of *negative* requirements such as unwanted or unplanned events and conditions. Typically, the safety lifecycle [2] starts by identifying negative requirements over existing system-level context. Safety requirements are then derived by choosing appropriate mitigation mechanisms to protect against the negative requirements identified. These safety requirements will in turn act as the constraints on the system and software design. Chosen mitigations may themselves bring new safety problems. New mitigations may thus need to be identified and safety requirements refined. The problem is complicated by the fact that the details of the system are often unavailable until the late stages of development. Hence, a key question is how to elicit and formulate the negative requirements along with the corresponding mitigation mechanisms in co-ordination with the architectural design process in an evolutionary manner.

Another vital aspect of safety is risk. From an engineering standpoint, there is no such thing as absolute safety. Safety is often defined as the measure of the degree of the freedom of risk under all conditions [12]. The basic tenet of evaluating safety-critical systems is thus to ensure that these systems present an acceptable level of risk balanced with their cost. Therefore, an important question is how to integrate risk assessment and cost benefit analysis with the safety design process.

Finally, safety is an emergent system property and it is not possible to take a single system component such as a software module in isolation to assess its safety. In practice, the emergent safety properties are enforced by a set of safety constraints upon the architecture. At the top level of design, these safety constraints are imposed upon the whole system (i.e., the system under design and its environment) and often expressed in an absolute functional form (e.g., 'must' or 'must not'). As the design process progresses, the safety constraints are eventually refined into other quality requirements such as performance and availability targets allocated onto the behaviours of relevant architectural components. Inevitably, our concern is thus how to capture such a linkage between safety and non-safety qualities.

2.2 Design for Safety

A large number of design techniques for safety have emerged in both research and practice. Safety is thus achieved by deciding upon the appropriate design techniques to be employed in a specific system context. In general, current practice advocates two classes of design approaches:

- *Process-based approaches.* Industrial safety standards such as IEC 61508 [2] prescribe a set of safety design techniques with respect to the classification of safety criticality. However, there is lack of practical guidance on demonstrating further how to exploit these techniques to tackle specific safety concerns. Moreover, most standards such as ARP 4761 [1] and IEC 61508 dictate the allocation of safety functions over software and hardware but fail to explore the cost/benefit tradeoffs behind allocation decisions.
- *Architectural patterns.* Architectural patterns have recently influenced the development of dependable systems. Examples of safety patterns can be found in Douglass' work [9]. Yet the coarse-grained nature of design patterns makes it difficult to reason precisely about the achievement of desired safety properties and the design tradeoffs involved [18].

Many advances have been made in the theory and principles of system and software safety, yet existing practice in architectural design for safety still remains ad hoc. We argue that this is due to lack of principled basis for choosing appropriate protection mechanisms and poor integration of system development process with the safety lifecycle. The work outlined in this paper follows by our previous work on safety tactics [18] and refines it by exploring the inter-dependencies between safety requirements, safety-related design decisions and architectures. In order for this approach to be successful, the following four challenges must be addressed:

- What is the precise meaning of safety concerns and mitigation approaches?
- How can you discover and evaluate these safety concerns with the aid of safety assessment activities?
- How can you identify and select mitigation approaches with respect to the safety concerns identified and tradeoffs involved?
- How do you compose the mitigation approaches selected into both the requirements specification and the architecture?

3 Proposed Framework

The aim of this framework is to provide practical guidance on identifying plausible architectural decisions and justifying the decisions made in an iterative and incremental manner. There are two important assumptions in the proposed approach. Firstly, our process assumes implicitly parallel development of requirements and architectures, as recognised by the Twin Peaks model [14]. Another assumption is the co-design of system and software architectures by means of architectural views. From the perspective of embedded system development, we argue that both the system and software architectures are key to realising dependability requirements. System architecture provides the system-level context from which the software architecture is built. Moreover, unifying the design of system and software architectures can effectively facilitate safety tradeoffs across the software/system boundaries. For example, system architecture may be designed to mitigate faults emerging from software architecture, and vice versa. The notion of architectural views provides an effective mechanism to restrict our attention on a selected portion of the system or software architecture. Views can be grouped in terms of architectural characteristics. Clements et al [6] define three common sets of views: module views, component & connector (C&C) views, and allocation views. Other common classifications can be logical and physical views [8], and Kruchten's 4+1 views [11]. The number of views needed is driven by the needs or concerns of stakeholders; architects are free to choose the views if applicable. The remainder of this section explains the key concepts in our approach and how they are organised in a decision-driven design process.

3.1   Conceptual Model

The conceptual model supporting our approach comprises three sets of information that are captured and manipulated in the design process: the core requirements set, deviation analysis set, and architecture set. More specifically, the core requirements set represents the system functionality and desired qualities, the architecture set reflects the current state of the corresponding architectural solution, and the analysis set regulates the decision-making procedure by providing a mechanism for identifying and evaluating potential quality concerns along with the mitigations that emerge in the design process. Figure 1 describes the conceptual model using UML notation [3]. The communication between the requirements and architecture domains is facilitated via the deviation analysis set (i.e., the identification of negative requirements, risks, and mitigation actions informed by design knowledge). Therefore the formulation of the deviation analysis set lies at the heart of our approach. We will now discuss the three sets in more detail.

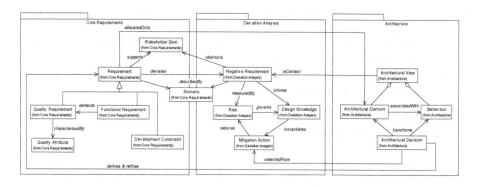

Fig. 1. The conceptual model

The Core Requirements Set

The core requirements set contains a set of essential requirements, which describe the related characteristics that a system is required to have. The root source of these comprehensive requirements is always the needs of the stakeholders, which are captured by the *Stakeholder Goal* entity. Requirements can be further categorised as functional requirements, quality requirements and development constraints. Functional requirements describe the required behaviours and features of the system. Quality requirements, collectively known as *quality attributes*, express the related characteristics of the system orthogonal to functionality. In practice, functional and quality requirements must exist together, as shown in Figure 1 by their participation in the *demands* relationship. Development constraints such as cost and resource budgets are system characteristics that will limit the whole system development choices available when attempting to meet the functional and quality requirements.

One valuable way of articulating functional and quality requirements is the use of scenarios (e.g., use cases [11] and SEI's quality-attribute-scenario framework [6] respectively). A scenario is simply a perceived story of the usage of a system under specific situations. Finally, the *derives & refines* relationship expresses the fact that requirements are often first stated in a general and abstract form, then restated in more detail as the design process progresses. This relationship explicitly links the requirements derived through design decisions made in the architecture set.

The Architecture Set

Within the architecture set, the system and software architectures are represented by a number of architectural views, each having a coherent collection of architectural elements with associated behaviours. While the views chosen and level of detail of a system may vary, at a minimum, the architecture set serves as a repository for architectural decisions made that will transform an abstract and provisional design solution into an intermediate solution and eventually into a detailed and stable solution. The transformation caused by architectural decisions can exist in the following two ways:

- The addition or removal of specific architectural elements (a.k.a., decomposition decisions)
- Reallocation responsibilities over existing architectural elements (a.k.a, allocation decisions)

As described in section 1, architectural decisions are decisions regarding design options identified in the deviation set.

Negative Requirements and Risks

Negative requirements have long been interest to the dependability community. Proper interpretation of negative requirements is critical to proper architectural solutions. In contrast with (positive) requirements, negative requirements describe the related characteristics that the system is not allowed to have, which otherwise together with specific conditions in the environment of the system will inevitably lead to the inability of the system to fulfil (positive) requirements, thereby obstructing the plan of achieving the stakeholders' goals. At an architectural level, the most significant classes of negative requirements are those leading to inability to fulfil the quality requirements, which we explicitly label *anti-quality requirements*. Example of anti-quality requirements can be system hazards (with respect to safety), system vulnerabilities (with respect to security), or bottlenecks (with respect to performance).

Regardless of the types of negative requirements, there is a common principle underlying them: i.e., causality. For example, what is the impact that results from a change? What causes an accident? There are three elements in causality: the cause, effect, and the causal agent who generates the cause [17]. Likewise, negative requirements can be articulated by means of scenarios. Inspired by the SEI's quality-attribute scenario framework, we here propose a negative scenario framework to capture anti-quality requirements. It consists of six parts:

- *Source*. The entity that generates the stimulus. The source is derived from a specific architectural element under consideration within a chosen view, which can come from the environment of the system or inside the system.
- *Stimulus*. An undesired condition or event that needs to be considered from the perspective of a specific quality. In our framework, the stimulus is identified by deviation analysis with the aid of proper guidewords.
- *Trigger*. The conditions under which the stimulus will be generated from the source. The trigger conditions are identified by deductive analysis performed over the chosen view. They may come from the propagation of other negative scenarios identified in the same view or be generated from the related views.
- *Environment*. The environmental conditions under which the stimulus will inevitably lead to the occurrence of the end effect. If these conditions do not exist, then by definition there will be no end effect.
- *End effect*. An undesired event that results in a specified level of loss or harm. The end effect must be defined with respect to the boundary of the same view from which the stimulus is identified.
- *Effect measure*. Typically the likelihood of the end effect, the severity, or their combination (i.e. risk). The values can be qualitative or quantitative.

There are several things to note about the expression of the negative scenarios. Firstly, the definition of a scenario depends upon the architectural context (i.e. the boundaries of existing architectural views and the current level of abstraction), as shown by the *inContext* relationship in Figure 1. From the perspective of an evolutionary system development process, it is necessary to proceed from a coarse view of the negative scenarios to a more refined view that provides a more satisfactory explanation, as the design process progresses. A typical example is the system decomposition, in which system-level scenarios are refined into component-level scenarios. Nevertheless, the evaluation of the *end effect* part is usually performed in a bottom-up manner. Table 1 illustrates anti-safety requirement "inadvertent deployment of thrust reverser" for an aircraft engine control system. This scenario is based upon the architectural context that an aircraft engine contains a thrust reverser as part of the aircraft braking function, which will be activated upon the arrival of specific airframe data. The *end effect* part of this scenario should be evaluated not only for the engine system level but also for the operational platform (i.e. at the aircraft level).

Secondly, the framework is inherently causal. Figure 2 illustrates the causal chain behind the framework. The effectiveness of architectural design for quality attributes thus lies at identifying where and how to 'break' this causal chain: e.g., to stop the generation of stimulus, or to prevent the propagation of the stimulus.

Thirdly, both the *stimulus* and *environment* parts can contribute to the *end effect*. Nevertheless, the *stimulus* is defined with respect to the environment of its source, and the environmental conditions are most likely normal events that cannot be eliminated by the designer. For that reason, conditions such as "airplane is in the air" should be recorded in the *environment* rather than the *stimulus* part. In many cases, we need to consider multiple environmental conditions such as normal and degraded modes in order to determine a full range of end effects.

Finally, each negative scenario inherently represents a *risk scenario*. Accordingly, a risk-based model can be built to support a rational decision-making process, as detailed in section 3.2. It is very likely that a scenario may have end effects on multiple attributes, all of which must be evaluated. For instance, a single system upgrade may affect not just modifiability but also performance, usability and safety. We thus need to measure the worst-case end effect (i.e. the most credible and critical one) as the *effect measure* part.

Table 1. The negative scenario – inadvertent deployment of reverser

Portion of Scenario	Possible Value
Stimulus	Inadvertent deployment of reverser
Source	Aircraft engine
Trigger	Invalid airframe data; airframe data transmission loss; engine commission failure
Environment	Airframe is in air
End effect	Physical damage to the engine; loss of controlled flight
Effect measure	Frequency: probable, Severity: catastrophic/critical

Fig. 2. The causal chain underlying the negative scenario framework

Mitigation Actions and Design Knowledge

A mitigation action represents an abstract design option for an architect that helps address a specific concern. In general, each attribute community has a collection of their own well-developed mitigation actions. Much work has been done in codifying design knowledge as the linkage between quality attributes and corresponding mitigation. For example, the SEI has codified a set of mitigation approaches (coined *architectural tactics*) with respect to six common system qualities such as performance in [6]. We added tactics for the safety attribute in [18]. However, the linkage between quality concerns and appropriate mitigation actions is still largely undefined. We observe that the mitigation actions are closely linked to the negative scenario framework. Broadly speaking, the adoption of an action is intended to offer protection against the occurrence of a specific negative scenario. This is achieved by controlling the causal factors (i.e., the *source, stimulus, trigger, environment* and *end effect* parts) behind the scenario. We represent this relationship in Figure 3. We thus propose four classes of mitigation approaches that are usually applied with the following precedence. Note that the design precedence does not imply just one of these classes should be taken. Rather, all are necessary unless the scenario has been mitigated sufficiently (e.g., the effect measure is within the tolerable region or broadly acceptable region in terms of ALARP model [2]).

1. *Elimination.* The aim of this class of actions is to remove the stimulus. It can be achieved by either removing the source of the stimulus or inhibiting all necessary trigger conditions of stimulus generation.
2. *Reduction.* This class of actions are used to reduce the occurrence of the stimulus. As a result, the end effect is less likely. This can be done by erecting barriers against the stimulus generation or inhibiting some of the trigger conditions.

3. *Resistance*. This type of mitigation is intended to stop the propagation of the stimulus into the end effect or switch to a desired system state. In many cases, the effectiveness of resistance actions lies at the detectability of the stimulus.
4. *Minimisation*. If the occurrence of the end effect is unavoidable, this class of actions provide options to reduce potential loss or harm. It is usually done by providing warning or contingency actions or facilitating emergency procedures.

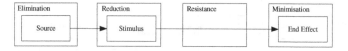

Fig. 3. Four roots of possible mitigation actions

From the above classification, a plausible design approach is to use the negative scenarios as primary to inform possible mitigation action candidates (i.e. architectural design space). In practice, the five parts of the scenario framework are not necessarily controllable. For the example scenario recorded in Table 1, effective mitigation options can be to reduce the occurrence of inadvertent deployment by validating airframe data and requiring data sample rates, or to detect and resist against the inadvertent deployment, or to minimise the potential loss by providing auto restow, since removing the engine or eliminating all trigger conditions is impossible. In this case, the *source* and *trigger* parts are bound. Parts not bound are considered free. To make an appropriate choice over various mitigation actions, a finer-grained view of mitigation actions is needed. We have codified the knowledge about mitigation actions in terms of the following six portions:

- *Applicability rules*. These rules specify how an action is related to a specific type of negative scenarios. Examples of factors involved can be, for example, the nature of the source (e.g., software, hardware or human), the type of the stimulus (e.g., timing or value failures), the characteristics of the environment (e.g., normal or degraded operational mode), or the value of effect measure (e.g., catastrophic or major). Hence, the task of specifying the applicability rule part is to articulate how the action is linked to a specific class of negative scenarios.

- *Usage conditions*. The usage conditions specify the conditions of the use of a specific action. For example, the use of sanity checking assumes the existence of known pattern of correctness or reasonableness. Some actions are dependent upon the application of other actions. The *voting* action, for example, requires that some form of redundancy has been employed in the view under consideration. In contrast, the use of some actions may imply further application of other actions. A common situation is the use of *detection* actions that are intended to detect a specific stimulus. Further action such as *recovery* is usually required upon detection. In short, usage conditions are specified to ensure the integrity of the proper application of an action.

- *Design parameters*. Many actions have a number of parameters, which determine how the desired mitigation is achieved. For example, in order to use the *redundancy* action, we must determine the number of redundant components, the level of diversity and the redundancy mode (e.g. passive or active redundancy). In practice, we may defer our decisions regarding the values of design parameters in later in the design process.

- *Vulnerabilities.* An action itself may bring about new quality concerns (i.e., negative scenarios). For example, the use of *voting* against value failures will raise a new reliability or safety problem: the robustness of the voting procedure, which can fail due to its underlying hardware or flaw in its algorithm. Codification of the issues can facilitate the next iteration of formulating negative scenarios.
- *Side effects.* An attribute-specific action often has impact on other attributes including business attributes such as cost. The side effects can be positive or negative. For the previous example of *voting*, this action has a significant negative impact on both performance and cost. If we choose to use *sanity checking* instead, then the negative impact on performance and cost is reduced.
- *Metrics.* The impact of each action should be measurable. The applicable metrics depend upon the type of the actions. For *elimination* and *reduction* actions, testability and process metrics are often appropriate. For *resistance* actions, the performance and availability metrics are most suitable. For *minimisation* actions, the usability metrics may be suitable.

Actions can be organised in a tree form. Figure 4 illustrates a set of safety-related actions whose root is the *reduction* action. The descendant nodes of the *reduction* action can be seen as possible refinements. Refinement is usually achieved by answering 'how' questions: e.g., how do we intend to eliminate the projected stimulus? If the stimulus is a design error, a suitable elimination mechanism could be *simplification*. If the stimulus is a random failure, we might use a more reliable hardware to replace the source (i.e., *substitution*). Hence, action refinement problem can be treated as the problem of searching and locating a proper node within the codified action tree.

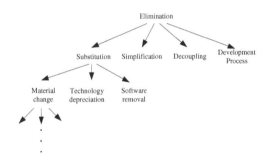

Fig. 4. A safety-related mitigation tree with elimination as the root

Having described what information is captured and how it is organised, in the next subsection we will describe our process in response to the three 'how' challenges identified in at the end of section 2.

3.2 The Process

We assume that the input to the proposed process is the available system information collated from the stakeholders, which includes both initial requirements and existing architectural context. The requirements set include both the core system functionality and desired quality attributes. The architectural information includes a number of essential views, along with the relevant behavioural models such as Use Case Maps (UCMs) [7]. These views (e.g., a context view) exist almost at the same time when the system functionality is known with some confidence. Some views (e.g., a deployment view) can be built when specific architectural assumptions have been made (e.g., uni-processor implementation). In essence, the process employs a cycle of scenario generation and design space formulation to take an initial set of essential requirements and iteratively refine them at the same time an architecture is developed incrementally. Figure 5 illustrates a process view of the proposed framework.

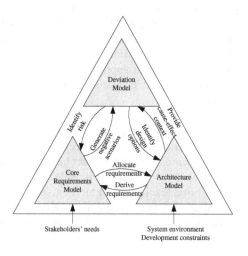

Fig. 5. The process model

The remainder of this section provides an overview of the process. The details of the process will be demonstrated in section 4.

Step 1: **Generate negative scenarios.** Identify possible deviations for each architectural element of a chosen view with the aid of an appropriate set of guidewords. The exact form of guidewords depends upon the quality attribute of interest. If performance is considered, for example, suitable guidewords could be *early* or *late*. As such, deviation analysis can be done in the form of failure analysis, threat analysis and change analysis, for availability, security and modifiability respectively. Both the causes and end effects of the deviations are then identified by deductive and inductive analyses, respectively.

Step 2: **Evaluate, prioritise and relate scenarios.** Evaluate the negative scenarios in terms of likelihood and severity. Rank the scenarios with respect to their risk levels. All top ranking scenarios must be addressed in the next step. Dependencies between scenarios should also be identified to help narrow down the plausible design space.

Step 3: **Identify architectural design space.** Determine the bound and free parts of a chosen scenario. Refine the architectural space via knowledge-based search. Determine the possible allocation options for each mitigation candidate. Even at the top level of the system design, an architect can still have choice over allocating mitigation responsibilities onto the environmental entities such as operators or the system under design. The mitigation candidates accompanied by allocation options form the architectural design space, from which the architect will make principled choices in the next step.

Step 4: **Choose architectural options.** Determine the benefits, cost, known vulnerabilities and side effects for each option. The benefits are mainly determined by the impact of the selected option upon the level of risk (i.e., the reduction of either the likelihood or severity part). The cost estimate is usually done by the aid of domain experts and past experience. The known vulnerabilities and side effects are identified in the codified design knowledge. Note that our method does not make decisions for the architects but simply aids them in elicitating and rationalising their decisions. The architect is free to choose specific option(s) for the purpose of balancing the potential costs against the benefits and residual risks.

Step 5: **Derive and formulate quality requirements.** Determine the exact portions of the negative scenario that a selected option is intended to address. Determine the corresponding action metrics with the aid of the codified design knowledge. Based upon the types of metrics, develop the corresponding quality requirements by means of the (positive) quality attribute scenarios.

Step 6: **Formulate architectural views.** Refine the existing architectural views and build new views if applicable, given the architectural decisions made and the set of quality requirements formulated.

Repeat the steps above. The process stops when all identified negative scenarios have been addressed sufficiently.

4 Case Study

The example concerns the design of a system consisting of a number of Automated Guided Vehicles (AGVs) that deliver pallets from an automated warehouse to machine tools as requested by an operator through a Central Control Computer (CCC). The most important system function here is pallet delivery. Five desired quality attributes are initially elicited from the stakeholders: safety, reliability, availability, modifiability, and performance. Among these attributes, the safety goal is the most important and mandates that the level of risk within the plant should be improved by the introduction of AGVs, as there have been three major injuries from the manually operated fork-lifts in the past 15 years. Alongside this safety goal, two safety constraints are identified for the operational platform:

• AGV must not enter the prohibited area.
• Correct pallets for the selected programme of machine tools must be used.

Given the system information available and architectural assumptions made (such as a map file stored in the AGV), we can formulate an initial architecture (e.g., context view, functional view and physical view). Figures 6 and 7 illustrate the physical view and behavioural model of the context view respectively.

The mechanics of our framework is demonstrated by two iterations of the design process.

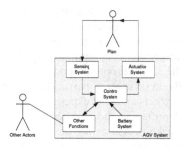

Fig. 6. An initial physical view

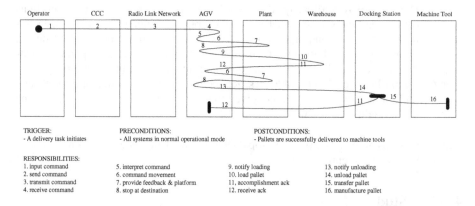

TRIGGER:
- A delivery task initiates

PRECONDITIONS:
- All systems in normal operational mode

POSTCONDITIONS:
- Pallets are successfully delivered to machine tools

RESPONSIBILITIES:

1. input command	5. interpret command	9. notify loading	13. notify unloading
2. send command	6. command movement	10. load pallet	14. unload pallet
3. transmit command	7. provide feedback & platform	11. accomplishment ack	15. transfer pallet
4. receive command	8. stop at destination	12. receive ack	16. manufacture pallet

Fig. 7. An initial UCM for pallet delivery with respect to the context view

Step 1: Generate Negative Scenarios

We began by relating existing architectural views to the QAs of interest. Practical guidance can be found in Rozanski & Woods's perspectives approach [16]. At this level, reliability and performance are closely related to the behavioural model, whilst availability and modifiability are usually linked to the physical view and functional view. Recall that the safety attribute is an attribute that exhibits its concerns via other attributes. We then performed deviation analysis over these views with respect to the corresponding guidewords. For each stimulus identified, the potential end effects are identified by inductive analysis (e.g., Event Tree Analysis [12]) to determine how the deviation can be propagated along the interconnections between the source of the stimulus and the remaining architectural components. The results can be violation of specific safety constraints or leading to specific accidents. Finally, we identified the trigger conditions by tracing back to the previous scenarios in the same view and examining the relevant architectural views such as the physical view. Table 2 illustrates part of the analysis results. It is likely that there is lack of sufficient information to fully predict the possible end effects in the early stages of development. A typical example is the scenario S1 in Table 2.

Step 2: Evaluate, Prioritise and Relate Scenarios

Based upon the understanding gained by both inductive and deductive analyses performed in the previous step, we then made simple conservative estimates of the likelihood and severity of each scenario. Sometimes, the likelihood estimate may be derived from historical data or through expert judgement. Arguably, in the early development process, it is only possible to make order of magnitude estimates of the likelihood and severity in a qualitative manner. Where there was uncertainty associated with scenarios such as S1, we simply skipped the corresponding estimation. We then determined their risk levels by means of risk classification [2]. The scenarios under evaluation were prioritised with respect to the level of risk calculated. Finally, we identified the dependencies between scenarios. Part of evaluation results are shown in Table 3. The most significant scenarios identified in this example are S22, S6 and S24. These must be addressed in the next step. For uncertain scenarios such as S1, they are still valid for design considerations in the next step, as they contribute to the most critical scenario S6.

Table 2. A subset of deviation analysis results

ID	QA	View	Source	Stimulus	Trigger	End Effect
S1	Reliability	UCM for pallet delivery	Operator	Incorrect user input	Human error	Erroneous command may be propagated through the use case path (N/A)
S6			AGV	Not go to the destination as requested	S1; AGV sensing failure; AGV c/s failure (s/w design error or processor fault); S22	Manufacturing is interrupted (anti-availability); AGV enters prohibited area (anti-safety)
S8			Warehouse	Load incorrect pallets	Warehouse control computer failure	Wrong loads delivered to machine tool (anti-safety)
S16	Performance		AGV	Late arrival	Inefficient navigation	Manufacturing is delayed (anti-performance)
S18	Availability	Physical view	AGV	Battery failure	Battery flat; wiring fault	Manufacturing is interrupted (anti-availability)
S22	Modifiability	Functional view	Plant	Layout change	Plant maintenance or business expansion	Rework of AGV software (anti-modifiability); AGV does not go to the destination as requested (S6)
S23		Physical view	AGV	Sensor upgrade	AGV maintenance	Rework of AGV software (anti-modifiability); Introduction of new fault (N/A)
S24	Safety	Context view	Plant	Obstacle present	Workers or other AGVs	Collision (anti-safety)

Step 3: Identify Design Space

In this step, we first determined the bound and free parts for each scenario. For the example scenario S6 in Table 3, the *source* part is bound, whilst the *stimulus* and *environment* parts are clearly free. The *end effect* part is also assumed to be bound, as there is almost nothing that can be done once AGV enters the prohibited area. We then identified the mitigation actions with respect to application rules and usage conditions. For S6, a suitable reduction action is *simplicity* that inhibits part of the trigger conditions (i.e., design errors of the AGV software system). For each candidate action, we also identified the associated possible allocation options. For the example of S8, an effective mitigation action candidate is *detection*, which in turns leads to two allocation options: whether to place onus on the AGV or machine tools to sense when the wrong parts are being delivered. Finally, we created the architectural design space by relating the candidate actions to allocation options. Table 4 shows a subset of the architectural design space for the scenario S6, accompanied by their purpose.

Step 4: Choose Architectural Options
The benefit of each option was determined in terms of its impact upon the frequency or severity measures of the scenario that it is intended to address. The known vulnerabilities and side effects of each option are also identified by the use of the codified design knowledge. Table 5 shows the cost-benefit analysis results of the architectural options in Table 4. At this point, we understood the benefits (i.e. the potential risk reduction), costs and side effects of each proposed architectural option, and decisions can thus be made upon judicious consideration of these options. For the example of S6, we chose the architectural options A1, A2 and A3 (i.e., checking whether AGV has attempted to enter prohibited area, and simplifying the design of the software modules and improving its ease of verification).

Table 3. A subset of scenario evaluation results

ID	Scenario description	Frequency	Severity	Rank	Contributor	Comments
S1	Incorrect user input	Occasional	N/A	N/A		Unknown consequence
S6	Incorrect AGV navigation	Occasional	Critical/ Catastrophic	2	S1, S22	
S8	Warehouse loads incorrect parts of pallets	Remote	Hazardous	6		We may need to assess the cost of damages of machine tools
S16	AGV late arrival	N/A	No safety effect	N/A		Commercial losses of interrupting manufacture are not considered
S18	AGV battery failure	Frequent	No safety effect	N/A		
S22	Plant layout changes	Probable	Critical/ Catastrophic	1		Depends on the actual plant layout
S23	AGV sensor upgrade	Probable	N/A	N/A		Unknown consequence
S24	Obstacle presents in path of AGV movement	Frequent	Critical/ Hazardous	2	S6	Collision in prohibited area could cause far worse injuries

Table 4. A design space for the negative scenario S6

Scenario	Design Space			
	Part addressed	Mitigation	Allocation	Intent
S6	Navigation design error	Simplicity	AGV c/s software	Correctness of the software design can be verified
	Processor fault	Redundancy	AGV c/s processor	The likelihood of random failures of redundant components is sufficiently low
	Incorrect navigation calculation	Sanity checking and fail stop	AGV c/s software	AGV position can be used to indicate possible violation of the safety constraint (i.e., whether AGV enters prohibited area)
		Comparison and fail stop	AGV c/s software or hardware	Value failures can be detected in case of discrepancy
		Voting	AGV c/s software or hardware	Value failures can be tolerated

Step 5: Derive and Formulate the Quality Requirements

For each architectural option chosen, we determined the quality requirements derived from the safety-related design decisions made in the previous step. For example, the use of architectural option A1. The portion being addressed here is the potential design error of the AGV software modules. The mitigation action in this option is *simplicity*. Thus suitable metrics of this action are testability metrics (e.g., path coverage). We then formulated the derived testability requirement in terms of stimulus and desired response, as shown in Table 6. The target value of the response measure is based upon the revised risk assessment by incorporating the risk reduction achieved by the selected option and often determined with the aid of domain experts. Table 7 shows the derived performance and availability requirements DR2 in response to chosen mitigation against S24.

Table 5. Cost effectiveness of architectural options

ID	Architectural Option	Impact	Cost	Vulnerabilities	Side Effects
A1	Simple design of AGV c/s software	The likelihood of design error is reduced by an order of magnitude	Low	Modern software systems are often inherently complex; no protection against underlying hardware faults	Modifiability: -low Performance: +medium
A2	Introduce redundant AGV c/s processor	The likelihood of processor fault is reduced by an order of magnitude	Medium	Common-cause failures such as power loss; no protection against software failures	Performance: -low
A3	Introduce a monitor that ensures AGV is stopped unless AGV is located within permitted area	The severity is reduced by an order of magnitude	Low	Monitor failures; Failures of the sharing resources such as sensor data and map file	Availability: -low
A4	Introduce two versions of navigation module and AGV is stopped if the two disagree with each other	The severity is reduced by an order of magnitude	High	Diversity of the two versions; Reliability of the comparison procedure; common-cause failure between the two version such as sensor faults	Availability: -medium
A5	Introduce three versions of navigation module and AGV is stopped unless two or more versions agree with each other	The severity is reduced by an order of magnitude	Very high	Diversity of the three versions; Reliability of the voting procedure; common-cause failure between the two version such as sensor faults	Performance: -low Availability: +high

Table 6. A derived software safety requirement DR1 against S6

Portion of Scenario	Possible Value
Source	AGV software module
Stimulus	Design error
Artefact	AGV software
Environment	Development time
Response	The correctness of each software module shall be testable
Response measure	Path coverage: 85%

Step 6: Formulate Architectural Views

In this step we refined existing architectural views. For example, in light of the derived requirement DR2, a new actor *Obstacle* is identified and added into the context view, In the physical view, the sensing system is decomposed into an obstacle sensing subsystem and position sensing subsystems, and the actuation system is decomposed into a braking subsystem and drive motors. The refined safety constraints (e.g., deadline and failure rate) are allocated onto the decomposed subsystems. New software-related views such as C&C view and deployment view were built in response to the chosen architectural options A1, A2 and A3. Figure 8 illustrates the initial C&C view. Behavioural models of the newly-added views were also created in response to the derived functions such as obstacle detection, map updating and monitoring. Figure 9 illustrates the UCM for obstacle detection and stopping. Again, the resolution of these views is necessarily coarse-grained and refinement will proceed in the next iteration.

Table 7. A derived performance and availability requirement DR2 against S24

Portion of Scenario	Possible Value
Source	Plant
Stimulus	Obstacle present
Artefact	AGV
Environment	AGV is moving towards the obstacle
Response	AGV shall detect the obstacle and stop the vehicle in time
Response measure	Deadline: 0.1second, failure rate: 2.5E-5 /hour

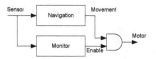

Fig. 8. A fragment of the C&C view (without consideration of other functionality)

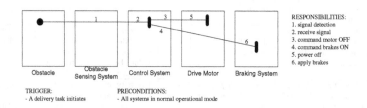

Fig. 9. UCM for obstacle detection and stopping

Second Iteration

In the second iteration, rather than repeat full-scale deviation analysis, we may choose to seek possible deviations over existing views that contribute to the failures of the chosen mitigation mechanisms in the first iterations: i.e., obstacle detection & stopping, map updating, and navigation monitoring. For the example of UCM in Figure 9, failures of either the obstacle sensing subsystem or control system are possible deviations that can lead to total loss of the stopping function. Further deductive analysis performed over the physical view revealed that battery failure (S18) is a possible cause of the control system failure. In this case, the scenario S18 that had been demonstrated to be 'safe' in the first iteration now has a new safety effect on the collision if it occurs when the AGV is approaching an obstacle. It is therefore necessary to trace back to the previous scenarios and revise them if new effects are discovered. Moreover, architectural assumptions (e.g., obstacle is detectable) made in the previous iteration need to be confirmed in this iteration. For instance, further studies reveal that the obstacles in the prohibited area such as AGV falling over edges may not be detectable. As such, we re-evaluated all elicited or revised scenarios and identified the most significant scenarios at this level, from which the decision-making procedure could be facilitated. For example, a decision was made to use dual redundancy to protect against the single point of failure of obstacle sensing. As a result, the obstacle sensing system is decomposed into a proximity sensing and bumper subsystem.

The number of iterations needed and scenarios generated range in terms of the size of the system and the risk acceptability criteria. For the medium-size systems such as the above AGV example, our experience shows that 4-6 iterations and 30-50 scenarios are quite likely. We would anticipate the number of scenarios to be larger for industrial-scale studies.

5 Discussion

In this section, we will discuss the major findings based on the preliminary results of our experiments. Related work is also discussed here for the purpose of comparison.

- *Application domain.* The proposed framework was developed for the safety-critical system domain. However, the generic nature of the framework (i.e. the negative scenarios and mitigation action model) makes it potentially applicable in other domains, such as security-critical systems and performance-critical systems, in which non-safety effects such as commercial loss and mission loss are also taken into account.
- *Role of negative requirements.* We feel that existing practice advocates stakeholder-centric requirements elicitation and there is little guidance on capturing negative requirements. Although quality requirements are initially elicited from the stakeholders, they are often by no means complete and precise. We argue that the notion of negative requirements offers an argumentative approach to interpreting and addressing quality requirements in a recursive manner. The essence of this perspective is an open-ended process of defining and debating the issues occurring in the achievement of quality requirements, thereby helping discover and enhancing existing quality requirements. Our approach is closely related to the misuse cases approach [4] in which negative requirements are identified by deviation analysis over existing use cases and captured in a form similar to use cases. New use cases are then derived in response to the mitigation against the identified misuse cases. However, this approach is defined solely in the functional context without consideration of architectural characteristics.
- *Design rationale.* Our framework is inherently consistent with existing argument-based design rationale techniques such as REMAP [15]. Our negative requirements are similar to their "issues" and mitigation actions are equivalent to their "positions". Negative requirements (i.e. issues) are identified by deviation analysis, which is strongly influenced by our recent work on failure modelling [19], and the design space is identified and controlled by means of causality and risk assessment. One missing step in our proposed framework is the linkage between risk model and quality-attribute model such as performance and reliability models, which determines how quality requirements can be derived with respect to mitigation actions chosen. The SEI has recently proposed a quality-attribute

reasoning framework [5] that unifies various quality attribute models. We anticipate that incorporation of this reasoning framework into our scheme will be
possible.

- *Risk assessment.* Within the proposed framework, the risk assessment is demonstrably qualitative. However, it is envisioned that a quantitative approach may
also be possible and would complement its qualitative counterpart. NASA provides a lightweight solution to quantitative risk assessment [10], which may be
incorporated into our framework.

- *Cost-benefit analysis.* We adopt the likelihood-severity matrix as the basis of
lightweight cost-benefit analysis, in which the ALARP model has been incorporated. Our findings reveal that the use of the matrix simplifies the analysis and
saves repeated analysis work in subsequent design refinements. A comparable
approach is the SEI's CBAM [6] in which benefits and cost are determined by the
agreement of the stakeholders. We argue that CBAM is a laborious effort-
intensive process and thus may be hard to apply many times over as part of an
evolutionary development process, though its analysis results tend to be more accurate and complete.

6 Conclusions

We have presented a concrete framework for eliciting and rationalising architectural
design decisions for safety-critical software systems. In particular, we have demonstrated how it is practical to elicit and formulate negative requirements using a
scenario framework to inform architectural design decisions and justify the rationale
behind them. Based upon the results of adaptations of the co-evolution of requirements and architectures to the safety domain, we justify the rationale for deriving
safety requirements that can then form part of the architectural design. Through provi-
sion of such a framework, we believe that there can be increased confidence in the selection of mitigation mechanisms.

References

1. ARP 4761: Guidelines and Methods for Conducting the Safety Assessment Process on
   Civil Airborne Systems and Equipment. Society of Automotive Engineers, Inc (1996)
2. IEC 61508 – Functional Safety of Electrical/Electronic/Programmable Electronic Safety-
   Related Systems. International Electrotechnical Commission (1998).
3. The United Modelling Language Specification 1.5. Object Management Group,
   http://www.uml.org
4. Alexander, I.: Misuse Cases: Use Cases with Hostile Intent. *IEEE Software*, 20 (1) (2003)
   58-66
5. Bachmann, F., Bass, L. and Klein, M.: Deriving Architectural Tactics: A Step toward Me-
   thodical Architectural Design. Tech. Report. CMU/SEI-2003-TR-004. SEI (2003)
6. Bass, L., Clements, P. and Kazman, R.: Software Architecture in Practice. 2nd Edition.
   Addison Wesley, Reading, USA (2003)
7. Buhr, R.J.A. and Casselman, R.S.: Use Case Maps for Object-Oriented Systems. Prentice
   Hall (1996)

8. Burns, A. and Lister, A.: A Framework for Building Dependable Systems. The Computer Journal, 34 (2). (1991) 173-181
9. Douglass, B.P.: Doing Hard Time: Developing Real-Time Systems with UML, Objects, Frameworks, and Patterns. Addison-Wesley (1999)
10. Feather, M.S., and Cornford, S.L.: Quantitative Risk-Based Requirements Reasoning. Requirements Engineering, 8 (4) (2003) 248-265
11. Kruchten, P.: The 4+1 View Model of Architecture. *IEEE Software*, 12 (6) (1995) 42-50
12. Leveson, N.G.: Safeware: System Safety and Computers. Addison-Wesley (1995)
13. Lions, J.L.: ARIANE 5: Flight 501 Failure. Inquiry Board report. Paris (1996)
14. Nuseibeh, B.: Weaving Together Requirements and Architectures. *IEEE Computer*, 34 (3) (2001) 115-114
15. Ramesh, B. and Dhar, V.: Supporting systems development by capturing deliberations during requirements engineering. *IEEE Trans. on Software Engineering*, 18 (6) (1992) 498-510
16. Rozanski, N. and Woods, Eoin: Software Systems Architecture. Addison-Wesley (2005)
17. Sosa, E. and Tooley, M. (eds.): Causation. Oxford University Press, New York (1993)
18. Wu, W. and Kelly, T.: Safety Tactics for Software Architecture Design. *Proceedings of the 28th Annual International Computer Software and Applications Conference (COMPSAC'04)*. IEEE Computer Society (2004) 368-375
19. Wu, W. and Kelly, T.: Failure Modelling in *Software Architecture Design for Safety*. ACM SIGSOFT Software Engineering Notes, 30 (4) (2005) 1-7

Runtime Prediction of Queued Behaviour

Nurzhan Duzbayev and Iman Poernomo

King's College London
Strand, London, UK, WC2R2LS
{nurzhan.duzbayev, iman.poernomo}@kcl.ac.uk

Abstract. Service-based software architectures are often modeled with queues and queuing networks. Such models are useful for performance evaluation and design. They can also assist in runtime maintenance and administration, but, in this context, it is often far more valuable to be able to forecast how QoS characteristics are likely to evolve in the near future. This is particularly important in cases where systems can be adapted to counter QoS constraint violations: in such systems, given predictions of likely future QoS characteristics, pre-emptive adaptation strategies can be implemented.

This paper outlines an approach to runtime prediction of QoS characteristics of queued systems. Predictions are computed by applying ARIMA forecasting techniques to basic properties of a queued model, and then using the model to predict complex QoS characteristics. We outline how our methods integrate into our implementation framework for monitoring and pre-emptive adaptation of web service based systems.

1   Introduction

Many service-based software architectures can be modeled with queues and queuing networks. Such models can are useful for the performance evaluation and design of a good software architecture. They can also assist in effective maintenance of an implemented system during runtime, even if original, model-based predictions of relevant characteristics are not met. For example, during the design of a system, we can use a queued model to compute the average number of requests in a queue by estimating the average rate of requests serviced and the average number of incoming requests per time unit. Then, when the system is implemented, if either of these rates deviates significantly from their estimation, we can still use the queuing theory calculation to determine the actual average number of requests in the queue. In this way, it is possible to calculate actual values of important quality of service characteristics at runtime by application of the queuing model.

However, for the purposes of maintenance and system administration, it is often far more valuable to be able to forecast how QoS characteristics are likely to evolve in the near future. This is particularly important for systems that can be reconfigured and adapted to counter QoS constraint violations. In such systems, given predictions of likely future QoS characteristics, pre-emptive adaptation strategies can be implemented.

C. Hofmeister et al. (Eds.): QoSA 2006, LNCS 4214, pp. 78–94, 2006.
© Springer-Verlag Berlin Heidelberg 2006

For example, consider a client web service using one of two functionally equivalent queuing server web services. By utilizing Universal Description, Discovery and Integration (UDDI) at runtime [16], it is possible to redirect the client's requests from one server to another. For the case of a single request, it would be preferable to redirect calls to the server that has the shortest queue length. In the case where a large number of calls make up a transaction that must be sent to the same server, then it may be preferable to redirect calls to the web service with the shortest *average* queue length (and so, the shortest average time for serving the transaction). The same situation holds in the case where an expensive UDDI lookup is required to search for equivalent web services: redirection should be done infrequently and the best overall server should be chosen. It is possible that one server might have the shortest current or average queue length, but, in a few minutes, the server will possess the longest queue, due to a steep increase in popularity. Performance of such an architecture could be further improved if adaptation was not based on current or average queue length, but on a *predicted* future queue length.

This paper outlines an approach to the prediction of QoS characteristics of queued systems. Predictions are computed from applying ARIMA forecasting techniques to basic properties of a queued model, and then using the model to predict complex QoS characteristics. Predictions are made with a confidence interval expressing the error associated with the measurement and prediction processes. We outline how our methods integrate into the MPA system for monitoring and pre-emptive adaptation of web service based systems, currently being developed by the Predictable Assembly Laboratory at King's.[1]

The paper proceeds as follows:

- Section 2 summarizes relevant notions from queuing theory.
- Our prediction and error analysis techniques are presented in section 3.
- An illustrate example is provided in section 4.
- Our implementation, the MPA system, is described in section 5, focusing on how prediction relates to monitoring and adaptation of web services using the Microsoft Windows Management Instrumentation framework and UDDI.
- Conclusions and related work are discussed in the final section.

2   Queued Communication Models

Queuing theory enables the mathematical analysis of queued communication between clients and a server (or set of servers) (see, for example, [7,17]). Such communication is commonplace in large-scale distributed systems, where the use of loosely coupled messaging permits messages to be sent asynchronously from multiple sources to the same component at the same time. Performance evaluation of such systems is essential, particularly when dealing with systems assembled through web services, as HTTP-based SOAP communication is susceptible to rapid performance deterioration.

---

[1] http://palab.dcs.kcl.ac.uk

We consider queued communication as in Fig. 1. A number of calls enter a queue per unit time. We write $X_i \geq 0$ for the random variable denoting the number of calls entering at unit time $i = 1, 2, \ldots$. Each call is numbered and served in some order. As soon as the server finishes servicing a call, it immediately starts to serve the next call (if there are calls remaining in the queue) and the served call leaves system. If repeated processing is necessary, a call joins the queue right from the beginning. The server is called *idle* when there are no calls remaining in the queue.

There is a range of different models of queued communication, each with well understood QoS benefits and disadvantages. Factors effecting the values of QoS characteristics for a particular model include the distribution of incoming requests, the servicing discipline (for example, randomly selected, incoming order or some priority discipline) and serving rate distribution.

Our prediction framework is parametrized with respect to the queuing model. Queue QoS characteristics are computed according to different formulae, according to the queuing model. In this paper we shall illustrate prediction of QoS characteristics with respect to the $M/M/1$ queuing model. This model is characterized by a Poisson arrival process and exponential service time distributions with a single server and a FIFO queue ordering discipline. We have defined prediction techniques for a range of commonly used queuing models (such as those involving a larger number of servers or more complicated serving disciplines such as Servicing in Random Order or Round Robin orders). The approach is analogous to that presented here.

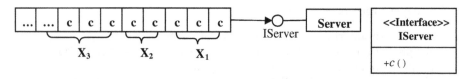

Fig. 1. A queued service. Invocations of the service's methods are queued, where each X_i is the number of invocations at unit time i.

2.1 Utilization and Related Properties

For queued systems, a central QoS characteristic is stability. A system is defined to be *stable* when each queued call is served within a required time-frame. It is *unstable* if there is a possibility that calls will not be served within the required time.

We compute stability via the notion of system utilization, defined as follows.

We assume each X_i is independent and equally distributed and with an average $\lambda = E[X_i]$, defining the average number of calls joining the queue per unit time. We assume that all calls have an average serving time $b > 0$ – this is the average unit time to process a single request. We consequently define the average service rate, the average number of requests that are served per unit time, to be $\mu = 1/b$.

Definition 1 (System utilization). *The utilization of a system, ρ is defined*

$$\rho = \lambda/\mu$$

where λ is average number of calls joining the queue per unit time and μ is the average service rate. No matter in which discipline the call servicing is, the system is stable if, and only if, $\rho < 1$ and unstable if, and only if, $\rho > 1$. In case when $\rho = 1$, the system is stable only when $X_i = X_j$ for all i, j.

Thus, a system is stable if it is able to process all calls arriving.

2.2 Quality of Service Characteristics

We shall concern ourselves with a set quality of service characteristics that are of importance to evaluating the efficiency of a M/1/1 system.

Theorem 1 (QoS Characteristics). *The following statements are true of a M/1/1 queued system:*

- *The probability of n requests being in a queue is*

$$P(n) = \rho^n P(0)$$

  where the probability of 0 calls in the system is $P(0) = 1 - \rho$.
- *The average number of requests in the system is*

$$E[N] = \sum_{n=0}^{\infty} nP(n) = \rho/1 - \rho$$

- *The average waiting time $E[W_i]$ for a request is*

$$E[W_i] = bE[N]$$

The proof can be found in, for example, [11].

Remark 1. It follows from the theorem that the total average time for a call spent in the system is $E[W] = E[W_i] + b$.

3 Queue Behaviour Forecasting

Given a system in which there are no trends in the number of calls made to a server or in the service time for a call, then the definition of ρ above provides the best means of predicting stability and QoS dependent characteristics.

While such situations are common, there are many contexts where trends in queue usage occur. For instance, if we are running a Google-like web service search engine, then, depending on various factors that influence the popularity of the service (our business plan, advertising strategies, the novelty and use of the service itself, etc), it is possible that there will be a genuine trend in the number of calls over time. In such a case, using an overall average to determine ρ will not provide the best immediate prediction of stability. It would be preferable to factor out earlier measures of calls (when the service was unpopular) and to emphasize the newer values, to predict if the system is likely to become unstable soon.

Trends and different seasonal variations need to be taken into account if we are to accurately forecast stability.

We consider the application of Auto-Regressive Integrated Moving Average (ARIMA) methodologies for the purpose of predicting QoS characteristics for queued systems. These methodologies take into account trends in a more sophisticated way than simple averages.

3.1   ARIMA Forecasting Strategies

One of the simplest strategies for time series prediction based on trends is to take an average of recent values of the time series, ignoring earlier values. This is the *simple moving average* technique. Here, the average is computed as

$$SMA(X_n, r) = \sum_{i=n-r+1}^{n} \frac{X_i}{r}$$

where r is cycle length and n is the total number of observations. This is essentially an arithmetic mean, but over a shorter cycle length than the total number of observations. Other similar approaches include associating weights with previous values in the time series, so that the forecasted next value depends more on the most recent value and less on the earliest value in the time series.

We consider so-called smoothing techniques that improve moving averages to incorporate previous errors in prediction (smoothing) and to detect seasonality. These techniques calculate averages over a given cycle. The difficulty of these techniques is determining the approach cycle length. If this cycle is short, then the probability of unacceptable noise increases, but we can determine trends in greater detail. When the cycle is long, we have less noise, but our predictions are less sensitive to trends in the system.

There are different techniques to measure seasonal changes and trends, and to get rid of their influence. In this paper, we apply the Holt-Winters procedure [5], because it is quite simple and provides a good illustration of ARIMA-based forecasting. (Similar ARIMA models could also be applied, depending on the context.)

The recursive definition of the formula over our time series (X_i) of calls per unit time is as follows. The Holt-Winters method uses three smoothing parameters α, γ and δ related to L_n (local level), T_n (expected trend), and I_n (seasonal index), related by the following formulae:

$$L_n = \alpha \left(X_n / I_{n-\Delta} \right) + (1 - \alpha) \left(L_{n-1} + T_{n-1} \right)$$

$$T_n = \gamma \left(L_n - L_{n-1} \right) + (1 - \gamma) T_{n-1}$$

$$I_n = \delta \left(X_n / L_n \right) + (1 - \delta) I_{n-\Delta}$$

Here Δ is seasonal interval. It depends from observation unit and season size (for example, if observations are monthly and seasons repeat annually, then Δ is 12). There are a range of techniques for determining the optimal smoothing parameters, depending on the domain of interest [10,5].

Given these values, the *predicted* number of calls arriving at time $n + k$ is defined in terms of a currently available set of observations $X_0, \ldots, X_n$:

$$\hat{X}_{n,k} = (L_n + kT_n) I_{n-\Delta+k}$$

for $k = 1, 2, \ldots, \Delta$.

Because of random behaviour of requests for the system, our predictions will never be perfect. Real values will lay somewhere near predicted value. It is therefore important to provide predictions with a confidence interval, defining probable maximal and minimal deviations of actual values from the prediction.

Let us assume that predicted number of calls will have an error of the form

$$\hat{X}_{n,k} = X_{n+k} + R_{n,k}^X$$

here $R_{n,k}^X$ is prediction error and X_{n+k} is actual number of calls that will enter into the system at $n + k$.

The confidence interval for $\hat{X}_{n,k}$ will then be

$$\left[X_{n,k}^{min}, X_{n,k}^{max} \right] = \hat{X}_{n,k} \mp \frac{\xi}{\sqrt{k}} \sqrt{Var \left\{ \sum_{m=1}^{k} R_{n,m}^X \right\}}$$

were ξ is a specified confidence level. For a 95% confidence interval, we let $\xi = 1.96$. The value of $X_{n,k}^{min}$ is treated as zero if it becomes negative.

3.2 Prediction of QoS Characteristics

Given the exponential smoothing prediction of call arrivals, it is possible to forecast M/1/1 QoS characteristics by substitution of predicted values of X into the formula for utilization. Confidence intervals are caclulated similarly.

We define the predicted utilization to be

$$\hat{\rho}_k = \hat{X}_{n,k}/\mu$$

We can determine the confidence interval for predicted utilisation in terms of predicted arrival rate's error, using the fact that the error of $\hat{\rho}_k$ will be $\hat{X}_n/\mu - X_n/\mu = R_n^X/\mu$:

$$\left[\rho_{n,k}^{min}, \rho_{n,k}^{max} \right] = \hat{\rho}_{n,k} \mp \frac{\xi}{\sqrt{k}} \sqrt{Var \left\{ \sum_{m=1}^{k} \frac{R_{n,m}^X}{\mu} \right\}}$$

Utilization prediction is useful in two cases:

- When there is a genuine trend towards instability. This is a serious problem for a queued system and pre-emptive notification can be very useful if an adaptation solution exists. For example, if a web service has a predicted instability, administration could refuse any more requests until the queue normalizes.
- When there is a "local" trend towards instability. A time series might have a globally stable utilization, but with locally unstable segments. That is, a queued system might be able to respond to all requests eventually, but at certain times, might have an unacceptably high number of requests compared to service time. This situation can also benefit from pre-emptive notification to inform an adaptation strategy.

The previous confidence intervals for a prediction are helpful for determining the certainty we have of a current predicted trend in utilization.

The $n + k$ predicted probability of i calls being in the system queue will be

$$\hat{P}_{n,k}(i) = (\hat{\rho}_{n,k})^i (1 - \hat{\rho}_{n,k})$$

and the average number of requests in the system queue

$$\hat{E}[N_{n,k}] = \hat{\rho}_{n,k}/(1 - \hat{\rho}_{n,k})$$

with confidence interval

$$\left[E_{n,k}^{min}, E_{n,k}^{max} \right] =$$

$$\hat{E}[N_{n,k}] \mp \frac{\xi}{\sqrt{k}} \sqrt{Var \left\{ \sum_{m=1}^{k} \frac{R_{n,m}^X}{\left(\mu - \mu \rho_{n,m} - R_{n,m}^X \right) \left(1 - \rho_{n,m} \right)} \right\}}$$

where the minimum values of the interval are at least limited by 0.

4   Example

To illustrate our predictive methods, we describe a simulated B2B web service based system. The queued server *WSDistributor* is a computer component distributor selling for example chips or monitors. There are 30 Client web services *WSAssembler*$_1$, ..., *WSAssembler*$_{30}$ that act as communication points to businesses that use the distributor for purchasing components which they then assemble into computers. Clients could make one of the following three types of call: makeOrder, cancelOrder or makeQuery. For the sake of simplicity, assume each call type has the same processing time.

The architecture of the system is shown in Fig. 2.

We implemented the distributor web service as an ASP.NET web service, running on a Xeon 1,7GHz server running Windows Server 2003 and IIS 6. We ran the Microsoft Web Application Stress tool on a Pentium M laptop to simulate various demand profiles, both random and noisy trends.

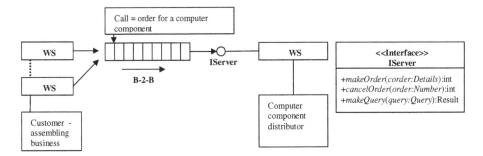

Fig. 2. Our B2B example

Fig. 3(a) shows an example simulation of incoming requests per minute for a noisy trend. Fig. 3(b) shows an overall average calculation up to observation time i (the most horizontal graph), against the 1-step-ahead exponentially smoothened prediction of calls at i. Confidence intervals for the prediction are represented by the faded lines.

In this example, it is clear that the probable time to process a call will not always be best given by the overall average. For example, the client WS's will make many more requests of the distributor during business hours, and probably no requests after business hours. In this case, the overall average is of little use in defining, for instance, an adaptation strategy involving server replication and load balancing. The exponentially smoothened version does a good job at filtering out noise and effectively identifies peak trends at the (181,201) and (301,341) intervals, at other points remaining very close to the overall average.

A more sensitive smoothened average could be obtained by changing the coefficients of the ARIMA equations: this would be useful if there are more subtle trends present in the time series. We should choose coefficients to avoid an overly sensitive average that identifies false trends. However, from the perspective of adaptation methods (describe in the next section), we need not be overly cautious: it is generally better to adapt a system to a few false trend predictions than have no adaptation in the face of genuine performance deterioration.

The QoS characteristics can be calculated with confidence intervals following the discussion of the previous section. An 18 point plot of predicted utilization is given in Fig. 4(a), together with a 95% confidence interval. Calculation of the utilization by means of the overall average will yield a value of around 0.275 at any point in time. In contrast, our predicted utilization reaches about 0.42 during the second peak. The overall utilization never reaches such a high level, and so overall stability is certain. However, while stability is maintained overall, it is more useful to understand where "local" instability can be found – sections where predicted utilization goes above 1. At such regions of the time series, while all calls may *eventually* be served, there is the potential for backlog which, if trends continue, would result in global instability. Observe that the 95% confidence interval for the utilization forcast is remains reasonably close to the forcast. The exception to this is at earlier points, when there are significant random fluctuations in the number of requests received, resulting in a greater error of the prediction. This illustrates the importance of computing confidence intervals, particularly when our source data is noisy and there is uncertainty about whether a trend exists or not.

An 18 point plot of predicted number of requests to be served in the queue is given in Fig. 4(b), together a 95% with confidence interval. The predicted number of calls in the queue never reaches 1: that is, we never predict there to be an unanswered request in the queue at any time. However, the predicted number of requests peaks between (150,190) interval. This also suggests a potential trend towards a backlog. If the predicted trend increased to an unacceptable level, there might be cause to adapt the system to pre-emptively eliminate too many calls waiting in the queue. Such adaptations are enabled through our MPA system, now described.

5   Monitoring and Adaptation Framework

We now outline how our approach to prediction operates together with monitoring and adaptation within the MPA (Monitoring/Prediction/Adaptation) system.

The architecture of the MPA system is given in Fig. 5. It comprises of three infrastructures: monitoring, prediction and adaptation. Systems are specified according to UML2 superstructure architectural metamodel that is extended to include QoS constraints, choice of queued communication models between components and adaptation policies in the event of QoS constraint violation. A system specification, consisting of an architecture, QoS constraints, queuing model and adaptation policies, is shared between the three infrastructures. Instrumentation of the implemented architecture is done according to the choice of constraints. Prediction follows the methods described in the previous section, with prediction strategies for QoS characteristics dependent on the choice of queued communication model. Adaptation follows the policies outlined in the specification based on current system predictions.

We have implemented our system in .NET, using its Windows Management Instrumentation API to assist in monitoring relevant system properties. However, because we adhere to the DMTF CIM (Common Information Model) standard [9] for instrumentation information exchange, so it is possible to adapt the monitoring and prediction infrastructures of our implementation to other environments. The adaptation engine is written using .NET's UDDI API, but its principle functions could also be adapted to any language capable of dealing with web services and UDDI.

5.1   Architectural Metamodel with Adaptation Policies

The framework requires that system models are written with respect to an extension of the UML metamodel. The metamodel identifies the architectural roles and relationships that are necessary to construct a model of the monitored system. A distinguishing feature of our metamodel is that it includes

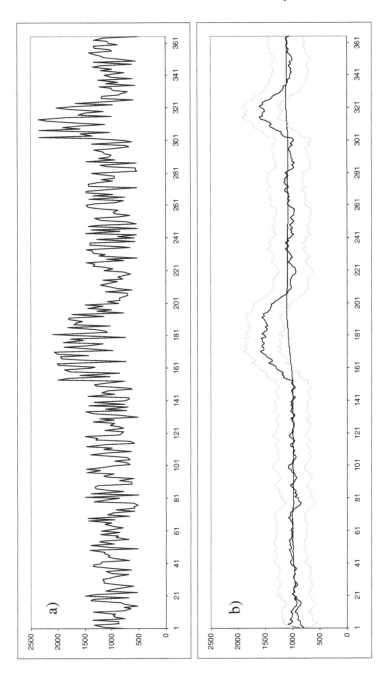

Fig. 3. (a) Observations of incoming stream. (b) Three-step prediction of load rate using exponential smoothing of incoming stream with 95% confidential interval, plotted against the arithmetical mean. The mean is the most constant of the graphs. (Horizontal axes denote time and vertical axes denote incoming stream load.)

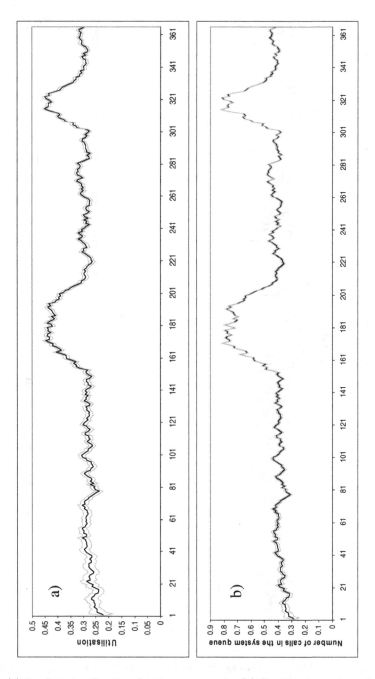

Fig. 4. (a) Predicted utilization for the case study. (b) Predicted number of calls in the queue for the case study. Both graphs have a 95% confidence interval.

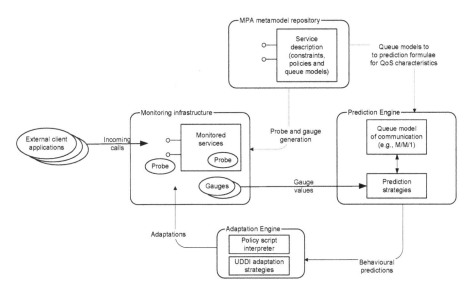

Fig. 5. The architecture of our monitoring, prediction and adaptation solution

- a QoS constraint language, based on the UML QoS profile [14], but extended to include a prediction construct, and
- an architectural adaptation policy language, that serves both as a specification of how an architecture should evolve in the face of QoS constraint violations, and also as a scripting language for the adaptation engine.

The metamodel is implemented using the OMG Meta-Object Facility and has an XML representation. Fig. 6 provides a visual representation of a small system written using the metamodel. Components and component connectors are defined as in the UML2 superstructure, but with tags that permit us to specify what interfaces are queued according to a particular queuing model. For example, *Distributor1* accepts calls along interface *IDist*, according to an assumed M/M/1 model. This queuing information is then used at the prediction stage to determine how to compute QoS characteristics of the queue.

A sugared extension of the OCL/UML-QoS is used to write constraints over queue QoS characteristics: for example we write $Prob(d.IDist.QueueLength > 5)$ for the probability that the queue length (an OCL property $QueueLength$) for calls to interface $IDist$ of a component d is greater than 5.

Importantly, we can also specify constraints over *future predictions* of characteristic behaviour. Constraints of the form A steps $:i$ are interpreted as meaning that a property A is predicted to hold i time units from the time of evaluation. For example,

$$Prob(d.IDist.QueueLength > 5) > .9 \text{ steps} : 10$$

means that, in 10 time units from the point of evaluation of the constraint, there will be at least 90% probability that the queue length will be greater than 5.

5.2   Performance Monitoring Infrastructure

The performance monitoring infrastructure layer is implemented using the Windows Management Instrumentation (WMI). The WMI is the core management-enabling technology built into the Windows 2000/XP/Server 2003 operating systems. WMI is an implementation of the Distributed Management Task Force's Web-Based Enterprise Management (WBEM) Common Information Model CIM standard [9], a platform-neutral language for defining application components and instruments. The WBEM standard as developed to unify the management of distributed computing environments, facilitating the exchange of data across a range of platforms.

Higher layers of the framework implementation interact with the monitoring infrastructure solely according to the CIM. Higher layers of our implementation could therefore be adapted to monitor systems operating under platforms and environments other than Windows and .NET, provided they possess WBEM compliant instrumentation technologies (for example, there are several open source platform independent Java implementations of WBEM).

The WMI enables instrumentation and plumbing through which Windows resources can be accessed, configured, managed, and monitored. Our framework essentially manipulates two kinds of WMI entities:

– *WMI events* enable a loosely coupled, subscription-based approach to monitoring important changes in an application. Windows and .NET provide a large base set of important events that can be monitored: for example, component activation, method calls and exceptions are available for monitoring as WMI events without the need for manual instrumentation. In addition, the developer can extend the WMI event model to accommodate domain-specific events.
– *WMI objects* are .NET components that are visible to a monitoring WMI program. They provide a data-centric view of an application. A developer can instrument a program by collecting a range of important data views of the program within a WMI object. The object is instantiated and resides within the same memory space as program. However, using the WMI API, a monitoring program can make inquiries about the WMI object, permitting instrumentation of the data.

The infrastructure enables the user to view the internal evolution of a target application, observing communication and interaction between its subcomponents, via user-designed instrument code that can be associated with various aspects of the application. Two kinds of instrument are used within our framework:

– *Probes*. These provide access to target key application data. These are implemented either as WMI objects or events. The monitoring infrastructure can access these at any time via pull-based collection (when given as WMI objects), or a loosely coupled, push-based subscription (when given as WMI events). Probes are generally directly linked to a service – they either form part of a service's methods or else are defined in a wrapper that intercepts calls to the service.

- *Gauges.* These use data from probes to compute *basic properties* that are of importance to determining QoS characteristics. For example, in the case of M/1/1 queues, we need a log of the arrival rate as it has evolved over time. This is provided by an arrival rate gauge. Gauges are external to monitored services, observing service behaviour through gathering of probe data.

The use of the WMI to perform monitoring does not affect the monitoring capability of our framework for non-.NET based service integration architectures. This is because the schema for WMI data transfer and event monitoring is the CIM, a platform-independent standard for describing the subsystems, networks, applications and services that make up an application. There are a range of different DMTF CIM event providers for most platforms – provided web service probes are written using these providers, we can monitor them using WMI.

The monitoring infrastructure imports a service architecture model to extract relevant application metadata: 1) Deployment data for individual services (location, interfaces, etc); 2) The initial architectural configuration of services (what usage connections exist between services); 3) The set of queued interfaces; 4) The basic properties that are necessary to compute values of the QoS characteristics used in the model.

A form of model transformation is necessary to develop instruments necessary to monitor the constraints defined in a given MPA model. Depending on the queuing model different WMI-based probes will be defined and attached to a service interface implementation. For example, in the simplest M/1/1 model, arrivals per second must be monitored, so a WMI-event probe should be generated to count the number of arrivals every second, and periodically update an gauge with this data. This approach is related to the model-based monitoring framework of [4] and is detailed in [3].

The monitoring infrastructure is generic: it provides a semantics for aspects of the metamodel that are open to interpretation. For example, the definition of a time unit can in fact be associated with any system activity by the monitoring infrastructure, leading to a range of possible notions of timing.

By using the infrastructure to link specification metamodels with instrumentation, our framework separates the concerns of building a nonfunctional metamodel that is appropriate for a particular domain from the concerns of building a monitoring system that checks constraints written in the metamodel.

5.3 Prediction and Adaptation Engines

The prediction engine shares the service architecture model with the monitoring infrastructure, obtaining relevant application metadata that will allow for communication between the two subsystems. The metadata also determines the prediction strategy.

- What interfaces are queued and, consequently, being monitored by the monitoring infrastructure.
- What basic properties are necessary to compute values of the QoS characteristics used in the model. This information is shared with the monitoring infrastructure and determines which gauges the prediction engine should subscribe to.
- What queuing model is being used by a service interface. This information is used to determine the appropriate QoS characteristic functions.

If a prediction (A steps : i) constraint is associated with an interface, then the prediction engine must subscribe to all gauges relevant to determining the true or falsity of A at any point in time. Gauges should contain a log information of values at previous time steps. Using this information, together with the queuing model specified for the interface, the prediction engine will predict if A holds i steps from the current state, following the style of computation described in the previous section.

The adaptation engine consists of a UDDI-based implementation of the policy language. The UDDI (Universal Description Discovery and Integration) provides classification to find the distributed Web Services (WS) by keyword matching. The UDDI version 3 allows searching WS using digital signatures.

Web service connections are changed dynamically whenever policy constraints are violated according to the data feeds from the monitoring and prediction infrastructure.

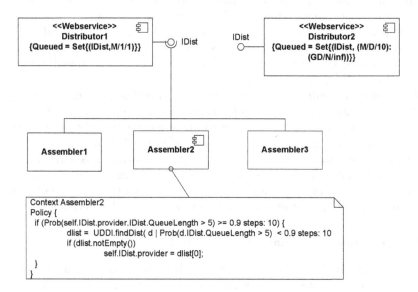

Fig. 6. A visual representation of a sample MPA architecture with a simple adaptation policy

6   Related Work and Conclusions

There are many systems that permit dynamic adaptation of architectures based on real time QoS information [2,1,19,6,15]. The work of [19] is most similar to ours, as they use UDDI and QoS information to assemble web service architectures of optimal performance. Adaptation has also been proven to be useful in a range of other contexts. For example, [1] defines a language of QoS policies for grid services that are enforced by means of adaptation mechanisms. A different approach to QoS adaptation is considered in [18] for the case of embedded systems. These systems do not involve forecasting of values as part of their adaptation strategies. The ARIMA methods need not only be applied to compute QoS queue characteristics. These strategies have the potential to be combined with such (non-queued) QoS-based runtime adaptation technologies.

The closest work to ours is Dinda's use of ARIMA techniques for host load prediction [8] of CORBA based systems and the performance prediction methods of [2] and [11]. The difference with that works is that we adapt ARIMA methods to queued models, instead of load time estimation models. The intention behind our MPA system is analogous to that of the Running Time Advisor of [8], but applied to widely distributed web service component architecture.

Further work on stability for more complicated queuing strategies is given in [12]. These results could be adapted to our context, to enable us to predict stability for systems involving multiple servers. A complete overview of different stochastic methods for analysis of queued systems is provided in [13]. The authors provide ten methods. Most of these methods have been contrived to be applied in different parts of science, but, to the best of our knowledge, have never was applied to predict behaviour of complex software.

Errors can occur in adaptation strategies based on prediction. We need to address the risk of such errors with respect to our prediction strategies. It will be interesting to see how these methods can be adapted to queues with service rejection. For example, we could consider models where service requests can be denied after entering a queue. Such models involve the probability of request refusal in addition to arrival and service rates. If request refusal is likely to exhibit trends over time, a second ARIMA forecasting strategy could be employed to predict refusal. Our methods could then be extended to the two prediction values to forecast the QoS characteristics we have considered for our simpler model.

The scalability and compositonality of our approach warrents further research, for application to larger queued systems built using several subqueues and queued networks, and entire distributed architectures built from queued components. This continuing investigation forms part of the first author's PhD work.

References

1. Rashid Al-Ali, Abdelhakim Hafid, Omer Rana, and David Walker. An approach for quality of service adaptation in service-oriented grids. *Concurrency and Computation: Practice and Experience*, 16(5):401–412, 2004.

2. Simonetta Balsamo, Antinisca Di Marco, Paola Inverardi, and Marta Simeoni. Model-based performance prediction in software development: A survey. *IEEE Transactions On Software Engineering*, 30(5):295–310, MAY 2004.

3. Kenneth Chan and Iman Poernomo. Model driven instrumentation for monitoring quality of service. In *Tenth IEEE International EDOC Enterprise Computing*, 2006. submitted, pending review.

4. Kenneth Chan, Iman Poernomo, Heinz W. Schmidt, and Jane Jayaputera. A model-oriented framework for runtime monitoring of nonfunctional properties. In *QoSA/SOQUA*, volume 3712 of *LNCS*, pages 38–52. Springer Berlin / Heidelberg, 2005.

5. C. Chatfield and M.Yar. Holt-winters forecasting: some practical issues. *The Statistician*, 37:129–140, 1988.

6. Luiz Marcio Cysneiros and Julio Cesar Sampaio do Prado Leite. Nonfunctional requirements: From elicitation to conceptual models. *IEEE Transactions On Software Engineering*, 30(5):328–350, MAY 2004.

7. Brian D.Bunday. *An introduction to queueing theory*. New York, Halsted Press, 1996.

8. Peter A. Dinda. Online prediction of the running time of tasks. *Joint International Conference on Measurement and Modeling of Computer Systems*, pages 336 – 337, MAY 2001.

9. DMTF. Common information model (CIM) specification, version 2.2, 14th June 1999. See http://www.dmtf.org/standards/cim_schema_v22.php.

10. Jr E.S. Gardner. Exponential smoothing: the state of the art. *Forecasting*, 2:1–28, 1985.

11. Paul J. Fortier and Howard E.Michel. *Computer Systems Perfomance Evaluation and Prediction*. Digital Press, 2003.

12. S. Foss and N. Chernova. On stability of a partially accessible multi-station queue with state-dependent routing. *Queueing Systems*, 1(29):5573, 1998.

13. S. Foss and T.Konstantopoulos. An overview of some stochastic stability methods. *Journal of the Operations Research Society of Japan*, 47(4):275–303, 2003.

14. Object Management Group. Uml profile for modeling quality of service and fault tolerance characteristics and mechanisms, http://www.omg.org/cgi-bin/doc?ptc/2005-05-02, 2005.

15. George T. Heineman, Joseph P. Loyall, , and Richard E. Schantz. Component technology and qos management. *International Symposium on Component-based Software Engineering (CBSE7), Edinburgh, Scotland*, May 24-25 2004.

16. Karsten Januszewski. *Using UDDI at Run Time, Part II*. Microsoft MSDN. http://msdn.microsoft.com/library/default.asp?url=/library/en-us/dnuddi/html/runtimeuddi1.asp (Accessed 4th of June, 2006).

17. L. Kleinrock. *Queueing Systems*, volume 1. New York, J. Wiley, 1975.

18. Praveen K. Sharma, Joseph P. Loyall, George T. Heineman, Richard E. Schantz, Richard Shapiro, and Gary Duzan. Component-based dynamic qos adaptations in distributed real-time and embedded systems. *International Symposium on Distributed Objects and Applications (DOA) , Agia Napa, Cyprus*, pages 1208–1224, October 25-29 2004.

19. Liangzhao Zeng, Boualem Benatallah, Anne H.H. Ngu, Marlon Dumas, Jayant Kalagnanam, and Henry Chang. Qos-aware middleware for web services composition. *IEEE Transactions On Software Engineering*, 30(5):311–327, MAY 2004.

Model Transformation in Software Performance Engineering

Antinisca Di Marco[1] and Raffaela Mirandola[2]

[1] Dipartimento di Informatica, Università di L'Aquila, L'Aquila, Italy
adimarco@di.univaq.it
[2] Dipartimento di Elettronica e Informazione - Politecnico di Milano, Milano, Italy
mirandola@elet.polimi.it

Abstract. Nowadays it is widely recognized the crucial role played in the software development process by the analysis of extra-functional properties (and especially performance) at the architectural level. To foster this kind of quantitative analysis we envisage the need to transform the performance model generation and analysis into a rigorous and sound discipline. To this end we intend to exploit the knowledge (acquired by other disciplines) in the area of model transformation, and import both reasoning and methodologies in the software performance engineering. In this paper we investigate the area of performance model derivation and analysis focusing on model transformation; we propose an initial taxonomy for the area of performance analysis at software architecture level and we delineate our suggestions towards a software performance model driven engineering.

1 Introduction

During recent years, the way software systems are designed and built is undergoing great changes. The main emerging trends are: the central role played by the software architecture concept in the software development; the model driven paradigm of development; and the attention given to the analysis of extra-functional properties during software development. Our work aims at merging these trends, as it intends to pursue the analysis of extra-functional properties (such as performance) at architectural level basing on model driven techniques. The software architecture approach to the design of software applications focuses on the high level modeling of an application in terms of coarse-grained components, interaction patterns among them and overall interconnection topology, abstracting away low level details [28]. The underlying idea is that better software systems can result from modeling and analyzing their relevant architectural aspects since the early phases of the development lifecycle. Analyzing the Software Architecture (SA) of a system aims at predicting the quality of the system before it has been built, to understand the main effects of an architecture with respect to quality requirements. This prediction, based on analysis methodologies applied to some suitable system model, can be exploited to drive decisions about what components and connectors should be used and how they should be architected so as to meet the quality requirements imposed on the design.

Out of any explicitly reference to model driven development, several models (and related tools) have been proposed so far for the analysis of extra-functional properties

C. Hofmeister et al. (Eds.): QoSA 2006, LNCS 4214, pp. 95–110, 2006.
© Springer-Verlag Berlin Heidelberg 2006

for software architecture, especially for SA described by UML diagrams [3,6]. The basic idea underlying these models (and tools) is the definition of a bridge between the architectural model and existing performance models. However, in these work the focus has been mainly on the "derived analysis model" rather than on the way of obtaining it.

At the same time, in the software engineering community the focus, in software development has been shifted from a code-centric approach to a model-centric approach with the definition and the adoption of the model driven development (MDD) paradigm, where the focus of model transformations is on a transformation path from high level to platform specific models (up to the executable code) of a software application. Model transformation has been actively investigated in the last years for what concerns the transformation from model-to-code considering both the derivation of intermediate models and the direct code generation. In this field some taxonomies of model transformation approaches have been defined to help a software developer choosing the method that is best suited for his needs [33,11,18].

However, to the best of our knowledge, only few work exist in the literature including in this model driven generation the analysis of extra-functional properties, such as performance [32]. Aim of our work is to exploit the knowledge in the area of model transformation and to import it in the software performance community in order to make the performance model derivation a rigorous and sound discipline rather than an art left to skilled people.

Indeed, carrying out the analysis of extra-functional quality attributes of a SA, can be seen as a transformation process that takes as input some "design-oriented" model of the software system (plus some additional information related to the extra-functional attribute of interest) and generates an "analysis-oriented" model, that lends itself to the application of some analysis methodology. However, defining such a transformation from scratch could be quite cumbersome, for several reasons; for example, the large "semantic gap" between the source and target model of the transformation, and the different target analysis notations one could be interested in to support different kind of analysis (e.g. queueing networks, Markov processes).

To alleviate these problems, we have launched a research initiative aiming at merging these trends, and in particular, we intend to change the focus in the area of performance model derivation, paying more attention to model transformation. As a first step towards this goal we propose an initial taxonomy of model transformation for the area of analysis of performance properties. Note that we do not intend to suggest a general classification for software performance engineering works (for this aspect we refer to [3,6]), rather we look at these works from the different point of view of model transformation to understand how to exploit these techniques for the performance model derivation. Furthermore we present a comparison among some of the existing approaches, and finally, starting from the analysis of the state of the art, we devise some guidelines that pave the way to software performance model driven engineering.

In this paper we present the first results we have obtained in this area. Our long term goal is the definition of a general framework for software performance model driven engineering, where it would be possible to choose which models and which transformation method apply for addressing a specific target problem.

We first present in section 2 the work in software performance engineering that uses model transformation, then we outline the key point of different transformation methodologies (section 3), and we customize them in the performance context (section 4) Then we present a comparison among the main classes of existing work (section 5) illustrating the lessons learned and presenting our first recommendation s(section 6). Finally we present conclusions and future work in section 7.

2   Software Performance Approaches in Model Driven Engineering

In this section we report the first efforts made to model driven engineering in the software performance domain. In particular we present: *(i)* two approaches from Petriu et al. that derive a Layered Queuing Network from UML diagrams realized by using XSLT language and graph transformation; *(ii)* some intermediate languages that have been defined to capture the relevant information for the analysis of non-functional attributes of component-based systems; and *(iii) Software Performance MDA framework* that extends the canonical view of the MDA approach to embed additional types of models allowing to structure a Model Driven approach keeping into account performance issues.

2.1   Petriu's Approaches

In [23,15] Petriu et al. propose several conceptually similar approaches where SA are described by means of architectural patterns (such as pipe and filters, client/server, broker, layers, critical section and master-slave) whose structure is specified by UML Collaboration diagrams and whose behavior is described by Sequence or Activity diagrams.

The approaches follow the SPE methodology and propose systematic methods of building LQN models of complex SA based on combinations of the considered patterns. Such model transformation methods are based on graph transformation techniques. We now discuss the details of two of these approaches.

In [23] SA are specified by using UML Collaboration, Sequence, Deployment and Use Case diagrams. Sequence diagrams are used to obtain the software execution model represented as a UML Activity diagram. The UML Collaboration diagrams are used to obtain the system execution model, i.e., a LQN model. Use Case diagrams provide information on the workloads and Deployment diagrams allow for the allocation of software components to hardware sites. The approach, to which we refer in the following as *Petriu1*, generates the software and system execution models by applying graph transformation techniques, automatically performed by a general-purpose graph rewriting tool.

The second considered approach proposed in [15] (that we name *Petriu2* in the following) uses the eXtensible Stylesheet Language Transformations (XSLT), to carry out the graph transformation step. XSLT is a language for transforming a source document expressed in a tree format (which usually represents the information in a XML file) into a target document expressed in a tree format. The input contains UML models in XML format, according to the standard XML Metadata Interchange (XMI), and the output is a tree representing the corresponding LQN model. The resulting LQN model can be in turn analyzed by existing LQN solvers after an appropriate translation into textual format.

2.2 Intermediate Languages

To reduce the complexity of the transformation task some intermediate languages have been proposed so far [14,25,16]. In this way, the direct transformation from source to target models can be split in a two-step transformation from the source model to an intermediate model, and then from the intermediate model to the target model.

The idea of defining a kernel language to reduce the complexity of a direct transformation from M different source metamodels to N different target metamodels has been considered, for example in [6], where (in a different context from extra-functional analysis) the kernel language is called a "pivot metamodel". A MOF [22] compliant kernel language specifically related to performance analysis called CSM, has been proposed in [25], with the goal of specifying intermediate models between design-oriented UML models with SPT annotations and performance models. The transformations from UML to an intermediate model and from it to different performance models (spanning layered queueing networks, extended queueing networks and stochastic Petri nets) are also presented in [16,24,34].

KLAPER kernel language [14] has been defined to capture the relevant information for the analysis of non-functional attributes of component-based systems, with a focus on performance and reliability attributes, abstracting away unnecessary details. The advantage of using KLAPER is that we have to devise only N+M instead of NM transformations. An additional advantage is that they could also be possibly simpler to devise than the direct transformations, as the intermediate model is likely to result "closer" to both the source and target models. In other words, KLAPER can be used to build an intermediate model that acts as a bridge in a model transformation path from design-oriented to analysis-oriented models. To integrate this kernel language into an MDD framework, leveraging the current state of the art in the field of model transformation methodologies, KLAPER has been defined as a MOF metamodel. Hence, it is possible to use the MDA-MOF facilities to devise transformations to/from KLAPER models, provided that a MOF metamodel exists for the corresponding source/target model. According to the MDD perspective, these transformations can be defined as a set of rules that map elements of the source metamodel onto elements of the target metamodel.

2.3 Software Performance MDA Framework

In [9] the authors extended the canonical view of the MDA [19] approach to embed additional types of models that allow to structure a Model Driven approach keeping into account performance issues.

The resulting framework (see Figure 1), namely SPMDA (Software Performance Model Driven Architecture), beside the typical MDA models and transformations, embeds new models and transformations that take into account the performance validation activities.

In order to keep performance aspects under control, three additional types of models and three additional types of transformations/relationships have been introduced. The new types of models are: CIPM, PIPM, PSPM.

CIPM - A Computation Independent Performance Model represents the requirements and constraints related to the performance. A good example of CIPM may be a Use Case Diagram annotated with performance requirements.

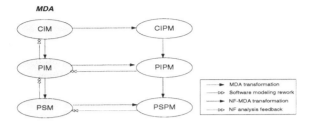

Fig. 1. The SPMDA framework

PIPM - A Platform Independent Performance Model is a representation of the business logics of the system along with an estimate of the amount of resources that such logics needs to be executed. The model must be computationally solvable, that means it should be expressed through a notation that allows performance analysis (e.g., Queueing Networks)

PSPM - A Platform Specific Performance Model contains the merged representation of the business logics and the platform adopted to run the logics. In a classical MDA approach a platform is represented from a set of subsystems and technologies that provide a coherent set of functionalities through interfaces and specified usage patterns (e.g. J2EE, CORBA, etc.). In a performance context a platform must also include the characteristics of the underlying hardware architecture, such as the CPU speed and the network latency.

The framework illustrates also the transformations and relationships among the models. The dashed arrows with single filled peak represent the additional transformations that we have introduced to tie MDA and SPMDA models. We distinguish between *horizontal* and *vertical* SPMDA transformations, as follows:

SPMDA horizontal transformation - It transforms a software model into the corresponding performance model at any level in the MDA hierarchy. In Figure 1 CIM→CIPM, PIM→PIPM and PSM→PSPM are horizontal transformations.

SPMDA vertical transformation - such transformations, differently to the ones in MDA, are intended to provide an input contribution to the horizontal transformation. Hence: CIPM→PIPM is a contribution to a PIM→PIPM transformation and, likewise, PIPM→PSPM is a contribution to a PSM→PSPM transformation.

Two types of arrows with double empty peak also appear in Figure 1 to give completeness to the software performance analysis process, and they represent the reverse paths after the performance analysis takes place. Dashed arrows with double empty peak represent the feedback that originates from the evaluation of a performance model. Continuous arrows with double empty peak are direct consequences of performance feedback. They represent the rework necessary on the software models to embed the changes suggested from the performance analysis.

3   Model Transformation Taxonomy

In a MDD framework, to decide which model transformation approach is most appropriate for addressing a particular problem it is necessary to answer some crucial questions such as: 1. identify "what" we want to transform; 2. identify "how" to perform transformation [18,11,33]

In the following we investigate some key points (mainly inherited from [18]), and suggest a number of objective criteria to be taken into consideration to provide concrete answers to the arisen question. Based on the answers, the software architect can then select the model transformation approach that is most suited for her needs.

3.1 What

The first point to be addressed concerns the *source and target models* of the transformation. Specifically, their:

- *Number*: a model transformation should be defined to handle multiple source models and/or multiple target models, and
- *Notations*: (i) the architectural language used to describe the source model, as it is from the software development process; (ii) the notation adopted for representing the target model.

Thus, basing on the notation in which the source and target models of a transformation are expressed, it is possible to distinguish between different kind of *Transformation*:

- *endogenous:* transformations between models expressed in the same language, and
- *exogenous:* transformations between models expressed using different language
- *vertical:* transformation that produces a target model at a different level of abstraction of the source model. Vertical transformation can abstract or refine the source model.
- *horizontal :* transformation that produces a target model at the same level of abstraction of the source model.

Moreover, another key point to be considered concerns the so called *technological space* (TS) [18] of the models. The transformation rules and tools should take into account the possibility that source and target models have different meta-metamodel. In this case the actual transformation is executed in the technological space of either the source or target model and some exporters and importers modules are provided to bridge the technological spaces.

3.2 How

To specify and apply a transformation, it is possible to apply knowledge from any of the major programming paradigms.

The major distinction between transformation mechanisms is whether they rely on a declarative or an operational (or imperative) approach. Declarative approaches focus on what needs to be transformed into what by defining a relation between the source and target models (e.g, [8]). Operational approaches focus on the how aspect, i.e., they focus on how the transformation itself needs to be performed by specifying the steps that are required to derive the target models from the source models (e.g, [33]).

In the following we give some examples of mechanisms (mainly declarative) that can be applied to perform model transformation,specifically, XSLT, graph transformation and QVT (for a detailed overview see [11,33]).

XSLT is a transformation technology based on XML. A transformation in the XSLT language is expressed as a well-formed XML document and describes a set of template rules for transforming a source document in a tree format (such as an XML file) into a result document described also by a tree. A template rule has two parts: a pattern (matched against nodes in the source tree) and a template (which can be instantiated to form part of the result tree). The target model of the transformation is separate from the source model and the structure of these two models can be completely different. Although, in the last years XSLT has gained a wide popularity, it is often consigned to deal with the lowest-level of model transformation due to its difficult readability and to the lack of acceptable error reporting. Furthermore, another point that can make difficult the application of XSLT as transformation language is its XML nature that entails source models described as tree, while models are more generally represented as graphs.

A *graph transformation* rule consists of a left hand side (LHS), which is a graph pattern consisting of elements constituting a precondition for the application of the rule, and a right hand side (RHS) which is a graph pattern containing the elements present after the application of the rule. Roughly speaking, such a rule can be applied to a host graph H as follows: when an occurrence of LHS is found in H, it is removed and replaced with a copy of RHS. For a detailed discussion on Graph Grammar and Graph Transformation see [5]. Solutions based on the graph transformation paradigm are often perceived by users to be too complex and hence have seen relatively little real-world usage [18].

The *QVT* (Query/View/Transformation) language is a OMG standard [21] whose purpose is to enable the transformation of MOF-based models [22]. MOF is the meta-modeling framework proposed by the Object Management Group (OMG) for the management of models and their transformations within the OMG "implementation" of the MDD paradigm, known as MDA (Model Driven Architecture) [19]. A QVT Transformation is composed of Relations. Each relation defines a bidirectional mapping between two (or more) domains for which the relation is defined. Each domain has a pattern, i.e. a configuration of object instances together with their mutual links and attributes that define the applicability conditions of a rule. A relation has a when clause and a where clause, containing a set of OCL statements, that are used to further constrain the applicability of the mapping rule (when clause), or to enforce the creation (or deletion) of certain elements that are found in the source model and that do not conform to the rule target pattern (where clause). We refer to [21] for further details.

4 Transformation Taxonomy for Performance Analysis

Quite recently, the academic community started to address the meta-modeling concept in the Software Performance Engineering (SPE) context [14,25]. Hence it is time to move towards Model Driven Engineering in SPE discipline and try to extend the usage of well established Model Transformation results in SPE domain.

By referring to the taxonomy outlined in the previous section we exemplify how the proposed dimensions can be customized in the SPE context for the "what" and "how" dimensions.

Let us start by considering the source and target models of a transformation in terms of *Number and Notations*. A model transformation should be defined to handle multiple source models and/or multiple target models. In general in SPE we have many-to-one model transformation (for example approaches that from a set of UML diagrams derives a Petri Net), and one-to-one model transformation. This is the case of using a source notation similar to the target notation, for example in case of using Petri Nets and Process Algebras as source models and stochastic extension of them as target model respectively. In this case the model transformation acts as a refinement of the source model where the target model is enriched with performance aspects.

In case of Klaper and CSM we may have many-to-one model transformations that translate different source models into Klaper/CSM model and then one-to-many model transformations that translate a Klaper/CSM model into a set of different performance models.

An additional point to be considered in the SPE context concerns the understanding and the classification of the amount and the type of information to embed in a software architecture in order to enable its validation versus performance properties.

Architectural languages often do not include information about the expected/ provided QoS. In these cases, it is fundamental to determine the information that is lacking in the software architecture description but crucial for the transformation of the SA into a performance model (examples of this information can be: number of invocations of a component within a certain scenario, service demand, etc). Some efforts in this direction can be found for example, in the introduction of UML profiles aiming at represent performance and QoS information [27,20].

Considering the kind of transformations we have:

– *Endogenous versus exogenous transformation*: Since SPE discipline aims at filling the gap among software and performance models in order to allow early performance validation of design decisions, the most SPE approaches are exogenous. Only few approaches are endogenous and are related to the ones having as source and target model petri net or process algebras.
– *Horizontal versus vertical transformation*: in SPE, the transformation are generally horizontal transformations where the performance model is specified at the same level of the software model. Sometimes the SPE approaches can require a first transformation-step where an abstraction of the source model is performed [26]. This abstraction aggregates a (large) number of source model elements according to certain rules. The aggregated groups are then mapped to a single target model element. Goal of this abstraction step is to reduce the complexity of the target model by maintaining the same representativeness level. In this case the transformation is a composition of both a vertical and a horizontal transformation.
– *Technological Space*: as already said, a technological space is determined by the meta-modeling used. There are several technological spaces, such as XML or MDA based on the usage of XML Schema or the MOF [22] as meta-metamodel respectively. In SPE context the meta-model of a source and target notation is in general

expressed in both XML and MOF. MOF is used to represent graphically the source and the target models whereas the transformational algorithms are implemented by using the XML technology. To bridge the gap among the different TSs the transformations are provided of exporters and importers as discussed by Mens and Van Gorp in [18]. However, in SPE the transformations are implemented with ad-hoc algorithms that use imperative programming languages instead of using XML or MOF translation mechanism such as XSLT and MOF translation language.

With respect to the "how" dimension of the taxonomy, in the SPE context the transformations are often implemented with *ad-hoc algorithms* that use imperative programming languages, however in several transformation methodologies and tools it is possible to devise a common underlying application schema/pattern. In this group of transformations the source architectural model is represented by a set of UML diagrams. These diagrams are annotated with ad-hoc or standard performance annotations and then exported in the underlying XMI/XML format. The transformation is then defined from the XML document of the source model to an XML model defining the target performance model (e.g., QN, PN, simulation). The transformation language is often JAVA or a similar imperative language. However, recently we experience that in some cases the transformations are defined using XSLT or graph transformation rules.

4.1 Characteristics of a Model Transformation

In SPE the model-to-model transformations are mainly realized by ad-hoc algorithms. However, we would like to reuse well established and tested transformation mechanisms existing in MDD. The success characteristics of transformation languages and tools as delineated in [18], can be imported quite easily in the SPE context:

- *Level of automation*: this dimension indicates if a transformation is fully automated or if it needs a human intervention. Of course a fully automated transformation is desirable in SPE.
- *Complexity of the transformation*: the complexity of the transformation is the degree of heavy-duty the transformation has. In general, the transformations in SPE have high complexity.
- *Preservation*: the preservation indicates how many aspects of the source model the transformation preserves in the target model. In SPE context, we can have several levels of preservation.
- *Ability to verify and guarantee correctness of the transformations*: we should prove that the transformations are correct and that do not introduce in the target model, for example, elements that have no correspondence with any element in the source model. This characteristic is always desirable in an model driven engineering.
- *Support for traceability and change propagation*: to support traceability the transformation tool needs to provide means to maintain an explicit link between the source and the target models. In SPE this characteristic guarantees the ability of the approach to feel back the source model with the results obtained from the analysis of the target (performance) model. Moreover, the support to change propagation allows to propagate directly the changes in the source model towards the target model. This is very important in SPE since the analysis results can suggest to the

developer some change over the source (software) model. Whenever the designer makes such changes, these are immediately reflected on the performance model.

- *Scalability*: the transformation tool should be able to deal with large and complex software model without sacrificing performance.

5   Comparison of Existing Approaches

In this section we first introduce some existing SPE approaches and then we compare them and the ones presented in section 2 by using the taxonomy for the SPE domain introduced in section 4. We name the considered approaches by using the name of the tools that implement them.

5.1   XPRIT-SPE·ED

In [29] the authors report their experience in building a complete path from software design to performance validation, based on existing tools that were not designed to interact with each other. The path reflects the Software Performance Engineering process model and consists of the following steps: 1) the UML software models is exported to an XMI/XML representation by using the Visual Paradigm UML Case tool; 2) a first software performance model is derived from the UML annotated model through the XPRIT tool [10]; 3) the software performance model is evaluated using the SPE·ED tool [31], which outputs are normally enough in early stages of design; 4) when more specific performance measures are needed, the model can be exported as a system performance model and analyzed with Qnap. The approach proposes and uses common XML based interchange formats, which allow multiple tools to be used to solve the models. The tools that perform model transformations are XPRIT and SPE·ED. XPRIT is made of two components: UML2EG, that allows to annotate Use Case and Sequence Diagrams and generate from the annotated diagrams an Execution Graph; UML2QN, that allows to annotate a Deployment Diagram and generate from the annotated diagram a Queueing Network representing the hardware platform where the software shall run. SPE·ED, by specifying the overhead matrix, syntheses the workload represented by execution graphs and parameterizes the queueing network of the hardware platform.

5.2   SAP·One

The Sap·One methodology has been introduced in [13] and it is conceived as a model-based approach to estimate the performance of software architectures. The prerequisites to apply the approach consist of modeling the software systems by means of UML 2 diagrams, as follows: modeling the system requirements through an Use Case Diagram, modeling the software architecture through Component and Sequence Diagrams. The UML diagrams are annotated with performance aspects by means of stereotypes of SPT Profile [27]. In particular, the information annotated is: (i) Component Diagram - service demand of each component service, scheduling policy of each component on pending service requests; (ii) Sequence Diagram - workload description, probabilities over the branching points, average number of loop iterations. The annotated diagrams are then transformed into a multichain QN as follows. Each component becomes a service center of the network, and its characteristics are extracted from the annotations illustrated above. The QN topology reflects the one of the Component Diagram. Each Sequence Diagram is processed to lump into a class of jobs (i.e. a chain) of the QN. A job traverses the network following the behavior described by the Sequence Diagram it comes from. The network workload is extracted from the annotations in the Sequence Diagrams [12].

5.3 UML-ψ

The approach proposed by Balsamo and Marzolla in [4] generates a process-oriented simulation model of a UML software specification describing the software architecture of the system. The used UML diagrams are Use Case, Activity and Deployment diagrams. The diagrams are annotated according to a sub-set of the UML SPT profile [27]. Such annotations are used to parameterize the simulation model. The approach define an (almost) one-to-one correspondence between the entities expressed in the UML model and the entities or processes in the simulation model. This correspondence allows easy report of the performance results back to the software specification that are annotated by means of UML SPT tag values. The approach has been implemented in the prototype tool UML-ψ (UML Performance SImulator).

5.4 ArgoSPE

In [7] the authors propose a systematic translation of Statecharts and Sequence Diagrams into GSPN. The approach consists of translating the two type of diagrams into two separate labeled GSPN. The translation of a Statechart gives rise to one labeled GSPN per unit where a unit is a state with all its outgoing transitions. The resulting nets are then composed over places with equal labels in order to obtain a complete model. Similarly, the translation of a Sequence diagram consists of modeling each message with a labeled GSPN subsystem and then composing such subsystems by taking into account the causal relationship between messages belonging to the same interaction, and defining the initial marking of the resulting net. The final model is obtained by building a GSPN model by means of two composing techniques. In [17] the authors extend the methodology by using the UML Activity diagrams to describe activities performed by the system usually expressed in a statechart as *doActivity*. Again, the activity diagrams are translated in labeled GSPN. Such targets model are then combined with the labeled GSPN modeling the statecharts that use the *doActivity* modelled by the activity diagrams. The authors implemented a java module to implement the GSPN generation. This approach has been implemented in ArgoSPE [2] tool that is a plug in of ArgoUML case tool [1].

5.5 Taxonomy Application

The dimensions we use to compare the considered approaches are the number of source and target models held from and the technological space used by the approaches, the automation degree and the complexity of the transformations, their degree of preservation, traceability and scalability, and finally the mechanisms used in the transformation.

Table 1. Summary of the methodologies

Approach	Complexity	Preservation	Traceability	Scalability	Technological Space	Model Transf. Mechanism
Petriu1 [23]	M	M	M/H	M		— Graph Transf.
Petriu2 [15]	M	M	M/H	M	XML	XSLT (relational?)
KLAPER[14]	M	H	M/H	M	MOF	relational (and graph transf.)
XPRIT-SPE·ED [29]	H	L	L	M	MOF/XML	ad-hoc
ArgoSPE [7, 17]	H	L/M	L	L	MOF/XML	ad-hoc
SAP·one [13]	M	H	H	M	MOF/XML	ad-hoc
UML-ψ[4]	L	H	H	M	MOF/XML	ad-hoc

We believe that the best approach is the one that present low complexity and high preservation, high traceability and high scalability. In general, preservation (i.e. the ability to preserve in the target model as many aspects of the source model as possible) and traceability (that measures the ability of the approach to trace the transformation steps from the source to the target model) are strictly related and they should have close values.

In table 1 we report the considered dimensions except for the number of source and target models held and the automation degree since all the approaches take in input many source models and generate one target model (many-to-one transformation), and present high automation.

In the table, the approaches are indicated in the first column by means of their name and reference. The values used from the third to the sixth column are discrete and belong to low (L), medium (M) and high (H). At this research stage we can only perform this coarse-grained classification of approaches since, in most cases, we can base only on the proposed description of the methods. A detailed comparison of the different techniques would require performing some common validation experiment and this is one of our medium-term objective.

All the approaches have as technological spaces XML or MOF or both. The first two, the ones proposed by Petriu et al., differ from each other only in the model transformation mechanism used to generate the performance model that are the graph transformation technology for the first and the XSLT language for the second. They present medium complexity, preservation and scalability, while the traceability is medium/high.

The third approach is the KLAPER language introduced in section 2.2. It has medium complexity and scalability, high preservation and medium/high traceability. The model transformation mechanism used to translate the source models into the target model is mainly relational even if the authors presented also a transformation that combines relational mechanism with graph transformation.

Differently from the first tree approaches the remaining ones are implemented by means of ad-hoc algorithms without following any MDD transformation mechanisms. The approach XPRIT-SPE·ED [29] has high complexity, low traceability, and medium scalability. The level of preservation is quite low, since the approach uses the software model to synthesize the workload the software provides over the hardware platform modeled by the performance model. The fifth approach in the table, instead, has high complexity, medium/low preservation and low traceability and scalability.

Finally the last two approaches present the same characteristics, except for the complexity where SAP·one [13] has an higher complexity with respect to UML-ψ [4]. Commonly, they have high preservation and traceability, whereas the scalability is medium.

6   Recommendation

As already discussed, at present, the introduction of extra-functional analysis at software architectural level is mostly handled by ad-hoc methods and tools whose key idea is to define a model transformation that takes as input some "design-oriented" model of the software system and (almost) automatically generates an "analysis-oriented" model that can be analyzed using traditional techniques. Figure 2 illustrates this kind of transformation: for each design model notation and for each analysis oriented notation, an ad-hoc transformation engine should be defined.

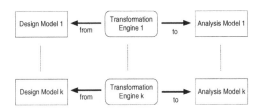

Fig. 2. Ad-hoc analysis-oriented model transformations

The idea we believe worth to pursue is to look at the construction of an analysis-oriented model as the result of a transformation from a design-oriented model integrated in the MDD paradigm for software system. In such a way, it is possible to exploit the MDD facilities to devise transformations from design models to analysis models and to render the transformation process automatic, sound and reliable based on well-established model transformation techniques. A key point in this paradigm is played by the existence of MOF metamodels [22]. According to MOF, a (meta)model is basically represented as a constrained labeled graph, where a given metamodel defines the "syntactic rules" to build legal models.

In such a way a transformation from a design to an analysis model is possible if a MOF metamodel exists for the corresponding models. According to the MDD perspective, these transformations can be defined as a set of rules that map elements of the source metamodel into elements of the target metamodel.

Figure 3 illustrates the target methodology based on the MOF metamodel; for the sake of simplicity we have illustrated a single step from design to analysis, however, it is possible to easily extend the approach by considering intermediate levels.

In this vision, the performance model derivation requires the definition of a MOF metamodel for both source and target models. In such a way the effort is shifted upwards towards the MOF metamodels definitions (that can be done once and for all for every notations) instead that in the definition and realization of ad-hoc methods that need to be designed and implemented for each design and analysis models.

Another interesting point that deserves further investigation is represented by the use and potentialities of the recently proposed intermediate models like KLAPER [14] and CSM [25] filling the gap between design and analysis models. Using these intermediate models it would be possible to reduce both the number and the complexity of the transformation to be defined.

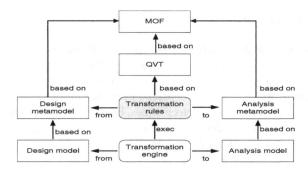

Fig. 3. Model Transformation in MDD

7   Conclusion

Notwithstanding it has been widely argued that the analysis of extra-functional properties (such as performance and reliability) should be performed from the design phase, this is still far to be a consolidated practice in the software development approach. In our view, the motivation can be partially found in the large "semantic gap" between design and performance models. To overcome this problem some methodologies and tool have been proposed for the automatic generation and analysis of software performance models. However, these methods lack of generality and are strictly related to specific design and analysis model notations. In this paper we proposed to view the performance model generation as a transformation in a MDD paradigm and to change the focus paying more attention to model transformation. To this end we proposed an initial taxonomy of model transformation in the software performance area; a comparison among some of the existing approaches and some recommendations towards software performance model driven engineering. The taxonomy lacks to consider other dimension that are very important for the SPE domain, such as accuracy of the generated performance model, the quantity of additional information needed in the transformation and so on. Our long term goal is the definition of a general framework for software performance model driven engineering, where it would be possible to choose which models and which transformation method to apply for addressing a specific target problem.

Acknowledgments

The authors would like to thank Vittorio Cortellessa and Vincenzo Grassi for helpful discussions on this topic.

References

1. ArgoUML – Object-oriented design tool with cognitive support. http://www.argouml.org/
2. ArgoSPE. http://argospe.tigris.org/
3. S. Balsamo, A. Di Marco, P. Inverardi, M. Simeoni, Model-based Performance Prediction in Software Development: A Survey, *IEEE Trans. on Software Engineering*, 30(5):295-310, 2004.

4. S. Balsamo, M. Marzolla, A Simulation-Based Approach to Software Performance Modeling, *Proc. Joint 9th European Software Engineering Conference ESEC& 11th SIGSOFT Symposium on the Foundations of Software Engineering FSE-11*, Helsinki, FI, sep 1–5, pp. 363–366, 2003.

5. Baresi, L. und Heckel. R, Tutorial Introduction to Graph Transformation: A Software Engineering Perspective, *In Proc. 1st Int. Conference on Graph Transformation (ICGT 02)*, Barcelona, Spain, LNCE 2505, October 2002.

6. S. Becker, L. Grunske, R. Mirandola and S. Overhage, Performance Prediction of Component-Based Systems: A Survey from an Engineering Perspective, LNCS 3938, 2006, to appear.

7. S. Bernardi, S. Donatelli, J. Merseguer, From UML Sequence Diagrams and Statecharts to analysable Petri Net models, *in ACM Proc. of WOSP2002*, Rome, Italy, pp. 35–45, 2002.

8. J. Bezivin, E. Breton, G. Dup, P. Valduriez, The ATL transformation-based model management framework, *Res. Report no. 03.08*, IRIN, Univ. de Nantes, Sept. 2003

9. V. Cortellessa, A. Di Marco, P. Inverardi, Software Performance Model-Driven Architecture, in Proc. of the 21st Annual ACM SAC - Track on Model Transformation. Bourgogne University, Dijon, France April 23 -27, 2006.

10. V. Cortellessa, M. Gentile, and M. Pizzuti. XPRIT: An XML-based Tool to Translate UML Diagrams into Execution Graphs and Queueing Networks (Tool Paper). in Proc. of 1st QEST01. 2004. Enschede, NL.

11. K. Czarnecki, S. Helsen, Classification of Model Transformation Approaches, *Proc. of OOPSLA03 Workshop on Generative Techniques in the Context of MDA*, 2003.

12. A. Di Marco, Model-based performance analysis of software architectures, Ph.D. thesis, University of L'Aquila, 2005.

13. A. Di Marco, P. Inverardi, Compositional Generation of Software Architecture Performance QN Models, *Proc. of WICSA 2004*, pp. 37-46, 2004.

14. V. Grassi, R. Mirandola, A. Sabetta, From Design to Analysis Models: a Kernel Language for Performance and Reliability Analysis of Component-based Systems, *in Proc. of WOSP05*, Palma de Mallorca, Spain, July 11-14, 2005, pp. 25 - 36.

15. G. Gu, Dorina C. Petriu, XSLT transformation from UML models to LQN performance models, In ACM Proc. of WOSP2002, Rome, Italy, pp. 227–234, 2002.

16. G. Gu, D.C. Petriu, From UML to LQN by XML Algebra-Based Graph Transformations, *in Proc.of WOSP 2005*, Palma, Illes Balears, Spain, July 11-15, 2005, pp. 99-110.

17. J. P. López-Grao, J. Merseguer, J. Campos, From UML activity diagrams to Stochastic Petri nets: application to software performance engineering, *In ACM Proc. of WOSP04*, Redwood Shores, California, pp. 25–36, 2004.

18. Tom Mens, Pieter Van Gorp, A taxonomy of model transformation, *Proc. Int'l Workshop on Graph and Model Transformation*, 2005.

19. J. Miller (editor), Model-Driven Architecture Guide, omg/2003-06-01 (2003).

20. Object Management Group: UML Profile for Modeling Quality of Service and Fault Tolerance Characteristics and Mechanisms. 2004. OMG document ptc/04-09-01.

21. OMG, MOF 2.0 Query/Views/Transformations Final Adopted Specification, *OMG Adopted Specification ptc/05-11-01* .

22. OMG: Meta Object Facility (MOF) 2.0 Core Specification, OMG Adopted Specification ptc/03-10-04, on line at: www.omg.org/docs/ptc/03-10-04.pdf.

23. Dorina C. Petriu, X. Wang, "From UML descriptions of High-Level Software Architectures to LQN Performance Models", *Proc. of AGTIVE'99*, LNCS 1779, pp. 47–62, 1999.

24. D.B. Petriu, M. Woodside, A Metamodel for Generating Performance Models from UML Designs, *in Proc. UML2004*, Lisbon, Portugal, Oct. 2004, LNCS 3273, pp 41-53.

25. D.B. Petriu, M. Woodside, A Metamodel for Generating Performance Models from UML Designs, *Proc. of UML Conference*, LNCS 3273, pp 41-53, (2004).

26. A. Sabetta, D.C. Petriu, V. Grassi, R. Mirandola, Abstraction-raising Transformation for Generating Analysis Models, *Proc. of Models 2005 Satellite Events*, LNCS 3844, pp. 217-226, 2005.

27. B. Selic (editor), UML Profile for Schedulability, Performance and Time, OMG Full Specification, formal/03-09-01 (2003).

28. M. Shaw, D. Garlan. Software Architecture: Perspectives on an Emerging Discipline. *Prentice-Hall* (1996)

29. Connie U. Smith, Catalina M. Lladó, V. Cortellessa, A. Di Marco, Lloyd G. Williams, From UML models to software performance results: an SPE process based on XML interchange formats, *Proc. of WOSP05*, pp. 87–98, Palma, Illes Balears, Spain, 2005.

30. C.U. Smith, L.G. Williams, Performance Solutions: A Practical Guide to Creating Responsive, Scalable Software, Addison-Wesley, 2002.

31. C.U. Smith and L.G. Williams, Performance Engineering of Object-Oriented Systems with SPEED, LNCS 1245: Computer Performance Evaluation, M.R.e. al., Editor. 1997, Berlin, Germany. p. 135-154.

32. A. Solberg, J. Oldevik, J.Aagedal, QoS-aware Model Transformation, presented at DOA 2004.

33. Laurence Tratt, Model transformations and tool integration, Journal of Software and Systems Modelling. Vol. 4(2), pp. 112-122, May, 2005.

34. M. Woodside et al., Performance by Unified Model Analysis (PUMA), *in Proc. of WOSP05*, Palma de Mallorca, Spain, July 11-14, 2005, pp. 1-12.

Traveling Architects – A New Way of Herding Cats

Aino Vonge Corry[1], Klaus Marius Hansen[1], and David Svensson[2]

[1] Department of Computer Science, University of Aarhus
Aabogade 34, 8200 Aarhus M
{apaipi, klaus.m.hansen}@daimi.au.dk
[2] Department of Computer Science, Lund University
Ole Römers väg 3, 223 63 Lund, Sweden
david@cs.lth.se
The PalCom Project
http://www.ist-palcom.org

Abstract. Making software developers work towards a common goal
may be likened to herding cats. If we further spread developers around
the globe, we run increased risks of being unable to design and impose
coherent software architectures on projects, potentially leading to lower
quality of the resulting systems. Based on our experiences in a large,
distributed research and development project, *PalCom*, we propose that
employing techniques from active user involvement in general (and from
participatory design in particular) may help in designing and sharing
quality software architectures. In particular, we present the *Traveling
Architects* technique in which a group of architects visit development locations in order to engage developers and end users in software architecture work. We argue that using techniques such as these may potentially
lead to higher quality of software architectures in particular for systems
developed in a distributed setting.

1 Introduction

Consider the following scenario, taking place in a distributed software development project, where development teams at different sites cooperate towards
forming a common architecture:

> *Two Traveling Architects, Mario and Lisa, visit a site in order to have
> a Traveling Architects workshop. The developers at the site have prepared
> a presentation of the end-users, the architectural requirements and the
> prototype they have imagined. At this site they work with rehabilitation of
> people who have had hand surgery. They have a number of scenarios that
> they want supported with a prototype, such as sharing of ideas between a
> group of rehabilitation patients.*
>
> *After the presentation, the developers go through the different parts
> of the prototype they want to build and discuss whether it would be ben-
> eficial to implement all of it. Lisa and Mario advice on the use of the*

C. Hofmeister et al. (Eds.): QoSA 2006, LNCS 4214, pp. 111–126, 2006.
© Springer-Verlag Berlin Heidelberg 2006

current common architecture, and note components that are candidates for placement in the project's toolbox of reusable components. They agree that some parts, such as the recording of video at consultations with physiotherapists, has to work in order for the end-users to be able to participate in the next application design meeting. Other parts, like the sharing of data over wireless net, could be simulated, because designing them wouldn't add to the common architecture.

During the meeting, Lisa and Mario create Unified Modeling Language (UML; [19]) diagrams of object and class models and sketch a documentation note on the prototype. After the meeting, the documentation note is finished and sent to the application developers to check for misunderstandings. Returning from the site, a meeting with other architects in the project is held in order to propagate the knowledge of the requirements and the input to the common architecture.

This is an example of the use of the Traveling Architects technique, taken from our work in the EC-funded Integrated Project PalCom [20]. PalCom explores the concept of *palpable computing*, denoting a new kind of ambient computing which is concerned with the above and other user-oriented challenges in complex and dynamic ambient computing environments. The two primary goals of the PalCom project are to explore the concept of 'palpability' and to design an open software architecture for palpable computing. In the following section we will present more about the project as a background, before discussing the Traveling Architects technique in more detail.

2   The PalCom Project

One of the subprojects in PalCom is the "Pregnancy and Maternity" project, where IT support for pregnancies is investigated. The vision is to equip pregnant women with a device called 'the Stone', which can support them during their pregnancy:

Alice comes home, greets her husband Bob and wants to show him something on a device she holds in her hand. The device has a very small screen and suggests using the TV as an external display. After Alice has accepted it, a film is shown on the TV. It is a recording from the ultra sound scan she went to that day because she is pregnant.

Since Alice is also diabetic, she has to measure her blood sugar level regularly. Her measurements are uploaded daily to the national Electronic Health Record (EHR) system, where experts will get a warning if the measurements are out of the ordinary. She has set the Stone to upload the data every night without her need to accept. One night the EHR system is unavailable. The Stone lets Alice know that is has tried to send the data without success. She then places it next to her computer, and the display is now on her computer screen. She points at the notification about the missed send of a message, and a graphical view of the connections is shown. On this she can follow the connections between devices and see that the Stone looses the connection with the EHR system at the EHR system installation and thus the problem lies at their end, not hers. She chooses for the Stone to try and contact the register until is succeeds and then let her know that it has succeeded.

When the Stone and its environment work as they are supposed to, the user does not have to think about the state of it or how it works. Only in situations where there is a usage breakdown should the user become aware that something should be changed and maybe decide how it should be changed. This visibility/invisibility trade-off is one of the challenges of PalCom.

In the situation where the Stone has to make use of external displays and keyboards, there is a composition of services and devices in the system. This composition happens dynamically and can be decomposed at any time, yet still keeping the system as a whole stable. Composition/decomposition and change/stability are also challenges in the PalCom project.

Twelve companies and universities from six European countries take part in PalCom. The research work is organized into sixteen work packages, and each of the partners are involved in several of them. The activities reported in this paper concern the connection between the work package responsible for the common PalCom architecture, and the *application prototyping work packages*, which work with prototypes at different sites, forming palpable computing in contact with its users.

Figure 1 shows the overall development strategy in the project: results from general design and architecture work influence the application prototypes, and vice versa, throughout the 48-month project.

The application prototyping work packages are the following:

– *WP7 On Site* supports the work of professionals working in the field, in particular landscape architects. One example of work is the prototype Site-

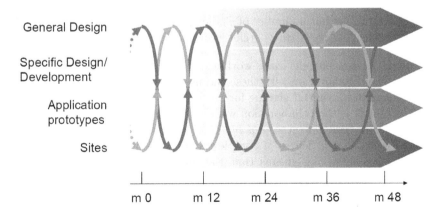

Fig. 1. Overall development strategy in PalCom

Sticks, which is used for location-based visual assessment at a construction site where a major European bank is building their new headquarters.

- *WP8 Major Incidents* supports first aid personnel at the site of a major incident, during ambulance transport of patients, and after having arrived at the hospital by the use of among others sensor networks. The work in this work package is carried out together with the hospital, the police and the fire department in Aarhus, Denmark.

- *WP9 Pregnancy and Maternity* creates application prototypes supporting women and their families during pregnancy and (early) maternity. The Stone, discussed above, is one of the WP9 prototypes.

- *WP10 Surgical Rehabilitation* builds prototypes in the context of rehabilitation after hand surgery, in cooperation with Malmö University Hospital. One example is a video recording prototype which explores tangible user interfaces in the context of physiotherapy consultation.

- *WP11 Care Community* supports disabled children and adults in rehabilitation, both at the hospital and, e.g., in the swimming pool. One prototype is the Active Surfaces, where a set of computerized tiles to be used in the swimming pool can be configured by a therapist for aid in various sequencing and positioning exercises. Another aspect of this work package is the research in incubator support. The Incubator prototype makes it possible for doctors to manipulate the position of a baby without opening the incubator, preserving the micro-environmental conditions inside.

- *WP12 Transient Locations* supports users seeking connectivity in ad-hoc and hybrid networks. The prototype RASCAL (Resilience and Adaptivity Scenario for Connectivity over Ad-hoc Links) makes use of agent technology for adapting to available network access resources and to get an overview of possible connectivity issues.

3   Introducing the 'Traveling Architects' Technique

The PalCom project has a number of challenges as alluded to by the above that are of high relevance to software architecture design in the project:

- *Distributed development teams* working with actual end-users at various locations. The collaboration with these end users at specific locations are crucial in understanding and designing for local work practice. One example (given in Section 2) is the collaboration with landscape architects.

- *An iterative, experimental, and incremental approach* to development. The project has a high degree of complexity, uncertainty and potential change of requirements. This means that the project employs agile development principles [11]. One consequence of this is that the software architecture is continually evolving and no full set of architectural requirements exists for the software architecture at a given point in time. Further, during our initial Traveling Architects work there were not always clear guidelines that could be readily presented to the prototyping teams. We could often only provide them with guidelines as to what direction the architecture should progress and whether their architectural requirements were addressed by others.

- *Limited central control* of software architecture design. Creating a software architecture in PalCom is in many ways a consensus-making process. With the outset in the central challenges of palpable computing on the one hand and concrete, usable application prototypes on the other hand, the architecture is gradually designed and evolved, catering for functional as well as quality requirements.

A Definition

To tackle such challenges, it was decided to form a team of architects that would be responsible for maintaining the architectural vision of PalCom by both working from the specific (application prototypes) and the general (the concept of palpable computing and architectural requirements) and for making sure that this vision was shared by all sites. In this way, the concept of 'Traveling Architects' was born. To be more precise, we define the concepts as follows:

> *Traveling Architects: a group of architects responsible for maintaining software architectural assets in a distributed development project by visiting development sites in order to design, evaluate, and enforce a software architecture in active collaboration with developers and possibly end users*

If we dissect the definition, a number of components are of interest in this context: "group of architects", "visiting", and "active collaboration".

With respect to the group of architects, the concept is related to the ArchitectureTeam pattern from Coplien's set of organizational patterns [8]. The main similarity is that they form a team of architects that can communicate about the architecture with each other and the groups of developers. In Coplien's ArchitectureTeam, the team of architects makes the initial architecture, which is not the case for the Traveling Architects. They spread the word of the evolving architecture and collects input to its evolvement. The decision of the concrete architecture is done in a team of architects of which the Traveling Architects are members. This team is built like an ArchitectureDefinitionTeam as described in Mezsaros' patterns [17].

The rationale for actually "visiting" remote development sites is closely connected to the rationale for "active collaboration" which is again closely connected to the concept of 'participatory design'. In fact, the Traveling Architects technique may be seen more generally as part of an attempt to employ participatory design techniques in software architecture work. Thus, we describe this concept and its potential relation to software architecture next.

Participatory Design and Software Architecture

Participatory design [13] is concerned with involving stakeholders (e.g., developers, end users, managers, or customers) of IT systems in the collective design of these systems. This is done for both moral and practical reasons [7]: Practitioners are the ones who need to live with the consequences of IT systems and they are the ones who have the real competence in what is to supported and who know the real, practical problems. Bringing diverse and indispensable competencies together is thus seen as a main part of doing systems development[1].

Concretely, design is often done collaboratively in workshop-like settings by users and designers/developers and informed by (ethnographic) studies of actual work practice [5]. The following Figure 2 illustrates the concepts at play:

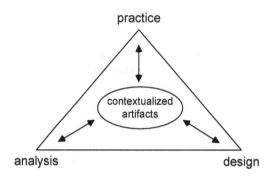

Fig. 2. Artifacts in participatory analysis and design (adapted from Mogensen and Trigg [18])

Here it is illustrated how analysis (e.g., work analysis through ethnography or participatory analysis), design (e.g., design of user interfaces), and practice (e.g., the work of users collaborating in design or analysis) communicate and collaborate through common artifacts. Such artifacts could, e.g., be user stories, sketches on whiteboards, or actual prototypes of applications. A number of techniques may be employed in order to work with and create these artifacts collaboratively: creating mock-ups, cooperative prototyping, future workshops [13], or use of situation cards [18] are examples of such techniques.

An example from PalCom is the use of participatory design at workshops in the *Pregnancy and Maternity* project. A number of healthcare providers involved in pregnancy were gathered at a workshop. They were given an introduction to the ideas formed by the designers. The ideas were based on field work done in the healthcare system and thus grounded in the work of the people present. The healthcare providers did not show great enthusiasm until we presented a concrete artifact to them. As an example of the Stone we had discussed with them previously, we had brought a PDA with a primitive application. The application could, e.g., send a Java program to a mobile phone in order to make it vibrate at given intervals. This was done in order to help the pregnant women do their birth preparation exercises. The healthcare providers responded to the artifact,

---

[1] Indeed some of the work on participatory design has influenced current thinking on software methods although techniques such as the On-Site-Customer of eXtreme Programming [4] has taken an analytical standpoint, removing practitioners from their work.

now suddenly understanding the concept and able to form new ideas also for extensions of functionality. The change in their attitude, when presented with an artifact, was remarkable. We have seen this effect numerous times in the PalCom project. Sometimes with applications, other times just with screenshots or natural artifacts, such as actual stones.

The main insight we use here is then that the same set of concepts as presented and illustrated above can be applied to the creation of *software architecture* rather than for the design of artifacts *directly supporting* work practice of users. Figure 3 tries to illustrate this. Here, the practice involved is that of developers (and perhaps transitively or directly that of end-users) including the designs they have produced, application architectures, prototypes etc. The artifact that is collaboratively being constructed is a software architecture in various forms: UML-based descriptions, architectural prototypes [2], verbal accounts continuously being given by developers and architects etc. The next sections will discuss the generalizability of the approach and then detail our experiences with the Traveling Architects approach and discuss concrete details of how to involve developers in the architecture work.

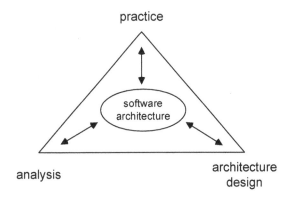

Fig. 3. Participatory design of software architectures

Generalizability

A natural question to pose is to which extent the PalCom experience is unique thus making the experience of the Traveling Architects only relevant to this particular project? Here, we point to two concrete examples of development efforts that have many of the same project characteristics as PalCom and that could thus reasonably use the presented techniques.

The first example is a set of projects aiming at realizing Danish EHR systems in all hospitals by 2006 [10]. Each of 14 Danish counties have had the responsibility of introducing an EHR system for the public hospitals in that county. This approach was chosen for multiple reasons: one was to be able to use various vendors in order to get vendors to compete on price and quality and another was that local hospitals have competent staff with partially local competences that need to be supported. One consequence of this choice has been that there has been no central control and thus no single software architecture (or integration platform) for all systems. This gives a number of challenges in integrating patient data from the systems, a particular twist to the problem being that the counties will merge to become larger units by 2007. Some of the issues of integrating the disperse systems are discussed in [14].

The other example comes from that of a globally distributed company that one of the authors worked with as part of an effort to build a series of prototypes for a global customer service system. The company had previously built a number of regional service systems. These were built regionally and built in order to support local practices well; customer interaction was, e.g., very different in Asia in terms of customer loyalty than in other parts of the world. Again, this led to (technical) problems when trying to enable service agents to provide service on a global basis among others due to the lack of a common architecture of the systems.

4   The PalCom Architecture

To give an overview of the PalCom open architecture that we refer to, we have included a part of our ontology for the architecture in Figure 4 (see [21]). The ontology may be thought of as a (very) logical view of the PalCom architecture, showing the concepts (and relationships) that are realized in the architecture. We do not intend this presentation to be exhaustive, but it gives a picture of what we are using to guide us in our work as Traveling Architects.

Going back to the scenario of Section 2, we see several of the concepts in the ontology in play. Alice is an *Actor* in a PalCom system. She makes use of several different *PalCom Assemblies*. One example is the Assembly formed between the Stone and the TV, which moves the displaying from the Stone to the TV screen for showing the recording from the ultra sound scan. A second Assembly comes alive when Alice connects the blood sugar measurement device to the Stone for storing measurement data, and a third one connects the Stone to the EHR system, managing the upload of data. The role of each Assembly is to coordinate a set of *Services*, communicating over *Communication Channels*. Each service is offered by one *Node*: the TV has a display service, the blood sugar measurement device has a measurement service, and the EHR system has a registry service.

The software implementation of the nodes is what distinguishes a *PalCom Node* from a *Non-PalCom Node*. The Stone is a PalCom node, because it hosts a *PalCom Runtime Environment*, which realizes the Stone's services through execution of *PalCom Runtime Components*. The TV, on the other hand, is a non-PalCom node. Its software does not run as PalCom Runtime Components, for reasons of legacy code or hardware restrictions, but its services are externally accessible in the same way as the services of the Stone.

Different kinds of restrictions in hardware are also targeted by the concept of *1st Order Resources*, which are associated with physical devices. Examples are CPU clock speed, memory, bandwidth and power. Taking these into account,

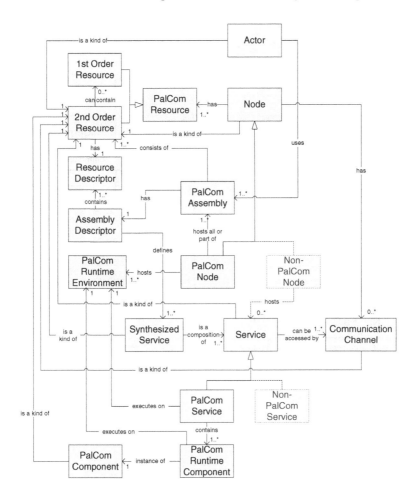

Fig. 4. PalCom concept ontology

together with *2nd Order Resources* such as Services, Nodes, and Actors, makes it possible for a PalCom Runtime Environment to adapt to varying resource conditions.

Figure 5 exemplifies how the different concepts may come together in a Pal-Com system. It can be seen how the Assembly XYZ references services on three different nodes. The *Synthesized Service* is a service that PalCom Node B offers on behalf of the Assembly, offering combined functionality not given by the individual services themselves.

5   Applying the Technique

The idea of Traveling Architects has been implemented during a period of about one year, in the second year of the PalCom project. In total, there have been eight

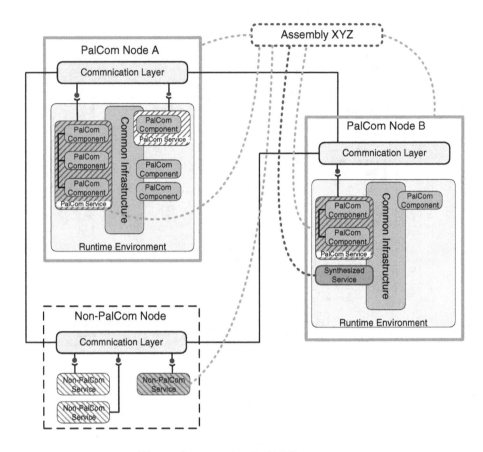

Fig. 5. An example of a PalCom system

meetings where the Traveling Architects have held workshops with the people from application prototyping work packages, and discussed the architecture of their respective prototypes in relation to the architecture. The general setup of the meetings followed the workshop example given in the introduction. On each occasion, the Traveling Architects team consisted of one or two people. There have also been general architecture meetings, where the Traveling Architects discussed their findings with the ArchitectureDefinitionTeam. Figure 6 shows the time line of the meetings and workshops. Next, we present experiences from these.

5.1 Techniques, Artifacts, and Meeting Types

The meetings and workshops have been organized in different ways, which has given experience from several types of situations that the Traveling Architects have experienced. Different aspects of our work as Traveling Architects were present to varying degrees in the different meetings.

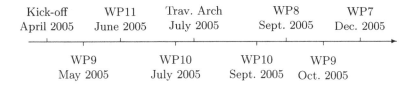

Fig. 6. Traveling Architects meetings

Within each site there has been iterative development based on participatory design. At the meetings we experienced the difference in the maturity of the development of application prototypes. This difference has also influenced the type of meetings held, the techniques applied, and the artifacts present.

Techniques. When interviewing the developers at the sites, we did not use an architecture-specific technique like ATAM [15] or QAW [1]. We performed a more ad-hoc, exploratory approach, partly because the prerequisites of the meetings were so different, partly because we wanted to free ourselves from restrictions in the beginning of the implementation of the concept. Some software development techniques were used, like the implementation of architectural prototypes [2]. When an idea had emerged, it was beneficial to implement and evaluate it before an application was based on it. We also used some of the activities described in RUP [12], e.g. the realization of use cases.

Artifacts. Since our task was to design, discuss, and document architecture, UML diagrams were used excessively to describe different views of the architecture. We had different stakeholders present at the meetings and they needed different views on the architecture, as described in [16]. At some meetings, where stakeholders such as end-users and ethnographers were present, we would draw the main use cases in order to determine if we agreed on the overall idea of the system. These use cases were later used to construct test cases to compare the architectural prototypes and applications with.

When other architects and some developers were present, we discussed the architecture seen from a module view with class and package diagrams. Other kinds of developers were more keen on discussing code snippets with the Traveling Architects or looking at allocation views of the design.

Whiteboards were often used as the common physical artifact in the center of the discussion. They have the benefit of enabling a number of people (there were often more than seven people at the meetings) to view the same diagram. Also, changing a figure or a diagram during a discussion is relatively easy on a whiteboard. We would potentially have benefited, though, from having tool support for our cooperative work as presented in [9].

Meeting Types. When we started the implementation of the Traveling Architects concept, we had imagined that the meetings would all be consisting of an aspect of documentation of the architecture and an aspect of designing architectures. Due to different challenges this was not what happened. At first this seemed frustrating, but eventually the need for Traveling Architects became more evident. The Traveling Architects just had a change of responsibility to often be more communicators than designers. These are examples of the types of meetings we have had:

- *Discovering architectural requirements*
  The developers had a somewhat clear view of the requirements of the application to be built, but they had not articulated them. The Traveling Architects thus had to distill from their knowledge what had architectural significance. Since the Traveling Architects are there to discuss architecture and often are not domain experts, this is not optimal.
- *Architectural reviews*
  The designers had documented the architecture before the meeting and we went through it together. This made the architecture more clear for the designers and gave the Traveling Architects real input for the PalCom architecture. A number of people interested in architecture met to discuss the architecture that we had defined at one of the prototype meetings. A lot of architectural discussions were triggered. This was interesting for most of the attendants but not so beneficial for the specific prototype architecture, because there were too many architects present.
- *Documenting architectures*
  A prototype had been implemented, but the process of developing it had been unstructured and there was no documentation of it. The Traveling Architects went through parts of the code together with the developers and documented the main parts.
- *Designing architectures*
  Some developers had clear architectural requirements and designing an architecture was a natural next step. This aspect in a meeting was very welcome.
- *Designing prototypes*
  A Traveling Architects meeting could be placed within a design meeting for a prototype to be built. It was useful to have a connection to the PalCom architecture in the discussion, but it was often difficult for the Traveling Architects to give input to the discussion about details in the specific prototype design.

6   Experiences

After some time as Traveling Architects, we look back at the work and the results, and we can see benefits of the work. Generally, the Traveling Architects' visits have worked as good opportunities for the prototype teams to discuss their architectures and have given valuable input to the PalCom architecture per se.

The work has given a number of benefits to the PalCom project, which we believe in themselves motivate the costs in terms of traveling and effort:

- The ArchitectureTeam has got hands-on experience with the prototypes.
- The knowledge of the status of the different prototypes has been spread within the project.
- The deeper insight into the prototypes made it possible for the architects to guide which requirements that are special for the different prototypes and should thus be focused on.
- There has been an increase in cross-partner collaboration.
- We have found new tools for the PalCom "toolbox", where development tools and software components are collected for use by other parts of the project. One example is a video streaming component developed in WP10, which was spotted as directly usable also in WP9.
- The architectures of the application prototypes have become clearer.
- Last, but not least, the software designs were documented.

We have also got an overview of the "hotspots" in the requirements and the architecture. These hotspots are issues spanning over several work packages, such as

- the location and role of the *Assembly Descriptor* in a PalCom system. The Assembly Descriptor specifies an assembly, which defines compositions of services and coordination between them.
- the sharing of data between services on the same device.
- the need for remote contingency handling, i.e. for dealing with errors that occur on other devices than the one an actor is interacting with.
- the distinction in PalCom between a *Service* and a *Resource.*
- the management and storage of data: when should it be handled locally, and when should we use a centralized model?
- the issue of partitioning a system into services of appropriate size and complexity.

In the challenging context of the PalCom project, the Traveling Architects initiative has helped keeping the focus on the architecture, and on the project as a whole. It has also helped speeding up the influences in both directions, between the prototypes and the architecture. Hopefully, in this way it has had a positive impact on the quality of the software architecture. Even though we do not have firm evidence of the way that the technique influences quality attributes, we speculate that the technique itself mostly influences architectural quality attributes (cf. the characterization of Bass et al.[3]) such as buildability and conceptual integrity. When speaking of conceptual integrity as it is described in [6] one normally refers to one system. In PalCom the situation is a bit different since there is no one system, on the contrary there exists an unlimited number of subsystems, that can stand alone or work with the others. And it is this strong challenge of construction of these small subsystems, that makes conceptual integrity important for PalCom. One major goal of the Traveling Architects is to achieve this conceptual integrity.

Enhancing system quality attributes (such as modifiability, availability, and performance) is probably more tied to the possible expertises of the individual architects traveling.

Moreover, It is a well known phenomenon that meeting face-to-face has advantages, compared to other types of communication, such as e-mail or phone conferences, see e.g.[22]. This is emphasized, e.g., in Coplien's patterns LockEmUpTogether and FaceToFaceBeforeWorkingRemotely [8] and was also experienced in our work as Traveling Architects.

Regarding the size of the Traveling Architects team, we feel that two persons was a good size, given the size of the prototype teams of about five persons. It is good not to be alone as Traveling Architect, and to be able to discuss things with the other architect directly at the meetings.

7   Conclusions and Future Work

Traveling Architects is clearly a promising technique. In the PalCom project, it has helped us work towards the definition of a common software architecture, with development teams spread across Europe. The setting is that the teams work in an iterative, experimental and incremental way, in close contact with end-users, and with limited central control. We have noted a number of concrete benefits already, of which the improved communication and spreading of knowledge in the project is the most apparent—the Traveling Architects have often been as much communicators as architecture designers. In the long run, we believe that our effort will lead to a higher quality of the software architecture.

We have seen advantages of applying concepts from participatory design to the creation of software architectures. Consciously working with UML diagrams, whiteboard drawings and code as artifacts has helped the active collaboration between architects and developers, and made the architecture more concrete for its users, the developers.

A number of different types of Traveling Architects meetings have been tried. Our conclusion here is that the documentation and design of architectures are the main ways of obtaining value from the meetings. What we had not expected, but what came as a positive side effect, was the communication of architectural requirements and ideas that were not already in use.

A relevant question is that of generalizability: can the Traveling Architects concept be successfully applied to projects other than ours, e.g. to industry-only projects? Yes, we believe it can. We have given two examples of large, distributed development projects with limited central control and iterative development strategies, where the technique could presumably have been successfully used. In particular, we think that the hands-on aspect of Traveling Architects is beneficial.

The first round of Traveling Architects has been exploratory and experimental. In our continued work, we plan to apply the technique more systematically. Now that we have more experience with it, we can put up clearer goals for each meeting, and apply more techniques from participatory design such as mock-ups, situation cards, or future workshops. In the end, we hope to be able to provide a strong, scientific evaluation of the technique of Traveling Architects.

Acknowledgements

The research presented in this paper has been partly funded by 6th Framework Programme, Information Society Technologies, Disappearing Computer II, project 002057 'PalCom: Palpable Computing – A new perspective on Ambient Computing' (http://www.ist-palcom.org).

References

1. M. R. Barbacci, R. Ellison, A. J. Lattanze, J. A. Stafford, C. B. Weinstock, and W. G. Wood. Quality Attribute Workshops (QAWs), 2nd edition. Technical Report CMU/SEI-2002-TR-019, 2002.
2. J. E. Bardram, H. B. Christensen, and K. M. Hansen. Architectural Prototyping: An Approach for Grounding Architectural Design and Learning. In *Proceedings of the 4th Working IEEE/IFIP Conference on Software Architecture*, pages 15–24, Oslo, Norway, 2004.
3. L. Bass, P. Clements, and R. Kazman. *Software Architecture in Practice*. Addison-Wesley, 2nd edition, 2003.
4. K. Beck. *Extreme Programming Explained: Embrace Change*. Addison-Wesley, 1999.
5. J. Blomberg, L. Suchman, and R. Trigg. Reflections on a work-oriented design project. In *Proceedings of PDC'94*, pages 99–110, 1994.
6. F. P. Brooks. *The Mythical Man-Month: Essays on Software Engineering*. Addison-Wesley, 20th anniversary edition, 1995.
7. M. Christensen, A. Crabtree, C. Damm, K. Hansen, O. Madsen, P. Marqvardsen, P. Mogensen, E. Sandvad, L. Sloth, and M. Thomsen. The M.A.D. experience: Multiperspective Application Development in evolutionary prototyping. In E. Jul, editor, *ECOOP'98 – Object-Oriented Programming. Proceedings of the 12th European Conference*, pages 13–40. Springer Verlag, 1998.
8. J. O. Coplien and N. B. Harrison. *Organizational Patterns of Agile Software Development*. Prentice Hall, 2004.
9. C. Damm, K. Hansen, M. Thomsen, and M. Tyrsted. Creative object-oriented modelling: Support for creativity, flexibility, and collaboration in CASE tools. In *Proceedings of ECOOP'2000*, pages 27–43, 2000.
10. The EHR Observatory. http://www.epj-observatoriet.dk/english.htm.
11. M. Fowler. The new methodology. http://martinfowler.com/articles/newMethodology.html, 2005.
12. D. Gornik. IBM Rational Unified Process: Best practices for software development teams. Technical Report TP026B, Rev 11/01, IBM, 2001.
13. J. Greenbaum and M. Kyng, editors. Lawrence Erlbaum Associates, 1991.
14. K. M. Hansen and H. B. Christensen. Component Reengineering Workshops: A low-cost approach for assessing specific reengineering costs across product lines. In *Proceedings of the 8th European Conference on Software Maintenance and Reengineering (CSMR 2004)*, pages 154–162. IEEE Press, 2004.
15. R. Kazman, M. Klein, and P. Clements. ATAM: Method for architecture evaluation. Technical Report CMU/SEI-2000-TR-004, 2000.
16. P. Kruchten. The 4+1 view model of architecture. *IEEE Software*, 12(6), 1995.
17. G. Meszaros. Archi-Patterns. In *Proceedings of the conference on Pattern Languages of Programming*, St.Louis, 1997.

18. P. Mogensen and R. Trigg. Using artefacts as triggers for participatory analysis. In M. Muller, S. Kuhn, and J. Meskill, editors, *Proceedings of the Participatory Design Conference (PDC) 1992*, pages 55–62. CPSR, 1992.
19. OMG. Unified Modeling Language specification 1.5. Technical Report formal/2003-03-01, Object Management Group, 2003.
20. The PalCom Project. `http://www.ist-palcom.org`.
21. PalCom. PalCom External Report 31: Deliverable 32 (2.2.1): PalCom Open Architecture – first complete version of basic architecture. Technical report, PalCom Project IST-002057, December 2005.
22. S. Teasley, L. Covi, M. S. Krishnan, and J. S. Olson. How does radical collocation help a team succeed? In *CSCW '00: Proceedings of the 2000 ACM conference on Computer supported cooperative work*, pages 339–346, New York, NY, USA, 2000. ACM Press.

A Practical Architecture-Centric Analysis Process

Antonio Bucchiarone[1,3], Henry Muccini[2], and Patrizio Pelliccione[2]

[1] Istituto di Scienza e Tecnologie dell'Informazione "A. Faedo" (ISTI-CNR)
Area della Ricerca CNR di Pisa, 56100 Pisa, Italy
antonio.bucchiarone@isti.cnr.it
[2] University of L'Aquila, Computer Science Department
Via Vetoio 1, 67010 L'Aquila, Italy
{muccini, pellicci}@di.univaq.it
[3] IMT Graduate School
Via San Micheletto, 3 - 55100 Lucca , Italy

Abstract. When engineering complex and distributed software and hardware systems (increasingly used in many sectors, such as manufacturing, aerospace, transportation, communication, energy and health-care), dependability has became a must, since failures can have economics consequences and can also endanger human life.

Software Architectures (SA) can help improving the overall system dependability, providing a system blueprint that can be validated and that can guide all phases of the system development. Even if much work has been done on this direction, three important topics require major investigation: how different analysis techniques can be integrated together, how results obtained with SA-based analysis can be related to requirements and coding, and how to integrate new methodologies in the industrial software development life-cycle.

In this paper we propose an architecture-centric analysis process which allows formal analysis driven by model-based architectural specifications. This analysis process satisfies the industrial requirements, since it is tool supported and based on semi-formal (UML-based) specifications.

1 Introduction

One of the most used definitions for software architecture is the following: *"The software architecture of a program or computing system is the structure or structures of the system, which comprise software components, the externally visible properties of those components, and the relationships among them"* [1]. Researchers in industry and academia have integrated the Software Architecture (SA) [2] description in their software development processes (e.g. [3,4]). However, putting SA in practice, software architects have learned that the SA production and management is, in general, an expensive task. Therefore the effort is justified if the SA artifacts are extensively used for multiple purposes helping on assuring the desired levels of dependability. Typical use of SA is as a high level design blueprint of the system to be used during the system development and later on for maintenance and reuse. At the same time, SA can be used in itself in order to *analyze and validate architectural choices*, both behavioral and quantitative. Thus, the problem of assuring as early as possible the correctness of a

C. Hofmeister et al. (Eds.): QoSA 2006, LNCS 4214, pp. 127–144, 2006.
© Springer-Verlag Berlin Heidelberg 2006

software system, occupies an ever increasing portion of the development cycle cost and time budgets.

Analysis techniques have been introduced to understand if the SA satisfies certain expected properties, and tools and architectural languages have been proposed in order to make specification and analysis rigorous and to help software architects in their work (e.g., [2]). Even if much work has been done on this direction, the application of such techniques into industrial systems can be still very difficult due to some extra requirements and constraints imposed by industrial needs [5]: first of all, we cannot assume that a *formal* modeling of the software system exists. What we may reasonably assume, instead, is a semi-formal, easy to learn, specification language. Moreover, the approach should be *time* reducing and *tool supported* (automated tool support is fundamental for strongly reducing analysis costs).

The main *goals* that industries try to catch by modeling and analyzing architectural specifications are:

g1: to produce highly-dependable systems, while limiting analysis costs and
g2: to create a suitable process, where architecture-level decisions may be aligned to requirements and propagated down to the deployed system.

Regarding *g1*, the SA community has observed, in a few years, a proliferation of architecture description languages (ADLs) [6] for rigorous and formal SA modeling and analysis and the introduction of supporting tools. Although several studies have shown the suitability of ADLs, industries still tend to prefer model-based (semi-formal) notations. In particular, since UML is the de-facto standard for modeling software systems and it is widespread adopted in industrial contexts, many extensions and profiles have been proposed to "adapt" UML to model software architectures (e.g., [7]).

Regarding *g2*, in the last few years there has been a lot of interest in understanding how SA may be integrated with the other phases of the software life cycle [3,4], and how results gained at a certain level may be propagated to lower levels [8]. However, an automated, tool supported process which permits to consistently move towards such development phases is missing. As a result, it is still very difficult to propagate results from one phase to another.

Software *model-checking* and *testing* are some of the most used techniques to analyze software systems and identify hidden faults. Unfortunately, both approaches suffer some limitations: while current testing techniques are typically of difficult automation, model-checking requires an adequate developers expertise and skills on formal methods. In summary, industries are not encouraged to use the above mentioned techniques: industrial requirements are not met by either selective or exhaustive analysis.

In this paper we propose an *architecture-centric design and validation process* which enables the validation of a software system during the entire life-cycle. The analysis process is architecture-centric, since it validates the architecture specifications with respect to requirements, and then uses the validated SA as the starting point for any other analysis. It combines model-checking and testing techniques: we apply a model-checking technique to higher-level (architectural) specifications, thus governing the state-explosion problem, while testing techniques are used to validate the implementation conformance to the SA model. We check and test the architecture and the system implementation with respect to architectural (functional) properties. This combination limits analysis costs and produces a highly-dependable system. The process is supported by automated tools, which allow formal analysis without requiring skills on formal languages. The analysis process satisfies industrial requirements, since it is tool supported, based on semi-formal (UML-based) specifications, and allows analysis to be performed even on incomplete models. We outline the theoretical description of the activities involved in the process, together with its realization in terms of existent analysis techniques and tools.

The following Section 2 describes our proposal, called hereafter MODTEST. Section 3 applies MODTEST to the Siemens C.N.X. system. Section 4 draws some considerations and gained advantages, based on the MODTEST application to Siemens C.N.X.[1] and TERMA GmbH[2] systems. Section 5 introduces some related works while Section 6 concludes the paper.

2   MODTEST **Goals and Overview**

A growing interest in software architectures characterizes the last decade. Indeed, many software companies have understood the importance of SA modeling in order to obtain better quality software reducing time and cost of realization. In practice the SA is used for multiple purposes: (i) some companies use the SA description just as a documentation artifact, (ii) others make use of SA specifications only for analysis purposes and (iii) finally many others use the architectural artifacts to make analysis and to formally or informally guide the design and coding process [9,10,2].

As stated before the SA design is an expensive task that requires time and effort. Thus the introduction of SA into an industrial development life-cycle is justified only by an extensive use of these artifacts able to produce adequate benefits, such as the production of good quality software reducing at the same time realization costs.

In case (i), SA documentation is produced, usually completely untied from the other phases. Typically, implementation-level modifications of the system are not updated to the SA architectural design. The result of this development process is that the SA design quickly becomes obsolete and drifts out from the implementation.

In case (ii) the SA specification is used to check design conformance to system requirements. In spite of the approach in case (i) at the end of the verification step the SA design is correct with respect to the requirements, thus preventing possible system errors deriving from SA choices. The SA, however, is not used to drive the next phases of the system development which are instead delegated to system designers expertise. As a consequence, the implementation of the system could not respect the SA design, and implementation and SA could represent different systems.

Case (iii), where the SA is exploited also to drive the next phases of the system development, represents the desirable solution to previous limitations. However, in order to become effective in industrial contexts, an aspect that cannot be neglected is the realization of *tools* to support the development process. Automation, in fact, is one of the most relevant means to reduce the time to market and to have a real benefit in the

---

[1] One of the Siemens R&D labs.

[2] The German subsidiary of TERMA, located in Darmstadt.

software development. Another problem that can hamper the integration of these approaches in a real industrial life-cycle is the use of formal and sophisticated languages. Formal ADLs, for instance, are powerful languages to specify and analyze architectures. They are tool supported and rigorous. However, they usually require formal languages skill and some training time.

MODTEST proposes an architecture-centric, automated, analysis process which satisfies main industrial needs (i.e., timeliness, informality, tool support), while combining SA-based testing and exhaustive analysis techniques (model-checking) to produce a highly-dependable system. MODTEST:

– permits to verify SAs and to produce high-dependable systems;
– makes use of semi-formal (UML-based) specifications that do not require knowledge on formal and sophisticated languages;
– is tool supported;
– brings together testing and model checking, two between the most used verification techniques;
– by introducing an architecture-centric process, bridges the gap between requirements, architecture and coding.

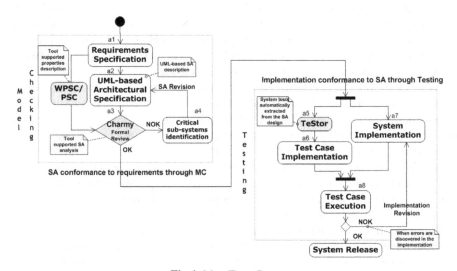

Fig. 1. MODTEST Process

Figure 1 shows the MODTEST architecture-centric analysis process. MODTEST includes two validation activities: validating SA specifications with respect to functional requirements through **model-checking**, and using such models and results to drive an SA-based code **testing** approach. In the model-checking phase we use the CHARMY model-checking technique to validate the architectural model conformance with respect to identified functional properties. In the testing phase we use a testing approach (supported by the TESTOR algorithm) which selects test cases driven by the architectural models and the model checking results. By combining these two approaches it can be *guaranteed that the architecture correctly reflects important requirements and the code conforms to the software architecture specification.* The key point of this process is that, if the SA does not conform to requirements, the SA is revised until a stable model is created (*SA revision*). Once the SA has been identified, both system tests and implementation are derived from it.

In more details (by referring to Figure 1):

- **Activity a1:** Requirements are identified, modeled and analyzed. One relevant problem that arises during the requirement engineering process is the result of failing to make a clear transition between different levels of requirements description. According to the terminology adopted in [11], the term "user requirements" is used to mean high-level abstract requirement descriptions and the term "system requirements" is used to mean detailed and possibly formal descriptions. Often in practice, stake-holders are able to describe user requirements in an informal way without detailed technical knowledge. They are rarely willing to use structured notations or formal ones. Transiting from user requirements to system requirements is an expensive task. In fact, we are speaking about decisions made during this early phase of the software development process, when the system under development is vague also in the mind of the customer. A good answer to this need is W_PSC [12], a speculative tool that facilitates understanding and structuring requirements. By means of a set of sentences (based on expertise in requirements formalization and on a set of well-known patterns [13] for specifying temporal properties used in practice) and classified according to temporal properties main keywords, W_PSC forces to make decisions that break the uncertainty and the ambiguity of user requirements. The output of W_PSC is a temporal property expressed in *Property Sequence Chart* (PSC [14,15]). PSC is a simple and (sufficiently) powerful formalism for specifying temporal properties in a user-friendly fashion. It is a scenario-based visual language that is an extended graphical notation of a subset of UML2.0 Sequence Diagrams (see Figure 2). PSC can graphically express a useful set of both *liveness* and *safety* properties in terms of messages exchanged among the components forming the system. Finally, an algorithm, called PSC2BA, translates PSC into Büchi automata[3] [16].

  W_PSC supports also the user on taking many decisions required transiting from requirements to architecture.

- **Activities a2-a3:** The SA is designed using the UML-based notation for SA modeling utilized in CHARMY [17].

  CHARMY [17,18] is a project whose goal is to apply model-checking techniques to validate the SA conformance to certain properties. In CHARMY the SA is specified through state diagrams used to describe how architectural components behave. Starting from the SA description CHARMY synthesizes, through a suitable translation into Promela (the specification language of the SPIN [19] model checker) an actual SA complete model that can be executed and verified in SPIN. This model can be validated with respect to a set of properties, e.g., deadlock, correctness of properties, starvation, etc., expressed in Linear-time Temporal Logic (LTL) [20]

---

[3] In our context, a Büchi automata is an operational description of a temporal property formula. It represents all the system behaviors that respects the logic of the specified temporal property.

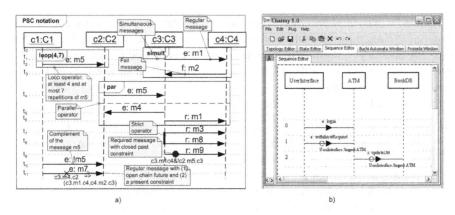

Fig. 2. PSC formalism and PSC as plugin of CHARMY

or in its Büchi Automata representation [16]. Instead of writing directly temporal properties that is a task inherently error prone, CHARMY is integrated with PSC and with PSC2BA that directly translates PSC specifications into a temporal property representation understandable by SPIN. The model checker SPIN, is a widely distributed software package that supports the formal verification of concurrent systems permitting to analyze their logical consistency by on-the-fly checks, i.e., without the need of constructing a global state graph, thus reducing the complexity of the check. It is the core engine of CHARMY and it is not directly accessible by a CHARMY user.

By using CHARMY, thanks to UML notation used for the system and properties specification, we have an easy to use, practical approach to model and check architectural specifications, *hiding the modeling complexity*.

– **Activity a4:** Whenever the SA specification does not properly implement selected requirements (NOK arrows), the SA itself needs to be revised. Thanks to the model-checker outputs, and following the CHARMY iterative process (described in [17]), we may identify specific portions of the SA which need to be better specified. Thus, starting from a first system SA high level abstraction, which identifies few main subsystems and a set of high level properties, we obtain a model that can already be validated with respect to significant high level behaviors. The subsequent steps are to zoom into the potentially problematic subsystems by identifying implied sub-properties.

– **Activity a5:** The sequence representing the properties validated through CHARMY is the input for TEst Sequence generaTOR (TESTOR [21]).

TESTOR allows us to extract test sequences from model-based specifications as produced by practitioners. A behavioral model of each component is provided in the form of UML state diagrams. Such models explicitly specify which components interact and how. Sequence diagrams are used as an abstract or even incomplete ("sketchy") specification of what the test should include. TESTOR takes in input UML state and sequence diagrams and synthesizes more detailed sequence diagrams (conforming to the abstract scenarios) by recovering missing information from state diagrams. Through the TESTOR algorithm we may identify traces of

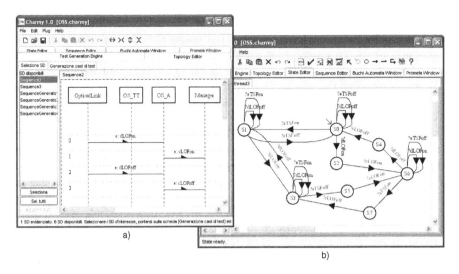

Fig. 3. Some screenshots of TESTOR and CHARMY

interest for testing the whole system or just a relevant subsystem. This guarantees a bigger synergy among model-checking and testing application. The output represents test sequences (which include a sequence of stimuli to the system under test, and the expected responses to those stimuli [22]) specified in the form of more informative scenarios. The TESTOR output represents test sequence specifications.

- **Activity a6:** Test sequences generated by TESTOR are used to identify test case implementations. These ones are produced out of TESTOR output. Test scripts may be then generated inputting TESTOR generated test specifications. For example starting from a test scripts database it would be possible to associate to a TESTOR's output the script(s) able to inject/detect the event itself into/out from the system under test.
- **Activity a7:** In parallel with the testing process, the SA is implemented. For this task we may use a java-based architectural programming language such as Arch-Java [23] or Java/A [24]. The basic idea of architectural programming is to preserve a software architecture throughout the software development process. For instance, in the analysis phase the components of an architectures are implied by the system boundaries of a use case model. In the design, architectures may be represented with UML component diagrams or by a model in an architecture description language. In the implementation, an architecture should be implemented in an architectural programming language, like Java/A or ArchJava.
- **Activity a8:** The test execution step, in our context, is implemented via the industrial in-use test execution process.

3   Applying MODTEST to the Siemens C.N.X. Development Process

In this section we apply the approach just described to a real system developed in Siemens C.N.X. Siemens C.N.X. is specialized in design and development of telecommunication equipments applied in transport networks, mainly based on Synchronous Digital Hierarchy (SDH) technology [25,26]. Siemens C.N.X. uses industrial design and production processes, which comply with clear and consolidated factory standards, in order to guarantee good quality levels able to satisfy market requirements.

We initially outline the standard telecommunication functional model as a way to formally describe the SA of telecommunication systems. Thus we select, among the set of relevant architecture components we apply the proposed approach, the Optical System (OS) application, as an example to show significant results. We consider only a simple part of the system in order to well explain how MODTEST works without distract with details of the case study that are out of the purposes of this paper.

In order to introduce the OS architecture in Section 3.3, we initially introduce the SDH System Architecture and background information needed to understand the case study architectural context (Section 3.1). In Section 3.2 we describe some of the requirements we analyzed with our approach. In Section 3.3 we describe the OS architectural model. Section 3.4 describes how we applied CHARMY to the OS architecture, while Section 3.5 illustrates the application of TESTOR. Finally, Section 3.6 describes how TESTOR results have been used to generate and execute test case implementations.

3.1   The SDH System Architecture

The "Functional Model" for an SDH system describes the way an equipment accepts, processes and forwards information contained in the transmission signal. Actually, it is a well defined standard by ETSI [25] and ITU-T [26] and it is widely used by telecommunication companies and providers.

The functional model is built around two specific concepts:

1. *network layering*, defining a client/server relationship between adjacent layers (i.e. each layer faces to a couple of adjacent layers: a server layer, which provides transport services to the current layer, and a client layer which uses the transport services the current layer provides);
2. *atomic functions*, specifying the behavior of each layer. Three basic atomic functions (connection, termination and adaptation) can be combined on the basis of combinational rules to completely model the layer processing and supervision functions.

In addition, "application functions" (performing equipment specific tasks) should reside at the top of a specific layer as shown in Figure 4.

A *network element* (NE), i.e. a node in the SDH network, is a stack of network layers, thus composed by many atomic functions and relevant application functions distributed in different layers. Many NE may be interconnected and each atomic function (in a specific layer in a NE) is directly related in a peer-to-peer connection to an identical function, in the same layer but in a different NE.

When this interconnected nodes and protocols are viewed at an architectural level, each NE is abstracted into an architectural component while a connector is used to simulate the (virtual) network connections. We are also able to identify a subsystem as a single application function, a single atomic function or a set of them composing a network layer, hiding the underlying levels using a "simple" (virtual) network connector simulating the relevant transport services.

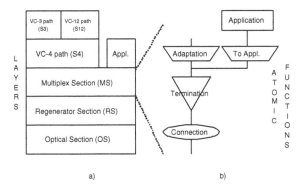

Fig. 4. a-b) SDH Layers and Atomic Functions

3.2 The Optical Session Requirements (Activity a1)

Based on the OS specification documents, we identified several functional requirements the system has to satisfy. Two of them are listed here down as an example:

- Requirement 1: when the atomic function called OS_TT detects a LOS defect, the LOS defect condition is reported as a failure to the Manager. Moreover, a dLOS active condition is reported to the OS_A using the "Trail Signal Fail" (aTSFoff) message;
- Requirement 2: if the atomic function OS_RS_A detects a LOF defect (dLOFon) and no dLOS occur, dLOF condition is reported as a failure (cLOFon) to the Manager;

Focusing on Requirement 1 we show, by using W_PSC, how to construct the PSC representing the property. By tacking into account the first part of the Requirement 1 (i.e., *when the OS_TT atomic function detects LOS defect (dLOSon)*), the first choice in which the user is guided is recognizing that the dLOSon message is optional. Thus, between the optional sentences offered by W_PSC, the user is asked to select the right sentence (i.e.: *If the message* $m1$ *is exchanged then ...*). Following the same reasoning the other two messages composing the requirement (i.e.: $cLOSon$ and $aTSFoff$) are recognized as mandatory. Thus selecting the appropriate sentences in the mandatory panel, the PSC representing the requirement 1, showed in Figure 5.a), is automatically generated.

Figure 5.b) shows the obtained PSC for Requirement 2.

3.3 The Optical Session Layer SA Model (Activity a2)

With the aim of validating the proposed approach to a real SDH-based Siemens TLC system, we here describe the Optical Section Layer (OS) subsystem and the related Automatic Laser Shutdown (ALS) safety feature. While the basic functionalities are described, some details are disregarded to make easy and effective this presentation.

Figure 6 illustrates the different components in the OS architectural configuration and their state machines.

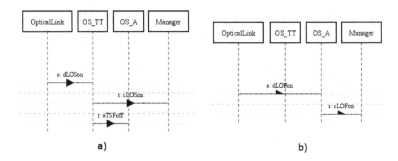

Fig. 5. PSCs for Requirements 1 and 2

The components Optical Link and Manager are external to the SDH NE. they abstract respectively the SDH network and the operator interface. The *OpticalLink* is used to inject failure conditions that can occur on transmission signals (i.e *Loss Of Signal* (LOS) and *Loss Of Frame* (LOF)). The *Manager* provides for provisioning commands and receives relevant system status reports (alarms, event notifications, etc.).

The main OS Layer components are:

The *Optical Section Trail Termination* function (OS_TT) which describes how the system processes and supervises the optical signal (OS_CI), translating it to (from) internal Adapted Information (OS_AI) format. This function detects the Loss Of Signal defect (dLOS), reporting the relevant failure (cLOS) to the Manager through the Management Information (OS_TT_MI) interface.

The *Optical Section to Regenerator Section Adaptation* function (OS_RS_A) makes available a reliable signal to (from) its client layer (Regenerator Section). Among other things, it checks for the Frame Alignment, reporting to the Manager a Loss Of Frame failure (cLOF) when the relevant defect (dLOF) is detected.

The *Automatic Laser Shutdown* function is a laser safety application defined by IEC 60825 and ITU-T G.664. Considering a LOS as a symptom of a optical cable break or disconnection, the ALS function switches off the laser transmitter to avoid possible human eyes injuries in case of accidental exposure to laser light. To recover the transmission, the laser is periodically, on automatic basis, or manually switched on checking if LOS condition clears during the reactivation interval.

3.4 CHARMY **Applied to the Optical Section SA (Activity a3)**

The requirements (properties) to be proven have been formalized in the form of CHARMY scenarios. Figure 5 shows how the first two requirements are expressed using the PSC notation for modelling scenarios. By using the CHARMY tool (PSC is also the notation used by CHARMY for properties specification), the scenarios are automatically translated into Büchi Automata while the architectural state machine models have been translated into Promela code. SPIN has then been run and no errors have been detected. This initial analysis gives us the assurance that the identified architectural model correctly reflects the expected behaviors. Now we can proceed with the implementation and testing steps of the proposed design process.

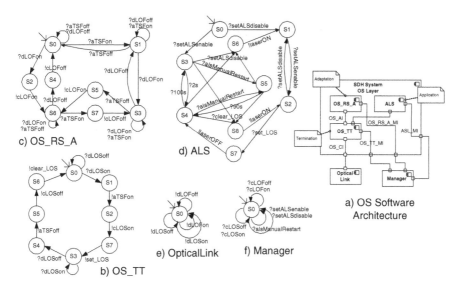

Fig. 6. OS components and state machines

3.5   TESTOR **Applied to the Optical Section SA (Activity a5)**

Taking in input the properties validated in CHARMY, TESTOR outputs more informative scenarios usable as test specifications. Figure 8 represents (one of) the TESTOR output for the scenario in Figure 5.b. In order to check the validity and the effectiveness of the proposed method, an extended comparison have been done between the TESTOR outputs and the relevant test cases specifications, as designed following the Siemens C.N.X. practice and currently applied to the SDH equipments of the Siemens SURPASS series. The test cases are expressed in a tabular way, like the example shown in Figure 7.

The first row represents the state the system needs to be to run the test. Usually, it coincides with the system initial state. Rows from two to five identify, in the second column the input actions, and the expected outputs in column three.

While our test specifications structurally resemble Siemens C.N.X. test specifications, from a semantical point of view some differences and considerations have to be outlined:

1. there is a direct relationship and high similarities between the scenarios produced in activity $a5$ by TESTOR and the relevant set of actions and reactions described, in natural language and tabular form, in the related Siemens C.N.X. test cases. Some differences derive from the level of details in the SA model (e.g. the outSD in Figure 8 does not concerns with LED's and alarm severity attribute);
2. both test approaches start from an initial system configuration;
3. TESTOR outSD's are SA based while Siemens C.N.X. tests are requirement based; by the way, since TESTOR itself uses the properties (i.e., requirements) to drive the trace selection, it is possible to find a basic correspondence between the two set of tests, identifying similar classification criteria;

Step Name	Description	Expected Result
1	Create a bi -directional XCONN: AU4CTP(A) O155 -2port 1 AU4CTP(B) O155 -2 port 2 ALS: disabled RScSSF Report: enabled MScSSF Report: enabled	No alarm on the SDH Analyser and LCT Led Major: off Led Minor: off
2	Alarm b y means SDH Analyser: LOS	LCT card1: LOS LCT card2: AU -AIS SDH Analyser: AU -AIS Led Major: on Led Minor: off
3	No alarm	LCT card1: No alarm LCT card2: No alarm Led Major: off Led Minor: off
4	Alarm by means S DH Analyser: LOF	LCT card1: LOF LCT card2: AU -AIS SDH Analyser: AU -AIS Led Major: on Led Minor: off
5	No alarm	LCT card1: No alarm LCT card2: No alarm SDH Analyser: No alarm Led Major: off Led Minor: off

Fig. 7. An excerpt of a Test Case Specification in Siemens C.N.X.

4. during a test, to interact with an SDH equipment, the external interfaces are manipulated and observed by means of instruments and terminals. Correspondingly, in the TESTOR scenarios, it is necessary to highlight the external agents (OpticalLink and Manager in our case study) used to simulate events on such interfaces;

5. generalizing the previous concept, TESTOR concerns also with the internal structure of the system (i.e. the system is not a black box). As a result, the selected tests take in care also the internal messages flow and state machine evolution. TESTOR should be refined to differentiate the named "System Functional Tests" (i.e. the ones that currently check the system compliance to the functional requirements looking at the system as a black box) with the "System Integration Tests" (taking in care the internal interaction between architectural components).

At the end, TESTOR is a promising approach, liable to further refinements and upgrading.

3.6 From TESTOR Outputs to Test Case Implementation and Execution (Activities a6-a8)

By reusing Siemens C.N.X. practices which allow the extraction of test case implementations from test case specifications, we may produce test case implementations out of our TESTOR output. Test scripts may be then generated inputting TESTOR outSDs.

Also in this case, a possible, future enhancement of the process is related to the (at list partial) automation of this step. Starting from a test scripts database (currently supported by a commercial tool) it would be possible to associate to an outSD event the related script(s) able to inject (detect) the event itself into (out) from the system under test.

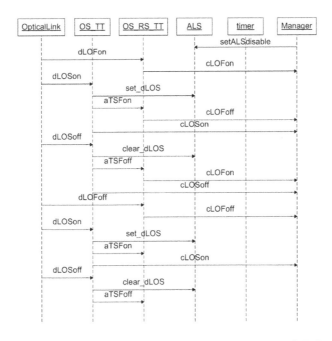

Fig. 8. One test case for Requirement 1 (Figure 5.a) as output of TESTOR

4 Considerations

MODTEST has been used to several industrial case studies with the scope to demonstrate that it satisfies main industrial needs (i.e., timeliness, informality, tool support) introducing the SA not only as a documentation artifact but as a design and analysis support. In fact, it realizes an architecture-centric, automated, analysis process which satisfies main industrial needs and supports the automatic generation of system test cases.

Based on our experience in applying MODTEST to the Siemens C.N.X. Optical Section System (OSS), presented in Section 3, and TERMA Gmbh Network Interface System (NIS) [27], the *main advantages* MODTEST exhibits are listed in the following:

- by applying model-checking at the architectural level we can *reduce the modeling complexity* and the *state explosion problem*. Moreover, whenever the SA requires to be modified, model-checking and testing results can be kept aligned;
- by using CHARMY we provide an easy to use, UML-based approach for model-checking, *hiding the formal modeling complexity*. In fact the knowledge on SPIN (the model checker used) is not required;
- the iterative model-checking approach identifies the most important properties to be validated, to refine the architectural model and finally to identify critical subsystems and focus on them;
- test specifications are identified from the architectural model (instead of directly from requirements) thus unifying some design steps, guaranteing consistency of the whole project and, virtually, eliminating the need of the review process;

- through the TESTOR algorithm we can identify detailed traces of interest for testing the whole system or just a relevant subsystem. This guarantees a strong and useful synergy between model-checking and testing application;
- MODTEST is automated: CHARMY, TESTOR, PSC, and W_PSC are implemented inside the same implementation framework. The tool may be downloaded from [17].

The *main limitations* consist in the initial investment required (in terms of time and human resources, to model and validate the system) and to tool support (since both CHARMY and TESTOR were initially developed as academic tools). We evaluated the effort required by the MODTEST process and we compared it with the traditional design process adopted by the actual development team in TERMA GmbH. The traditional process used in TERMA for the NIS system requires about 970 man per hours. This process does not consider exhaustive analysis and considers only a brief test phase. The introduction of the MODTEST process in TERMA GmbH required an effort of approximatively 700 man per hours. This effort is removed when an adequate expertise and knowledge on the application context, analysis techniques and tool support is reached. The real overhead we experienced in this NIS project is about approximatively 300 man per hours due principally to the design phase and successively reviews.

It is important to note that modeling and analysis effort will be re-paid with a better documented architecture, easier system maintainability, and improved alignment among validation techniques. Finally we expect that other projects can factorize the design effort and the expertise that is obtained by using the instruments that compose MODTEST can reduce the overhead required by the MODTEST process.

5 Related Work: Software Architecture-Based Development Process in Industrial Context

Many research topics may be related to our research. For the sake of brevity, we report here relevant research papers on *Software Architecture-based development Process in industrial context.*

In the research area of Software Architecture much work is oriented on architectural specification and analysis in an industrial context. In [9] a description of the state-of-practice in industry is introduced, related to the use of software architecture. It is based on a set of observations and analysis of interviews, and a workshop with chief architects from companies.

In [28] the authors extensively describe the experience gained with the embedding of architectural support in three organizations. They focus on architectural support in the area of software architecture recovery, visualization, analysis and verification.

In [10] the nature of SA and SA design in an industrial process is investigated.

In the Unified Software Development Process (UP) [29], an architectural specification embodies a collection of views created in different phases. In the Hofmeister, Nord and Soni' book on applied software architecture [3], an architectural specification is composed by four different views: *conceptual, module, execution,* and *code.* In the "architecture-based development" proposed in [4], the authors present a description

Company	System	System or Software Architecture	SA Role	Tool support	Reference
ABB	Industrial Robots	Software	Design and Code	Partially	[9]
Ericsson AB	Radio Access Network	System	Design and Code	Partially	[9]
TietoEnator Telecom & Media	Radio Based Station	Software	Design and Code	Partially	[9]
Volvo Construction Equipment	Volvo CE equipment	System	Design and Code	Partially	[9]
Volvo Car Corporation	Diagnostic System	Software	Design and Code	Partially	[9]
Bombardier Transportation	Train Communication Network	System	Design and Code	Partially	[9]
Philips	Digital telephony systems	Software	Design and Code	Partially	[10]
Mobile Software Company	Mobile Terminal Software	Software	Design, Code and Validation	Partially	[28]
Siemens C.N.X.	Optical Session Application	Software	Design, code, conformance and Testing	From requirements to testing	This paper
TERMA GmbH	Network Interface System	Software	Design, code, conformance and Testing	From requirements to testing	This paper

Fig. 9. Comparison

of an architecture-centric system development where a set of architecture requirements is developed in addition to functional requirements and the architecture is analyzed through the Software Architecture Analysis Method (SAAM). The process comprises six steps: i) elicit the architectural requirements (expressing quality-based architectural requirements through quality-specific scenarios), ii) design the architecture (using views), iii) document the architecture (considered as a crucial factor in the SA success), iv) analyze the architecture (with respect to quality requirements), v) realize and finally, vi) maintain the architecture. The requirements are informally validated, the architecture is specified through different views, The architecture is analyzed through the Architecture Tradeoff Analysis Method (ATAM). This process differs from traditional development in which SA is used for design perspectives since it focuses on capturing system qualities for analysis.

KobrA (Component-based Application Development) [30] is a software process- and product-centric engineering approach for software architecture and product line development. KobrA uses a component-based approach in each phase of the development process, it uses UML as the modelling language, it exploits a product line approach during components development and deployment, and it makes a clear distinction between the Framework Engineering stage and the Application Engineering stage (typical of product line developments).

For completeness, we also cite TOGAF [31], a detailed method and a set of guidelines to design, evaluate and build enterprise architectures, and Catalysis [32], a methodology that makes special emphasis on component-based development.

In Figure 9 we can see the relation between MODTEST (the last two rows) and the others methodologies. This relation is based on the role of the SA in the development process, the automatism of the tool supporting and in which level the architecture is used (system or software). We can conclude this paper saying that MODTEST is a tool-supported process that can be used for each phase of software development and that uses a software architecture as a key point. In fact the process starts from the requirements and through the software architecture produces the test cases and software code of the application guaranteeing well-conformance relations in each step.

6   Conclusions

Software architectures represent the first, high-level, step in the design of a software system. When it is used for analysis purposes, it needs to take into considerations both requirements and implementation.

The main original aspects of our work can be summarized as: integration of analysis techniques at the software architecture level, investigating how these techniques can be applied together spanning from functional requirements analysis to code testing, how the software architecture is used to perform these integration, how these approaches satisfy the main industrial needs (i.e., timeliness, informality, tool support), and finally how the automation of every steps of the process and the introduction of it in real case studies has improved the entire development and testing process currently in use.

MODTEST is tool supported since it is based on CHARMY and TESTOR already implemented and released. Nevertheless these tools are initially developed as academic tools and are not completely ready to be used in industries. This represents one of causes of the overhead required to introduce MODTEST in industrial development life-cycles (see Section 4). Even if this overhead is justified by the gained software quality, which is vital for dependable systems, it can be successfully reduced by improving the tools that compose MODTEST. For this reason as future work we plan to develop new versions of CHARMY and TESTOR improving our industry collaborations in order to have mature products. An aspect that must be not neglected is to have real relations with current UML distributions commonly used in the industry world. First results are already obtained thanks to CHARMY extensions that permit to open models made with UML distributions and an ADL UML-based, called DUALLY [33], that we are developing.

Acknowledgements

The authors wish to thank Siemens C.N.X. and Terma GmbH for their contribution with the case studies. This work is supported by the PLASTIC project: Providing Lightweight and Adaptable Service Technology for pervasive Information and Communication. Sixth Framework Programme. http://www.ist-plastic.org.

References

1. Pressman, R.: Software Engineering - A Practitioner's Approach. McGraw-Hill, Singapore (1987; 28-29)
2. Bernardo, M., Inverardi, P.: Formal Methods for Software Architectures, Tutorial book on Software Architectures and Formal Methods. SFM-03:SA Lectures, LNCS 2804 (2003)

3. Hofmeister, C., Nord, R., Soni, D.: Applied Software Architecture. Addison-Wesley (1998)
4. Bass, L., Clements, P., Kazman, R.: Software Architecture in Practice, second edition. SEI Series in Software Eng. Addison-Wesley Professional (2003)
5. Bertolino, A., Marchetti, E., Muccini, H.: Introducing a Reasonably Complete and Coherent Approach for Model-based Testing. (In: Testing and Analysis of Component-Based Systems Workshop, Tacos 2004)
6. Medvidovic, N., Taylor, R.N.: A Classification and Comparison Framework for Software Architecture Description Languages. IEEE TSE **26**(1) (2000)
7. Medvidovic, N., Rosenblum, D.S., Redmiles, D.F., Robbins, J.E.: Modeling Software Architectures in the Unified Modeling Language. ACM TOSEM **11**(1) (2002)
8. STRAW '03: Second Int. Workshop From Software Requirements to Architectures (May 09, 2003, Portland, Oregon, USA)
9. Mustapic, G., Wall, A., Norstrom, C., Crnkovic, I., Sandstrom, K., Andersson, J.: Real world influences on software architecture - interviews with industrial system experts. In: Fourth Working IEEE/IFIP Conference on Software Architecture, WICSA 2004. (2004) 101–111
10. Bril, R.J., Krikhaar, R.L., Postma, A.: Architectural Support in Industry: a reflection using C-POSH. Journal of Software Maintenance and Evolution (2005)
11. Sommerville, I.: Software engineering (7th ed.). Addison-Wesley Longman Publishing Co., Inc., Boston, MA, USA (2004)
12. Autili, M., Pelliccione, P.: Towards a Graphical Tool for Refining User to System Requirements. In: 5th GT-VMT'06 - ETAPS'06, to appear in ENTCS. (2006)
13. Dwyer, M.B., Avrunin, G.S., Corbett, J.C.: Patterns in property specifications for finite-state verification. In: ICSE. (1999) 411–420
14. PSC Project: PSC web site. http://www.di.univaq.it/psc2ba (2005)
15. Autili, M., Inverardi, P., Pelliccione, P.: A scenario based notation for specifying temporal properties, 5th International Workshop on Scenarios and State Machines: Models, Algorithms and Tools (SCESM'06), Shanghai, China. ACM press (2006)
16. Buchi, J.: On a decision method in restricted second order arithmetic. In: International Congress on Logic, Method and Philosophical Sciences. (1960)
17. CHARMY Project: Charmy Web Site. http://www.di.univaq.it/charmy (2004)
18. Inverardi, P., Muccini, H., Pelliccione, P.: Charmy: an extensible tool for architectural analysis. In: ESEC/FSE-13: Proceedings of the 10th European software engineering conference, New York, NY, USA, ACM Press (2005) 111–114
19. Holzmann, G.J.: The SPIN Model Checker: Primer and Reference Manual. Addison-Wesley (2003)
20. Manna, Z., Pnueli, A.: The temporal logic of reactive and concurrent systems. Springer-Verlag New York, Inc. (1992)
21. Pelliccione, P., Muccini, H., Bucchiarone, A., Facchini, F.: TESTOR: Deriving Test Sequences from Model-based Specifications. (In: Proc. 8th Int. SIGSOFT Symposium on Component-based Software Engineering. May 2005. LNCS 3489) 267–282
22. Hartman, A.: Model Based Test Generation Tools. Technical report, AGEDIS project Downloads (2002)
23. Abi-Antoun, M., Aldrich, J., Garlan, D., Schmerl, B., Nahas, N., Tseng, T.: Improving System Dependability by Enforcing Architectural Intent. In: ICSE 2005 Work. on Architecting Depend. Systems. (2005)
24. Hacklinger, F.: Java/a - taking components into java. In Proc. 13th ISCA Int. Conf. Intelligent and Adaptive Systems and Software Engineering (IASSE'04) (2004) 163–169
25. ETSI EN 300 417: Transmission and Multiplexing (TM); Generic requirements of transport functionality of equipment. Eur. Telecom. Standards Institute (2001)

26. ITU-T G.783: SERIES G: Transmission Systems and Media, Digiral Systems and Networks - Digital terminal equipments - Principal characteristics of multiplexing equipment for the synchronous digital hierarchy. Int. Telecommunication Union (1997)
27. Cardone, M.: Experiencing Architectural Analysis in Industrial Contexts. Master's thesis, Computer Science Department, University of L'Aquila, Italy (2005)
28. Smolander, K., Hoikka, K., Isokallio, J., Kataikko, M., Makela, T.: What is Included in Software Architecture? - A Case Study in Three Software Organizations. In: 9th IEEE International Conference on Engineering of Computer-Based Systems. (2002) 131–138
29. Jacobson, I., Booch, G., Rumbaugh, J.: The Unified Software Development Process. Addison Wesley, Object Technology Series (1999)
30. Atkinson, C., Bayer, J., Bunse, C., Kamsties, E., Laitenberger, O., Laqua, R., Muthig, D., Paech, B., Wüst, J., Zettel, J.: Component-Based Product-Line Engineering with UML. Addison-Wesley (2001)
31. TOGAF 8: The Open Group Architecture Framework. http://www.opengroup.org/ architecture/togaf/ (2005)
32. Souza, D.D., Wills, A.C.: Objects, components, and frameworks with UML. The Catalysis approach, Addison-Wesley (1998)
33. Muccini, H., Inverardi, P., Pelliccione, P.: DUALLY: Putting in Synergy UML 2.0 and ADLs. (In: 5th IEEE/IFIP Working Conference on Software Architecture (WICSA 2005))

Embedded Systems Architecture: Evaluation and Analysis

Bastian Florentz and Michaela Huhn

Technical University of Braunschweig, 38106 Braunschweig, Germany
{florentz, huhn}@ips.cs.tu-bs.de
http://www.ips.cs.tu-bs.de

Abstract. Short innovation cycles in software and hardware make architecture design a key issue in future development processes for embedded systems. The basis for architectural design decisions is a transparent architecture evaluation.

Our model-based approach supports a uniform representation of hierarchies of quality attributes and an integration of different architecture evaluation techniques and methods. We present a metamodel for architecture evaluation as a basis for the precise description of the quality attribute structure and the evaluation methodology. By modelling architecture evaluation, the relationships between architectural elements and quality attributes and interdependencies between quality attributes can be represented and investigated. Thereby, the architecture exploration process with its evaluations, decisions, and optimizations is made explicit, traceable, and analyzable.

1 Introduction

The evaluation of architecture has become an important part of software and system design. The early stage of design in which architecture development takes place shows its impact to the whole design process as well as the software or system at its life time. A lot of effort is invested in making architectural decisions to ensure high quality architectures. An accurate and target-oriented definition of the architecture is just one step in the right direction. The evaluation of architectures to ensure conformance to design goals is another.

We define a metamodel for the description of architectures in the embedded system domain as well as for the definition of architecture evaluation. The common basis of components and connectors allows for analysis of the architecture regarding quality attributes and associated evaluation techniques. This explicit representation and documentation of the architecture evaluation leads to increased traceability and comprehension of architectural decisions. These are essential not only for the justification of certain decisions but in particular for their traceability and reusability.

Short time-to-market requires the reuse of existing and reliable components and architectures to quickly derive and compose new dependable software and system architectures. With their long life cycles, embedded systems can profit

C. Hofmeister et al. (Eds.): QoSA 2006, LNCS 4214, pp. 145–162, 2006.
© Springer-Verlag Berlin Heidelberg 2006

from high quality architectures and their comprehensible, traceable evaluation. Additionally, with explicit requirements and restrictions already available in the early stages of design, embedded systems are predestined for a precise description of their architecture; and architecture evaluation has high potential to lead to concrete architecture design advices. Such advices of how to understand, build, or change an architecture, and actually the whole system design, are based on analysis of relations between architecture and evaluation elements. The investigation of analysis results with the goal to derive architectural decisions and uncover optimization potential will be one main topic of our research.

In Section 2, the terminology used in this paper is described. Section 3 introduces the metamodels of architecture, evaluation, methodology, and analysis. The approach is applied to an embedded system cut-out in the case study of Section 4. The benefits of using the metamodel especially with respect to analysis results are presented in Section 5. Section 6 concludes.

2   Terminology

As our field of interest is slightly more general than pure software systems, a brief review of the most relevant terms follows.

Architecture evaluation is directed to software, as well as to system architecture in this paper. Embedded systems, consisting of hardware short of resources and software realizing the system's functionality, build the center of interest.

A *quality attribute* (called quality characteristics in ISO/IEC 9126 [1]) is a quality goal that the system under consideration at least meets the quality level given in the requirements. The *quality attribute DAG* (or *QADAG* for short) represents a hierarchical structuring of the quality attributes as a **d**irected **a**cyclic **g**raph. In our setting, a quality attribute (1) may be decomposed into (sub-)attributes or (2) consist of an evaluation technique in combination with scenarios and constraints. An example of a quality attribute is the maximal bus load that arises from a particular application in a distributed controller network. The bus load may be a subattribute of the system performance.

An *evaluation technique* associated with a quality attribute describes exactly how to evaluate the architecture regarding the quality attribute while considering of the attached scenarios and constraints.

A *scenario* represents specific examples of current and future uses of a system that are relevant for architectural design [2]. A constraint is a restriction on the design space.

An *evaluation result* is generated by applying an evaluation technique. The result of an arbitrary unit can be assigned by an *interpretation* to a quality rate.

The *quality rate* (or quality rating in [1]) is an interpreted evaluation result to a value between 0 and 100% representing the ratio of meeting the requirements represented by a quality attribute. The quality rate is also known as *utility* in the economic view of CBAM [2]. A quality rate of 100% represents the best ratio of meeting the requirements, where as a quality rate of 0% represents the worst ration of meeting the requirements. It is possible to add a so called K.O. -flag (or just K.O. for short) to a quality rate. This means that the quality of the architecture, regarding a proper quality attribute, is not acceptable for the system to be working or even buildable. In this case, the quality rate is 0%.

The ISO/IEC 9126 standard [1] defines a framework for evaluating software product quality based on six quality attributes (called quality characteristics in ISO/IEC 9126) namely functionality, reliability, usability, efficiency, maintainability, and portability. Furthermore, guidelines for their use, i.e. the evaluation process, are part of the standard. An evaluation process model is given, which we do not adopt directly, but use analogously in great parts. Thus, software product evaluation can be done using the ISO/IEC 9126 standard. For specific needs in certain application domains, most parts of the standard can be used but some details may not totally fit. Additional definitions (e.g. subcharacteristics) will be needed, although suggestions for such subcharacteristics are given informally in the appendix of the standard.

ISO/IEC 9126 refers to embedded systems as software in use. Here, embedded systems are the center of interest for architecture evaluation which slightly moves the view on the relevant quality attributes. Nevertheless, this approach can be applied to more or less pure software architectures, as well.

Performance of an embedded system is a measurement of appropriate utilization of short resources by software functions under certain conditions. ISO/IEC 9126 has a strong relation to the software part and calls this quality attribute *efficiency*.

In many domains, millions of units of an embedded system are produced and sold. Thus, the hardware costs of each unit take precedence over the design costs which are shared among all of them. In the following, *costs* are meant to be the estimated costs per unit.

The *maintainability* of an architecture can be decomposed into changeability, portability, etc. These subattributes are directed to the system in use in ISO/IEC 9126 ([1]). The embedded systems we are addressing are only modified in a very restricted manner after installation (in the moment software flashes only). The maintainability concerns the reuse of existing architecture components in new systems and other contexts and configurations as well as the possibility to port them to other hardware platforms. Actually, the maintainability considers the system under development and not the installed units.

3   Metamodels for Architectures and Their Evaluation

Besides a coarse metamodel for an embedded system architecture, we present a metamodel for architecture evaluation and the methods to evaluate an architecture and to analyse the evaluation. Most of these models are based on components and connectors (cp. [3], [4]). For reasons of class naming conventions and to keep names short, the names of the classes can differ from the usual spelling, e.g. *communication line* will be `CommLine` in the diagrams. All metamodels are given as UML class diagrams.

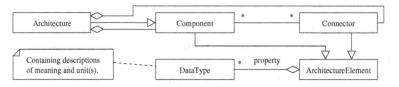

Fig. 1. Components and connectors view as basis for metamodels

Both, components and connectors are architecture elements which may contain properties represented by data type instances. The concrete data types depend on the architecture element and are used to specify relevant information for the architecture evaluation like memory size, worst case execution time (under stated conditions), costs, and so on. Figure 1 contains the basis for the architecture metamodels described in the following section. An architecture contains components and connectors that may be linked to one another. Additionally, an architecture is a component itself to ensure hierarchy in architectures in the sense of connecting architectures. However, we will not use this subclass relation in this paper. Architectures or parts of them are directly linked to one another. See the mappings, for example, in which the components of function architecture and hardware architecture are connected via connectors of the mappings that are architectures in themselves, because architecture elements may be contained in several architectures. Thus the architecture component and architecture connector relations are aggregations and no compositions which ensure exclusivity for the containing object.

3.1   Embedded Systems Architecture Model

Our embedded system architecture model is inspired from the architectural descriptions used in the automotive domain [5]. The *function architecture* describes the logical structuring of functions that communicate via virtual connections between provided and required signals (see Figure 2).

The *hardware architecture* that provides a network of controllers, sensors, and actuators (all devices, see Figure 4) communicating via communication lines, e.g. buses (see Figure 3). Sensors provide signals, actuators require signals. Controllers are devices that are able to compute and therefore to host functions. Sensors and actuators are not.

The system architecture is completed by a mapping of the functions on controllers and a communication mapping of signals to communication lines. Although a concrete bus configuration or protocol etc. is rarely known at this point of development, the signals are mapped to communication lines and buses to estimate their utilization as a first step. Figure 5 shows the metamodels of

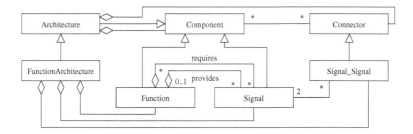

Fig. 2. Metamodel function architecture

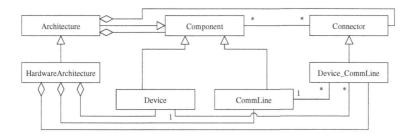

Fig. 3. Metamodel hardware architecture

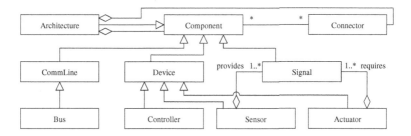

Fig. 4. Metamodel hardware devices

both mappings. Components to be mapped are shown in the lower part of the figure. The function architecture and the hardware architecture in combination with the mappings (both architectures, too) build a system architecture.

We omitted the depiction of the architecture elements properties in the metamodels for function architecture, hardware architecture and the mappings. In Section 4, some examples for properties are given. Actually, a property is a data type with unit and name and maybe some utilities for handling its values.

For the moment, we consider the function architecture to be invariant. It will serve as the common basis on which different system architecture variants are compared. The hardware architecture, the function mapping, and the communication mapping are variable in the system architecture's design.

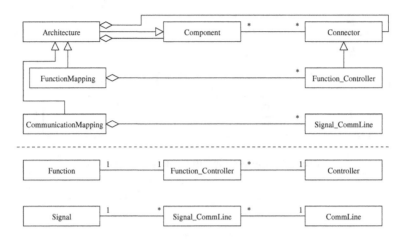

Fig. 5. Metamodels for mappings

3.2 The Architecture Evaluation Model

The metamodel for architecture evaluation and methodology is twofold. The first part is the evaluation model which has already been introduced as the quality attribute DAG in the terminology section. In this section we will give some detailed information on the quality attribute DAG's metamodel. The second part is a classification of the quality attributes to support execution order decisions regarding the evaluation techniques to be applied in a architecture evaluation. This part will be introduced informally with a short example in Section 3.3.

The basic elements for architecture evaluation are quality attributes. They are structured in a **directed acyclic graph**, called quality attribute DAG or QADAG for short. The structure is built on a composite pattern. Figure 6 depicts the hierarchical composition of quality attributes. Each quality attribute may have several associated scenarios and constraints to specify the requirements that have to be considered for architecture evaluation. We use scenarios to express what may happen to a system in its lifecycle (see Kazman et al. [6] and [7]). Scenarios specify requirements relevant for architecture design decisions in most cases. An example from the automotive domain is that system architects have to be aware of late changes for certain hardware components. Semiconductor suppliers may announce at any time that some product is discontinued soon and substituted by a defined set of successor products (which partially differ in their properties). Another scenario may anticipate the evolution of the system in future series. To specify restrictions and requirement changes that immediately refer to the evaluation of the quality attribute, constraints are assigned to an attribute. Examples for a constraint are that only certain vendors or technologies must be considered.

While a leaf quality attribute of the QADAG has an evaluation technique specifying how to evaluate an architecture with respect to this attribute, a composite attribute has a joining technique to specify how to join the evaluation results of

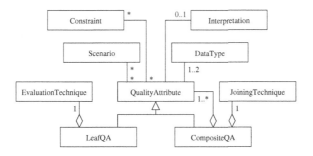

Fig. 6. Metamodel quality attribute DAG

the subattributes. The evaluation results (`DataType` in the metamodel) may be raw evaluation data of an arbitrary unit or the interpretation of the result to the quality rate (again `DataType`). Therefore, interpretation instances are necessary to map the values to the quality rate (see Section 2). In addition to the interpretation to a value between 0% and 100% quality rate, the interpretation may result in a K.O. This means that a system based on an architecture evaluated to K.O. in at least one quality attribute will not work or be buildable. A K.O. result will be propagated to the root of the DAG representing the architecture evaluation itself immediately. In this case, the architecture variant is ruled out and any further evaluation of this variant can be canceled. The requirements represented by a quality attribute are based on the evaluation or joining technique, the scenarios and constraints, and the interpretation of the evaluation result. The evaluation or joining technique, in combination with the interpretation, can give a concrete representation of the requirements.

The joining techniques may need some weight information specifying the relative importance of a subattribute for a composite quality attribute (see [8]). But, not every joining technique has to be based on this weight. For an example see the joining of hardware costs in the case study (Section 4), which does not work on quality rates but sums up the raw evaluation value (hardware costs per system unit). Therefore, we allow for joining not yet interpreted evaluation results which is necessary in the embedded systems domain.

3.3   Evaluation Methodology

An instance of the quality attribute DAG (e.g. Section 4) built in conformance to ISO/IEC 9126 or any other domain specific architecture evaluation definition represents the architecture evaluation itself. In addition to the architecture evaluations structure, the methodology is not yet defined by the QADAG. A first idea of the execution order is given. It is clear that subattributes have to be considered before any superior quality attribute. But, the partition of the DAG in quality attributes may give another hint for the evaluation techniques' execution order. In the embedded systems domain, technical requirements represented in e.g. the performance quality attribute are evaluated first because they are able to rule out variants by K.O. evaluations. We especially want to support one main goal of evaluation methodologies, i.e. efficient architecture evaluation of normally several variants. We call an architecture evaluation efficient if inadequate variants are ruled out early in the overall evaluation, where early means that as little as possible evaluation effort has been done. Next to the preferred evaluation regarding quality attributes capable of rejecting a variant, further information is necessary to define an efficient methodology. Therefore, we suggest a set of formal quality attribute classifications that can be extended according to the application domain's requirements.

K.O.-attribute
> *description:* May a quality attribute lead to a rejection of an architecture variant because of contained restrictions regarding the evaluation techniques?
> *classes:* no, direct, indirect (containing direct or indirect K.O.-attributes)

availability of evaluation
> *description:* Some evaluation techniques can be performed by experts only (based on experiences or measuring). Others are available in form of implemented algorithms, which leads to a higher availability. There are evaluation techniques based on simulation or formal analysis, too.
> *classes:* Expert know how, expert measuring, simulation, formal analysis, algorithm on special hardware, etc.

effort of evaluation
> *description:* Effort of the evaluation, or in case of an available algorithmic description, a complexity measure.
> *classes:* based on person time

The classification of quality attributes can help to identify the quality attribute most useful to increase efficiency of the overall evaluation by preferring K.O.-attributes and such with high availability and low effort.

3.4   Evaluation Analysis

Figure 7 contains the metamodel for describing dependencies between the architecture elements and between architecture elements and quality attributes (via results representing data type instances). These dependencies can be used for detecting and explaining, e.g. reciprocal influences of the same architecture

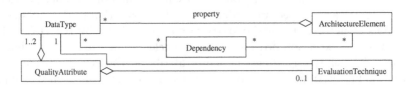

Fig. 7. Metamodel for dependencies

elements on some quality attributes which may lead to a no-win situation. Sensitivity and trade-off analysis (see Kazman et al. [7] or Lung and Kalaichelvan [9]) can be input for these dependencies, as well as output of their examination. An example for the benefits of these considerations is given in Section 5.

4 Case Study

The case study is an automotive system cut-out close to reality, a power window system. The structure of the QADAG depends mainly on the application domain and the goal to be achieved by system's development. The case study's QADAG is an example of embedded systems in an early design phase. In later phases, a more detailed evaluation can be performed based on more quality attributes defined for more detailed system architectures.

Although the case study originates from the embedded systems domain, which has a strong relation to hardware, the approach can also be adapted to more software related systems as already state in relation to the ISO/IEC 9126 standard. Therefore, the quality attributes have to be adapted to domain specific needs. In some cases, an extension of the metamodel may be useful to describe specific software architecture parts of the application domain, which does not affect the applicability of the approach in general.

4.1 The Architecture to Be Evaluated

The functionality of the power window system is contained in Figure 8 as a UML object diagram. It shows the logical composition of the system's functionality (the function architecture) extended by sensors and actuators as sources and targets for signals. The boxed area contains the functions instances of the function architecture. An explicit depiction of the signals is omitted in this figure. But the lines between the function, sensor, and actuator instances are an abstraction where to send the provided or where to get the required signals.

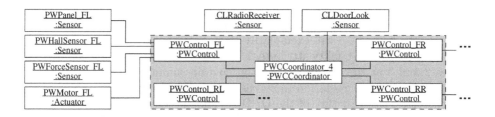

Fig. 8. Function architecture with sensors and actuators

The functions will be mapped to two hardware architecture variants as shown in Figure 9. The communication mapping, i.e. the mapping of signals to communication lines, will be done implicitly, while no variation in the concrete architectures is possible here. The main difference of the variants are the number and dimensioning of the controllers and their networking. Variant I is a legacy system with a CAN bus for future integration of further sub-/systems. Variant II is a system with a single controller, designed for reducing the permanently growing number of controllers in automotive systems development. The legend of Figure 9 refers to the metamodels (see the underlined terms). The communication mapping is omitted.

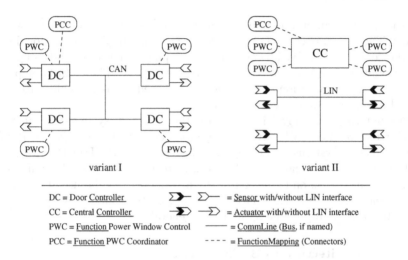

Fig. 9. The case study systems

Table 1 contains properties of the functions, the controllers, and the sensors and actuators needed for architecture evaluation. Applying approaches described in [10], [11], [12], and [13] will help to get more detailed input for as well as output from performance evaluation.

The quality attributes of the architecture evaluation are hierarchically organised in the quality attribute DAG of Figure 10. The doubly outlined rectangles represent composite quality attributes, the singly outlined rectangles represent leaf quality attributes which have directly associated evaluation techniques not shown in the figure. We will exemplarily show how to evaluate the architecture regarding some of the quality attributes and how to handle the evaluation results. Tables 2 and 3 at the end of this section contain summaries of the evaluation results and their interpretation to overall evaluation results, the systems' quality. Therefore, the structure of the QADAG and the tables is alike. Additional information on the QADAG, i.e. the weights of subattributes, is explicitly given in the tables.

4.2   Communication Performance

The performance of the communication network can be estimated in early design phases by taking the communication lines' capacities and the signals' specifications into account. Actually, we assess the maximal load of a bus not considering

Table 1. Architecture properties

Function Power Window Control (PWC)					
memory req RAM	8 kbyte		memory req ROM	12 kbyte	
required signals			provided signals		
signal type/instance	width	cycle	signal type/instance	width	cycle
ReqManOpen	1 bit	20 ms	OpenWindow	1 bit	20 ms
ReqManClose	1 bit	20 ms	OpenWindowSmoothly	1 bit	20 ms
ReqAutoOpen	1 bit	20 ms	CloseWindow	1 bit	20 ms
ReqAutoClose	1 bit	20 ms	CloseWindowSmoothly	1 bit	20 ms
ReqCentralOpen	1 bit	100 ms	StopWindow	1 bit	20 ms
ReqCentralClose	1 bit	100 ms			
WindowEnabling	2 bit	100 ms			
Clamp15	3 bit	100 ms			
WindowPosition	8 bit	100 ms			
CounterPresure	8 bit	100 ms			
Function Power Window Control Coordinator (PCC)					
memory req RAM	6 kbyte		memory req ROM	8 kbyte	
required signals			provided signals		
signal type/instance	width	cycle	signal type/instance	width	cycle
Clamp15	3 bit	100 ms	WindowEnabling (4x)	2 bit	100 ms
ReqDisableRearWindows	1 bit	100 ms	ReqCentralOpen (4x)	1 bit	100 ms
ReqDoorLockOpen	1 bit	100 ms	ReqCentralClose (4x)	1 bit	100 ms
ReqDoorLockClose	1 bit	20 ms			
ReqRadioOpen	1 bit	20 ms			
ReqRadioClose	1 bit	20 ms			

Controller properties			Sensor and actuator costs		
	DC	CC		standard	smart
RAM capacity	32 kbyte	64 kbyte	power window panel	€ 2.00	€ 4.00
ROM capacity	32 kbyte	64 kbyte	hall sensor (position)	€ 1.00	€ 3.00
costs	€ 15.00	€ 20.00	force sensor	€ 1.00	€ 3.00
			window motor	€ 5.00	€ 7.00

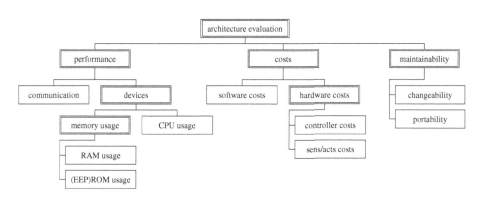

Fig. 10. Quality attribute DAG for embedded systems

message specifications or detailed scheduling strategies which are rare in early design phases. We use a simple scheduling algorithm of Liu and Layland [14] to evaluate the network's maximum utilization

$$U = \sum_{i=1}^{m} (C_i/T_i)$$

with U as the utilization, C_i as the time needed for the transmission of signal i, and T_i as the transmission cycle of signal i. Based on the object diagram in Figure 8, the provided signals of the functions as well as of the sensors are taken into account. Additionally, required signals with no source in the systems cut-out (e.g. Clamp15) are added to the estimation. With the direct connection of the sensors and actuators to the controllers in variant I, the bus traffic is about 1150 bit/s. The connection of the sensors and actuators to the controller via the LIN bus in variant II leads to a traffic of 3750 bit/s. This results are netto data without communication overhead and delays, the computed traffic is doubled to achieve a more conservative estimation, which will be adequate at this design level. With assumed transfer rates for CAN at 125000 bit/s and LIN at 19200 bit/s and the conservative estimation we achive a utilization of 1.8% for variant I and 39% for variant II. In this example, we firstly assessed the maximal bus load and then considered the buses' specifications and not the other way around which does not exactly represent the scheduling algorithm's execution but (1) is more demonstrative and (2) nevertheless conform to the algorithm's idea.

The utilization may be interesting for an expert. To make the result comprehensible for everybody, it needs to be interpreted. Figure 11 illustrates how to interpret the results. This interpretation step has to be done for nearly every evaluation result without some exceptions (e.g. hardware costs). For brevity, we omit the explicit presentation of other evaluation results.

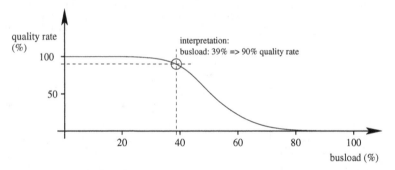

Fig. 11. Interpretation of the busload

4.3   Hardware Costs

The costs for controllers and sensors/actuators is given in Table 1. The costs for the hardware installed in the systems of Figure 9 can be assessed by adding up the hardware piece's costs with its application quantity in a concrete hardware architecture. Thus, the costs for controllers and sensors/actuators can be assessed what will be done separately to establish a more precise evaluation of the system's changeability. Because only the total hardware costs per unit are important for the costs quality attribute we need to join the evaluation results of the two hardware costs subattributes before interpreting them. Actually, the hardware costs in variant I are higher than in variant II, but an interpretation of the quite high costs for smart sensors and actuators may have ruled out this variant.

4.4   Maintainability

While maintainability of a software system is considered in ISO/IEC 9126 [1], the need for maintainability is slightly different in the automotive domain of embedded systems. Although there is need for runtime maintainability, too, we concentrate on the maintainability of the systems and their components in respect to be reusable as a changed system (changeability) or in other architectures for e.g. a new product family (portability).

Especially in the automotive domain, this kind of changeability is needed to cover a whole product family with limousine, coupé, etc. which may need four or only two power windows. Therefore, the system performance and its subattributes are direct input to quality attributes like changeability. Because of the high utilization of variant II, the changeability is evaluated more pessimistic ('maybe' → 50%).

Like defined in ISO/IEC 9126, portability is influenced by conformance to standards. In the automotive domain, the AUTOSAR approach defines standardized interfaces to certain layers to ensure portability of the software components. Thus, the conformance of all components to AUTOSAR is subattribute to portability, although the components will not be ported in the systems life time but in the design time. For this case study, we assume that the AUTOSAR conformance for variant II cannot be granted and will be evaluated as 'critical'.

4.5   Evaluation Results

The evaluation results are summed up in Tables 2 and 3. The subattributes's weights are specified for each quality attribute having subattributes. One exception is the hardware costs attribute which has no weights assigned because the evaluation results are not joined as weighted quality values but as raw evaluation results. The overall result advantages variant II because its costs are less than the costs of variant I. In the automotive domain, costs are the strongest quality attribute (see their weight). Some discussion about how to evaluate and how to come to an architectural decision can be based on the explicit presentation of the evaluation result and their integration to the overall result. The current architecture evaluation and its overall result are traceable and the trade-off between costs and maintainability can be made visible. In this case, a discussion of the pros an contras may lead to the advantage of variant I in case of a planned reuse of the system or at least parts of it. Additional costs may be compensated by saving development expenses in other projects.

5   Benefits of Analyzing the Architecture Evaluation

By modelling the architecture evaluation, the dependencies between the quality attributes and particular design decisions can be made explicit and analyzed further.

We illustrate the benefits of such an dependency analysis in an abstract example depicted in Figure 12. Let us consider two quality attributes (QA) named

Table 2. Architecture Evaluation Variant I

Architecture Evaluation Variant I (4xTSG with CAN)					
58.6%					
-					
30		100		15	
performance		costs		maintainability	
100%		40%		100%	
-		-		-	
100	100	50	100	100	100
comm.	devices	SW	HW	chng.	port.
100%	100%	100%	10%	100%	100%
1.8%	-	-	€ 96	granted	granted
	100	100	-	-	
	memory	CPU	ECUs	s/a	
	100%	100%	-	-	
	-	-	€ 60	€ 36	
	100	100			
	RAM	ROM			
	100%	100%		*(weights)*	
	43.8%	62.5%		QA name	
				quality rate	
				result	

Table 3. Architecture Evaluation Variant II

Architecture Evaluation Variant II (ZSG with LIN)					
68.4%					
-					
30		100		15	
performance		costs		maintainability	
80%		70%		35%	
-		-		-	
100	100	50	100	100	100
comm.	devices	SW	HW	chng.	port.
90%	70%	100%	55%	50%	20%
39%	-	-	€ 88	maybe	critical
	100	100	-	-	
	memory	CPU	ECUs	s/a	
	80%	60%	-	-	
	-	-	€ 20	€ 68	
	100	100			
	RAM	ROM			
	90%	70%		*(weights)*	
	59%	87.5%		QA name	
				quality rate	
				result	

A and B where A is performance-oriented and B cost-oriented. Their evaluation and thus their quality rate (QR) shall depend on the same architecture element represented on the x-axis. For instance, when you evaluate a processor, then usually you have to pay for better performance characteristics, thus the quality rate for the cost-oriented attribute will decrease. The dependency between both quality attributes regarding the architectural interpretation is represented by their evaluation results' quality rate interpretation shown as graphs. To come to an overall good quality result, the sum of both attributes quality rates has to be considered (see the upper left coordinate system and the upper right containing the optimum of the weighted normalized sum). Let us assume, that the weight of cost-oriented quality attribute is decreased after a first discussion in the architecture exploration process, to enable the decision for a more expensive performance oriented design variant. The break-even point shifts slightly, however, not far enough to reach the next performance level in the lower left coordinate system (let quality attribute A's quality rate graph be left-continuous). However, with the explicit knowledge of the quality attributes' sensitiveness, the weighted and normalized sum can be recalculated and a more expensive but better perfoming architecture is recognized as the optimum.

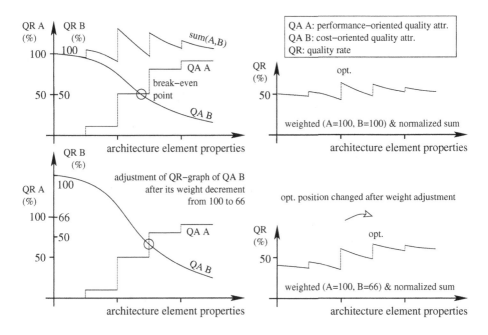

Fig. 12. Analysis of quality rate optimum

Remember: The y-axis scale of attribute B was stretched to 150% of its size because of a loss(!) to 66% of the original weight. By stretching the y-axis, the weight relation is equalized. That means that 100% quality rate of attribute A are assigned to 66% of attribute B, which was the intention of decreasing the weight of attribute B. Although the scale of the y-axis of attribute B persuades the reader that it has more weight, this leads to a loss in the break-even point analysis like shown in the example.

6   Conclusion

We have shown how to apply an evaluation model, the quality attribute DAG, in the embedded systems domain. The example of hardware costs has shown, that the quality attribute DAG is capable of handling domain specific quality attribute compositions as well as abstract compositions via the weighted joining of interpreted evaluation results, i.e. quality rates. With this structured and explicit combination of quality attributes, the architecture evaluation becomes traceable, and therefore reusable and analyzable. In addition to the benefit of documentation, the consideration of dependencies between architecture and evaluation model and between the evaluation model's elements increases the traceability of architectural decisions. Especially in the embedded systems domain, where requirements and restrictions often are technical and accurate, the analysis of dependencies is quite helpful to understand architectural decisions as well as the inner and overall evaluation results.

The approach was developed in close cooperation with the system architects from the electric/electronic development department of the Volkswagen AG. In this domain, the architectural design is - compared to our approach - made on a much more informal level so far with respect to both, the architectural descriptions and the evaluation process applied. Nevertheless, our approach has been applied in the development department, already, to check the usability and expressiveness of the evaluation result. Therefore, a prototypic tool has been implemented for importing/building the architectures, performing the evaluation, and presenting the results. For first applications and presentations of out approach (and tool) we got quite good feedback of the system architects as well as of management staff. Thus, further applications are planed with more complex case studies.

6.1   Related Work

Several approaches deal with the evaluation of software architecture. There is much work done on comparison of this approaches (see Ali Babar and Gorton [15], Ali Babar et al. [16], Bergner et al. [8], Dobrica and Niemelä [17], Ionita et al. [18], and Reussner and Hasselbring [12]). Some of them can be adapted to specific domains or integrated with other approaches. They are classified into qualitative, quantitative, and hybrid methods (see Bahsoon and Emmerich [19]). Our approach aims to (1) the integration of several architecture evaluation methods or techniques, (2) the comparison of several architecture variants, and (3) the analysis of relations within the evaluation model, the quality attribute DAG.

The integration of a set of techniques is considered in most approaches just by supporting different quality attributes. We extend the evaluation models used in most approaches for a more detailed integration of the quality attributes and their evaluation results, which we found out to be necessary, applying our approach in the embedded systems domain. In this domain, several quite different but not totally independent quality attributes need to be integrated. A difference of our approach to DoSAM [8] is the more thoughtful integration of the evaluation results of the same unit and dimension (see the hardware cost quality attribute for example).

The comparison of a set of architecture variants requires a method to keep the complexity of the architecture evaluation in limits. Actually, the complexity of each single technique cannot be affected, but their execution can. As extension to SACAM [20] and DoSAM, which both support comparison of architecture variants, we explicitly support a structured execution of a set of evaluation techniques to handle the evaluation complexity.

Furthermore, we extend the evaluation model for expressing interdependencies between the quality attributes. This helps to make architectural decisions traceable and therefore reproduceable/reusable and justifiable.

6.2 Future Work

We plan to extend our work in the direction of evaluation analysis. We want to detect dependencies by comparing evaluations of several architecture variants and derive new dependencies from known ones. Thus, further as well as indirect dependencies can be uncovered which can be useful for guiding the architecture exploration process and for increasing the traceability of architectural decisions. Furthermore, the impact of changing the quality attributes' weight is one way to modify an architecture evaluation as shown in Section 5. Additional investigation on these impacts will be done to predict the impact of such changes more explicitly. This will help to guide discussion about weight changes. Thus, discussions about changes with low potential of solving architecture no-win situation can be avoided and time is safed for more promising discussions.

References

1. ISO: ISO/IEC 9126 Information technology - Software product evaluation - Quality characteristics and guidelines for their use (1991) First edition.
2. Bass, L., Clements, P., Kazman, R.: Software Architecture in Practice. Addison-Wesley Longman Publishing Co., Inc. (1998)
3. Clements, P., Bachmann, F., Bass, L., Garlan, D., Ivers, J., Little, R., Nord, R., Stafford, J.: Documenting Software Architectures: Views and Beyond. Addison-Wesley (2002)
4. Hofmeister, C., Nord, R., Soni, D.: Applied Software Architecture. Addison-Wesley Longman Publishing Co., Inc., Boston, MA, USA (2000)
5. Florentz, B.: Systemarchitekturevaluation: Integration unterschiedlicher Kriterien. In: 26. Tagung 'Elektronik im Kfz'. (2006)
6. Kazman, R., Abowd, G.D., Bass, L.J., Clements, P.: Scenario-Based Analysis of Software Architecture. IEEE Software 13(6) (1996) 47–55
7. Kazman, R., Klein, M.H., Barbacci, M.R., Longstaff, T.A., Lipson, H.F., Carriere, S.J.: The Architecture Tradeoff Analysis Method. In: ICECCS. (1998) 68–78
8. Bergner, K., Rausch, A., Sihling, M., Ternité, T.: DoSAM - Domain-Specific Software Architecture Comparison Model. In: QoSA-SOQUA. Volume 3712 of LNCS. (2005) 4–20
9. Lung, C.H., Kalaichelvan, K.: An Approach to Quantitative Software Architecture Sensitivity Analysis. IJSEKE 10(1) (2000) 97–114
10. Happe, J.: Predicting Mean Service Execution Times of Software Components Based on Markov Models. In: QoSA-SOQUA. Volume 3712 of LNCS. (2005) 53–70
11. Koziolek, H., Firus, V.: Empirical Evaluation of Model-Based Performance Prediction Methods in Software Development. In: QoSA-SOQUA. Volume 3712 of LNCS. (2005) 188–202

12. Reussner, R., Hasselbring, W.: Handbuch der Software-Architektur. Dpunkt Verlag (2006)
13. Wandeler, E., Thiele, L., Verhoef, M.H.G., Lieverse, P.: System Architecture Evaluation Using Modular Performance Analysis - A Case Study. In: ISoLA. (2004)
14. Liu, C.L., Layland, J.W.: Scheduling Algorithms for Multiprogramming in a Hard-Real-Time Environment. J. ACM 20(1) (1973) 46–61
15. Babar, M.A., Gorton, I.: Comparison of Scenario-Based Software Architecture Evaluation Methods. In: APSEC. (2004) 600–607
16. Babar, M.A., Zhu, L., Jeffery, D.R.: A Framework for Classifying and Comparing Software Architecture Evaluation Methods. In: ASWEC. (2004) 309–319
17. Dobrica, L., Niemelä, E.: A Survey on Software Architecture Analysis Methods. IEEE Transactions on Software Engineering 28(7) (2002) 638–653
18. Ionita, M.T., Hammer, D.K., Obbink, H.: Scenario-Based Software Architecture Evaluation Methods: An Overview. In: ICSE/SARA. (2002)
19. Bahsoon, R., Emmerich, W.: Evaluating Software Architectures: Development, Stability, and Evolution. In: AICCSA. (2003)
20. Stoermer, C., Bachmann, F., Verhoef, C.: SACAM: The Software Architecture Comparison Analysis Method. Technical Report SEI/CMU-2003-TR-006, SEI (2003)

Parameter Dependent Performance Specifications of Software Components[*]

Heiko Koziolek, Jens Happe, and Steffen Becker

Graduate School Trustsoft
University of Oldenburg Germany
Chair for Software Design and Quality
University of Karlsruhe, Germany
{koziolek, happe, sbecker}@ipd.uka.de

Abstract. Performance predictions based on design documents aim at improving the quality of software architectures. In component-based architectures, it is difficult to specify the performance of individual components, because it depends on the deployment context of a component, which may be unknown to its developers. The way components are used influences the perceived performance, but most performance prediction approaches neglect this influence. In this paper, we present a specification notation based on annotated UML diagrams to explicitly model the influence of parameters on the performance of a software component. The UML specifications are transformed into a stochastical model that allows the prediction of response times as distribution functions. Furthermore, we report on a case study performed on an online store. The results indicate that more accurate predictions could be obtained with the newly introduced specification and that the method was able to support a design decision on the architectural level in our scenario.

1 Introduction

Performance is an important quality attribute of a software architecture. It can by characterised by metrics such as response time, throughput, and resource utilisation. In many existing systems, the reason for bad performance is a poorly designed software architecture [15]. Performance predictions based on architectural descriptions of a software system can be performed before the implementation starts, thereby possibly reducing costs for subsequent refactorings to fix performance problems. It is the hope that such early analyses support the decision for design alternatives and reduce the risk of having to redesign the architecture after performance problems have been diagnosed in the implementation.

Component-based software architectures are well-suited for early performance predictions, if information needed for performance evaluation has been specified for each component by its developers. As component developers cannot know in which context their components will be deployed [8], these performance specifications should be parameterisable for different hardware resources, required services, and usage contexts to allow accurate predictions [3].

---

[*] This work is supported by the German Research Foundation (DFG), grant GRK 1076/1.

C. Hofmeister et al. (Eds.): QoSA 2006, LNCS 4214, pp. 163–179, 2006.
© Springer-Verlag Berlin Heidelberg 2006

In many performance prediction approaches, the component specifications are parameterisable for different usage contexts only by allowing to specify probabilities for the possible requests to the component's provided services (e.g., [4,17]). It is often neglected that component services can be called with different parameters, and that these parameter can have a significant influence on the performance of the architecture.

The dependencies between parameters of a component service and its performance have to be made explicit by *component developers* in the specifications to allow accurate performance predictions. *System architects* can then adjust performance predictions to the expected usage profile. In some cases, the dependencies between parameters and performance might be intricate and hard to specify, for example if a service first performs complex computations on a parameter value an then changes its performance depending on the results. Furthermore, parameters might be complex objects or even other components, for which a reasonable specification is difficult. However, in this paper a first step to integrating parameters into performance specifications of software components shall be taken. Parameters considered here can be of a primitive or composite data type.

A notation based on extensions to the UML SPT profile [12] is provided to specify the dependencies between parameters and performance. This profile allows annotating UML diagrams with performance-related information. As many existing performance approaches already use this profile (e.g., [4,11]), they could also benefit from the extensions presented in this paper. Tools evaluating annotated UML diagrams could be changed with low effort to incorporate the extensions. Another advantage of the UML-based notation is the familiarity of the developers, who often already know the UML language. However, the concepts underlying the approach presented here are not bound to the SPT profile and might be carried over to other notations (e.g., future performance related profiles).

The contribution of this paper is a modelling notation for parameter dependent performance specifications for software components and an according analytical performance prediction model. Unlike most performance prediction models, we explicitly incorporate the influence of parameters on resource demand as well as on the usage of external services in our predictions. A case study, in which response times for a design alternative of a component-based software architecture are predicted, is provided to illustrate the benefits of this approach.

The paper is organised as follows: Section 2 describes the modelling in our performance prediction approach and focuses on parameter dependencies. Section 3 shows the necessary computations, and Section 4 explicitly lists the assumptions underlying the approach. The case study of a performance prediction for an component-based on-line store is provided in Section 5. Section 6 points out related work, while Section 7 draws conclusions and sketches future work.

2   Modelling Component Performance

Several models from different developer roles are used for the prediction of the performance in a component-based architecture in our approach. The architecture itself is modelled with a UML component diagram by the system architect. For each component, the component developers provide a specification, which will be described with more detail in the next paragraphs. Components are associated with system resources by system deployers using UML deployment diagrams. The user behaviour is modelled with activity diagrams, in which each action represents the invocation of an entry-level component service by a user.

All models are combined and completed by the system architect, who performs the predictions supported by tools. For this prediction approach, it is intended to use a development process model outlined in [9]. In the following paragraphs, component specifications, needed annotations, parameter characterisations, and modelling of resource demand are elaborated on.

2.1   Components and Service Effect Specifications

Software components are black-box entities with contractually specified interfaces. *Provided* interfaces publish services of the component. *Required* interfaces specify which external services are needed by the component. Moreover, in this approach a component specification contains a so-called *Service Effect Specification* (SEFF) for each provided service [13]. It describes how the provided service calls the services specified in the required interfaces. Here, a service effect specification is modelled with UML activity diagrams, where each action represents a call to a required service of the component. Activity diagrams are better suited for composition than sequence diagrams, as each external service call could be modelled with an additional activity diagram that is the SEFF of another component. In the example in Fig. 1, component c provides the service a and requires the services x, y, and z. The service effect specification for service a on the right hand side shows that, upon invocation, service a first calls service x, and then either service y or z before it finishes execution.

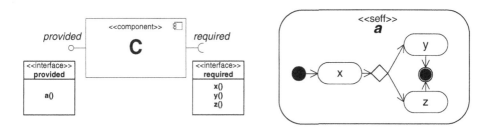

Fig. 1. Component C, Service Effect Specification for Service a

2.2   Annotations

To predict the performance of components, additional information is required in the specification, such as transition probabilities on branches, the number of iterations for each loop, arrival rates of requests, and resource demands (i.e., the time an actions is expected to execute on a resource). This additional information is included into the SEFFs by annotations according to the UML SPT profile [12]. Each action and transition is annotated with the stereotype <<PAstep>>. The tagged values of the profile (e.g., to specify resource demands, transition probabilities, repetitions of steps etc.) can be used as described in the profile specification. Two extensions to the SPT profile notation are defined in the following (Tab. 1), to better reflect the influences of different usages of the architecture in the model.

Table 1. Redefined Tags

Tag	Type	Multiplicity	Domain Attribute Name
PArep	PAloopValue	[0..*]	Step::repetition
PAparam	PApar	[0..*]	Step::parameter

First, we redefine the tag `PArep` of the UML SPT profile allowing to either specify a mean value or to associate percentiles to the number of loop iterations. To ease the later analysis, loops are always modelled with the tag `PArep` here. Following the approach in [10], cycles within the activity diagrams indicated by backward transitions are not allowed. Loops have to be made explicit whenever they are used. This can be done in three ways. First, by annotating an arbitrary behaviour call node with a `PArep` tag and taking the called activity as loop body. Second, by using loop nodes provided in UML 2.0 as basic element. The loop node allows explicit modelling of the loop initialization, the repetition test and the loop body. Third, by using expansion areas in UML 2.0, which specify a set of actions that are executed iteratively on a collection of input objects. We use loop nodes and expansion areas in our examples later on.

```
<loopValue>        ::= ( <type-modifier>, <integer> )
<type-modifier>    ::= 'mean' | 'percentile', <real>
```

Tagged Value Type Definition 1: PAloopValue

Second, we define a new tag `PAparam` to characterise parameters of component services. The signature of a component's service specifies formal parameters. However, for QoS analyses, we need probabilistic characterisations of the actual parameters that the formal parameters can be bound on during runtime by the users.

2.3 Parameter Characterisation

Three forms of parameters can be distinguished. *Input* parameters are arguments passed to a provided service of a component. *Output* parameters are the return values of these services. *Internal* parameters can be global variables or configuration attributes of a component. All these forms of parameters may have different influences on the performance of a component:

- **Resource Usage:** Parameters can influence the usage of the resources present in the system executing the component. For example, the time for the execution of a service that allows uploading files to a server depends on the size of the files that are passed as input parameters.

- **Control Flow between Components:** Service effect specifications describe how requests to provided services are propagated to other components. The transition probabilities or number of loop iterations in service effect specifications can depend on the parameters passed to a service.
- **Internal State:** Input parameters can be stored as global variables within a component, thus becoming internal parameters and altering the internal state of the component. Later, they can be used by computations of other provided services of the components and then influence resource usage or control-flow between components.

In the following, we consider primitive types (e.g., boolean, int, short, char) and composite types (e.g., String, List, Tree, Hash, Object). Other forms of parameters like streams or pointers are excluded here. It is useful to characterise parameters not only with constant values but with probability distributions. In the following specification of the tag PAparam, we allow modelling probabilities distributions over the value, the subtypes, the number of elements, the byte-size, and the structure of a parameters.

- **Value:** By providing a probability distribution for the value of a parameter, its input domain is partitioned into multiple subdomains. For example, for an integer-parameter x the domain can be partitioned into two subdomains with $x \leqslant 0$ and $x\ 0$ depending on its influence on the performance of the component. The system architect can then specify a probability for each subdomain.
- **Subtypes:** Different subtypes can be passed to a service that has specified some supertype in the signature of a provided service. For example, a generic service drawing graphical objects might have a different response time depending on the type of objects passed to it (e.g., simple circle vs. complex polygon). In this case, it is useful to specify a probability distribution over the subtypes and to neglect the value of the parameters.
- **Elements:** For composite data types, it is more difficult to find subdomains over the value domain. The performance-influence of collections like array, tree, or hash can sometimes be characterised simply by the number of elements. Thus, it may be appropriate for such parameters to specify probability distributions over the number of elements.
- **Size:** Parameter values might also be passed between different servers thus creating a communication delay. The delay can best be analysed if the *byte-size* of the parameter is specified. To refine the specification a probability distribution for the size could be specified. Note that modelling the overall size of a parameter is appropriate if the inner structure of the parameter is unknown and the number of elements cannot be determined.
- **Structure:** Additionally, the *structure* of collections (sorted, well-formed, balanced, etc.) can have an influence on performance (e.g., presorted arrays are usually sorted quicker than unsorted arrays). Thus, a component developer could specify the behaviour of a component's service depending on the structure of a parameter passed to it.

For a single parameter, several of these characterisations could be specified. For more complex parameters like objects it might be necessary to first decompose them into more primitive types and then characterise these types. Besides specifying probability distributions, it may be convenient to specify mean values, constants, minimum or maximum values for parameters.

To model parameters in SEFFs, object nodes (represented as pins on actions) from UML 2.0 activity diagrams can be annotated with the newly defined tag PAparam (see tag definition 2). The string-value for <paramValue> is a representative characterisation of the subdomain of the value (e.g. "0 *value* 10") or can be used to specify a constant value (e.g. "foo"). The integer-value for <paramSize> specifies the number of bytes of the parameter, while the integer-value for <paramElements> models the number of elements in a collection. Finally, the string-value of <paramStructure> can be used to make any statement about the structure of the values in collection (e.g. "presorted" or "unsorted"), if it has an impact on performance (e.g. in sort-operations).

```
<paramStr>            ::= ( <property-modifier> )

<property-modifier> ::= <paramValue> | <paramType> | <paramSize> |
                        <paramElements> | <paramStructure>

<paramValue>          ::= 'value', <valueModifier>, <string>
<paramType>           ::= 'type', <valueModifier>, <string>
<paramSize>           ::= 'size', <probModifier>, <integer>
<paramElements>       ::= 'elements', <probModifier>, <integer>
<paramStructure>      ::= 'structure', <string>

<valueModifier>       ::= 'const' | 'min' | 'max' | 'percentile', <real>
<probModifier>        ::= 'mean' | 'sigma' | 'kth-mom', <integer> | 'max' |
                          'min' | 'percentile', <real>
```

Tagged Value Type Definition 2: PAparam

The dependency between a parameter and resource usage or control flow between components can be specified by using scalar variables of the tagged value language (TVL) of the UML SPT profile. The same variable can be used in a PAparam tag and another tag (e.g., PAprob, PArep, PAdemand, etc.) to model a dependency.

For example, in Fig. 2, a collection is passed to service a as parameter P1. The component developer has specified that the number of loop iterations of the required service y is three times the number of elements ("3*$P1elements", where $P1elements is a scalar variable of the TVL) of the collection passed to service a in parameter P1. Once the system architect specifies the number of elements in the collections the expected users will pass to the service, the number of external calls is also specified via the dependency.

In the same example, the type of parameter P2 is integer. The component developer has specified that, depending on whether values of P2 are smaller or larger than 100, either the required service y or z are called, because the transition probabilities of to these service depend on the variable specified for the parameter. The transition probability from x to z is specified as a difference to turn the cumulative percentiles into a probability.

Furthermore, parameter P3 is a binary large object. The component developer has specified that service a takes this parameter and returns parameter P4, which is 100 Bytes larger than parameter P4.

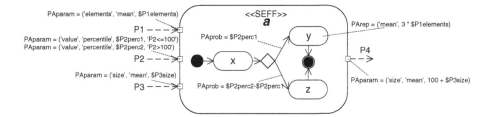

Fig. 2. Annotated Service Effect Specification for Service a including parameters

Note, that it is only necessary to characterise parameters if they indeed influence the performance. Most parameters do *not* change resource usage or alter the control flow between components, and their characterisation can be omitted. Characterising every parameter of the services in a complex component-based architecture would require too much effort and not support performance analysis. What parameters have to be characterised because of their influence on performance has to be defined by the component developer. So far, this task has to be done manually. However, it is conceivable to develop tools for the reverse-engineering of existing components to help component developers in obtaining the necessary specifications in a semi-automatic way. This is part of our future work.

3   Computing Component Performance

To calculate the response time for a service invocation, the resource demand of the service itself and the resource demands of required services have to be added. Resource demands are specified as probability mass functions (PMF) in our approach for a more refined modelling, and the necessary computations for combining these functions are described in the following. More detailed description of the computations can be found in [7,10].

To conduct the computations, first the annotated activity diagrams are transformed into stochastic regular expressions, which are described in [10]. The mapping is straightforward: sequential executions are mapped to sequential expressions, control flow branches are mapped to alternative expression, and loops are mapped to single expressions with a distributions function for the number of iterations. The PMFs modelling the resource demand are annotated to each expression. So far, forks and join in activity diagrams are not supported by this approach. The abstract syntax tree of the resulting stochastic regular expressions is then traversed and the following computations are performed for each control flow primitive.

Sequence: The PMF for successive service invocations can be computed as the convolution of the single PMFs:

$$x_{R_1 \cdot R_2}(n) = x_{R_1} \circledast x_{R_2}[n]$$

Alternative: The PMF for a branch in the control flow can be computed as the sum of the PMF weighted by the transition probabilities:

$$x_{R_1+R_2}(n) = p_1 x_{R_1}[n] + p_2 x_{R_2}[n] \text{ (average case)}$$

Loop: As we have also specified a PMF for the number of loop iterations with the PArep tag, the random variable for the resource demand of a loop is (ln is the PMF for the number of loop iterations):

$$X_{R^l} = \begin{cases} X_R & \text{with probability} & l(1) \\ X_R + X_R & \text{with probability} & l(2) \\ \vdots & & \\ \sum_{i=1}^{N} X_R & \text{with probability} & l(N) \end{cases}$$

with $N \in \mathbb{N}_0$ and $i \in N : l_i \geq 0$. The corresponding PMF for the loop has the form:

$$x_{R^l}(n) = \sum_{i=1}^{N} l(i) \circledast_{j=1}^{i} x_R[n]$$

For the computation of the convolutions of the PMF, we use discrete Fourier transformations (also see [7]). The total response time obtained by analysing a stochastic regular expression can be fed into performance models like queueing networks to calculate the response time of a service in presence of multiple users in the system. These models also include contention delays of the requests into the response time.

4   Underlying Assumptions

The limiting assumptions of the prediction model concern the availabilty of data and the mathematical model. A tradeoff can be observed: if the mathematical assumptions are relaxed, more information about the system is required and vice versa. Furthermore, we discuss the limitations of the presented approach in the following.

Availability of Data: Service effect specifications have to be available for all services provided by a component. They have to be enriched with execution times, transition probabilities, loop iterations etc., and this information has to be specified by the component developer without knowing the usage context and deployment environment of the component. For the component developer, this can be a hard task that needs to be supported by tools guiding the estimation of resource demands or measuring the required data for existing components.

If a parameter influences the performance of a service, subdomains for its input values have to be identified by the component developer. This can be done by looking at boolean expressions of branches and loops that depend on the parameter (or one of the parameters that was derived from it). For example, the expression $(x < 5)$ implies a partitioning of the values of x into two subdomains: $x > 5$ and $x \leq 5$. For both subdomains, the system assembler can specify probabilities that are mapped to the branching probabilities according to the expected usage profile. As for the creation of SEFFs, it is the hope that the subdomains of parameters can be derived from a component's source code in a semi-automatic way.

Mathematical Assumptions: The stochastic regular expressions used in our prediction model are based on Markov chains. Therefore, some of the assumptions of Markov chains are inherited. The Markov property (the probability of going from state i to state j in the next step is independent of the path to state i) is present in our model, but has been weakened for loops. We explicitly model (arbitrary) PMFs for the number of loop iteration. Therefore, our prediction model is not bound to a geometrical distribution on the number of loop iterations like classical Markov models (also see [6]).

Branching probabilities are modelled in dependence on a service's input parameters. Thus, we still assume that the past history of the service's execution does not influence the branching probabilities. However, we allow parametrising these probabilities by characterisation of parameters of a service, thus enabling more realistic predictions for different usage contexts.

Many analytical performance prediction approaches assume that execution times are exponentially distributed, which significantly eases the analysis. However, the measurements of our case study in section 5 show that, often times, execution times are not exponentially distributed. For this reason, we used arbitrary distribution functions which reflect the actual system behaviour more accurately.

However, it is assumed that execution times are stochastically independent. This is a result of the convolution used to combine the execution times of sequential services. When convolving two PMFs, the result reflects all possible combinations of execution times. In reality, the execution times of sequential services might be dependent. For example, if the execution of one service is slow due to a high system load, the execution of another service will be slow as well. Such a dependency is not reflected by our model.

Further Limitations: Our approach is a first step and still embodies some limitations that shall be adressed in future research. The *scalability* of the approach is still unknown as up to now we have not analysed a large-scale industrial size software architecture.

The *parameter modelling* is limited to primitive and composite data types, and parameters like streams or pointer are not supported.

So far, only one user request is modelled in the system at the same time, thus, *contention* for resources by concurrent requests is neglected in this approach. However, the results of our analyses can possibly used as input parameter for performance models such as queueing networks, which support contention analysis. Moreover, we do not support modelling components that start *threads* during the execution of their services, as we cannot analyse forks and joins in the control flow.

5   Case Study

In the following we report on a case study to validate to applicability of our approach. The performance of a component-based on-line store for music files (WebAudioStore) is analysed. Parameters influence resource usage and inter-component control flow in this application, so the store is well suited to be modelled with our approach. Simplifying the analysed architecture aids in understanding the case study. However, the considered case is exemplary. Many similar cases could occur in an industrial sized architecture, whose analyses would be support by our method as well.

The architecture of the WebAudioStore has been modelled and implemented, so that measurements based on the implementation and predictions based on the specification can be compared. In this case, the performance prediction aims at supporting a design decision regarding an architectural alternative. The aim of the case study is to validate the applicability and usefulness of the proposed prediction model. Thus, the following questions have to be answered:

1. Does the prediction model favour the design with the lowest response time and, thus, support the right design decision?
2. How much do the computations based on component specifcations deviate from measurements based on an implementation?

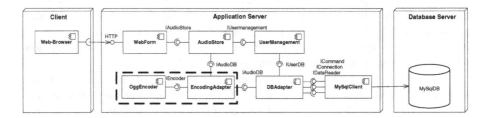

Fig. 3. WebAudioStore Architecture

5.1   Original Architecture

The simplified architecture of the WebAudioStore can be found in Fig. 3. Note that the components within the dashed box indicate an extension described in Section 5.2. Clients can buy and sell music files in the store via a web interface. To sell files, MP3-files can be uploaded to the store. It is possible to upload multiple files, so that complete albums can be offered. The files are stored in a MySQL database located on a different server than the application. Clients connect to the store using DSL lines (128 KBit/s Upload), the application server is connected to the database server with a dedicated line with a throughput of 512 KBit/s.

Fig. 4(a) shows the usage scenario for uploading files to the store. Note that only the parameter dependencies are included in the illustration. Additional specifications necessary for the performance prediction like the service's resource demand are omitted in the illustration to allow an easier understanding. Users select several files from their hard drives and click the upload button afterwards, which initiates a service of the WebForm component. This is the performance critical service, since the files are copied to the database during this action.

Its SEFF (see Fig. 4(b)) indicates that the service HandleUpload of the component AudioStore is called as often as the number of files selected by the user. Thus, the inter-component control flow is influenced by a parameter provided by the user. The service HandleUpload (see Fig. 4(c)) calls services of the component DBAdapter (via the interface IAudioDB), which transmits the files to the database server by executing SQL queries. The size of the files influences the response time of this scenario.

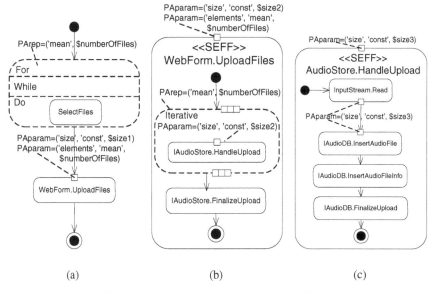

Fig. 4. Scenario for the Use Case "Upload Files"

The system architect can take these specifications provided by the component developers and instantiate the included variables with data from the usage scenario. In the scenario considered here, users usually upload eight to twelve MP3-files with a size of 3.5 to 4.5 MBytes. These files are encoded with a bit rate of 192Kbps.

The response times for this scenario are too slow and shall be improved transparently for the clients, so that they can use the store as usual.

5.2   Design Alternative: Compression

It is suggested to reduce the response time of the "UploadFiles" use case by applying the Fast Path performance pattern [15]. Thus, an additional compression component interface) is put between the DBAdapter and the AudioStore (dashed box in Fig. 3). By reducing the size of the uploaded audio files, the time for the network transfer between application server and database server is reduced. For the compression, a component using the OGG Vorbis encoder (component OggEncoder) shall be used that reduces the file sizes by one third by converting the MP3-files with a bitrate 192Kbps to OGG-files with a bitrate of 128Kbps. It is included into the architecture using the adapter EncodingAdapter that implements the IAudioDB interface. Because the audio quality of OGG-files with lower bitrates is better than the one of MP3-files, there are no significant quality losses expected. However, re-encoding the MP3-files costs a certain amount of time. With a performance prediction, it is analysed whether the time saved by reducing the network traffic outweighs the time for the encoding.

The component developer of the OggEncoder component has specified that the size of the output parameter of the EncodeFile service is $\frac{2}{3}$ of the input parameter's size (Fig. 5(b)).

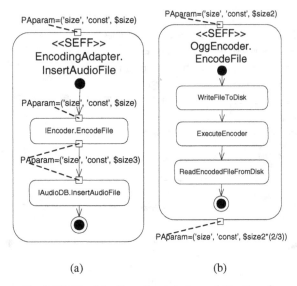

(a)   (b)

Fig. 5. SEFFs of the EncodingAdapter and OggEncoder

5.3 Computations

Before answering the question which design alternative is rated best, we present how the computation process works and what input data was used for the example of the design alternative employing compression.

From the usage profile, it is known that the size of the input files is 3.5, 4, and 4.5 MB with a probability of 0.1, 0.6, and 0.3 respectively. The system assembler uses this information to estimate the execution times of the compression (Fig. 6(a)) and the transfer of the compressed file to the data base (Fig. 6(b)). For the estimation of the latter, the the compression rate of the OggEncoder has to be considered.

Both functions contain relatively few values and can easily obtained by either measurement or estimation. However, an integrated approach requires that both PMFs are derived automatically from the size of the input files and service specifications. For this paper, it is assumed that these values are delivered by the system assembler.

The encoding (EncodeFile) and transfer (InsertAudioFile) to the database are executed sequentially as shown in the SEFF of service EncodingAdapter. InsertAudioFile (Fig. 5(a)). To compute its execution time, the convolution of both PMFs is computed.

5.4 Results

Fig. 7 shows its result compared to the actual measurements. Even though the predictions match the measurements pretty well, they look a little bit "blurred". This is a result of the convolution that computes all possible combinations of its input functions and, therefore, assumes their independence. This assumption does not hold in this case: If the file is large, both compression and transfer to the database will consume more time. To achieve more accurate results, this dependency needs to be reflected in the model.

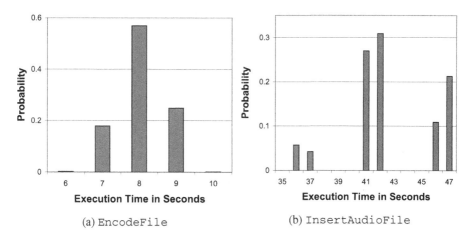

(a) EncodeFile   (b) InsertAudioFile

Fig. 6. Probability mass functions used as input

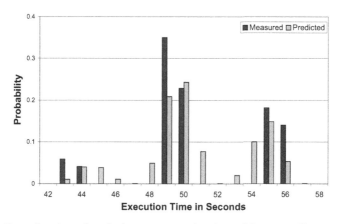

Fig. 7. Execution time of method InsertAudioFile of the EncodingAdapter

Knowing the execution time of the EncodingAdapter.InsertAudioFile the execution time of the service HandleUpload of the WebAudioStore component is set to the same PMF, since the execution times of FinalizeUpload and InsertAudioFile are below one second and are thus set to zero.

As the last step, the execution time of the service UploadFiles of the WebForm component is determined using the computed values as input. The execution time of FinalizeUpload is assumed to be zero. The usage profile contains information on the value distribution of parameter numberOfFiles. This is used for the computation of the loop execution time. It is known, that eight to twelve files are uploaded by the users with a probability of 0.1, 0.1, 0.2, 0.4, and 0.2 respectively. This directly influences the number of loop iterations as expressed by the PArep tag in Fig. 4(b). Fig. 8 shows the resulting prediction in comparison to the measurements. The curve

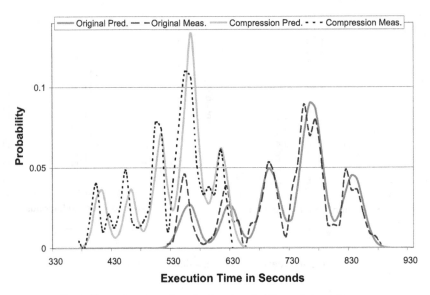

Fig. 8. Execution time of method `UploadFiles` of the `WebForm`

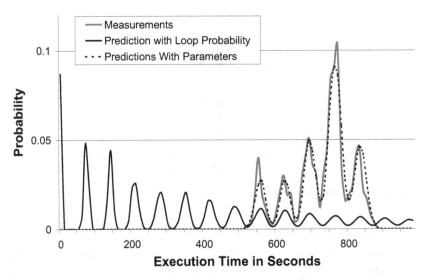

Fig. 9. Execution time of method `UploadFiles` of the `WebForm`

is not an exact fit, but represents its structure pretty well. For the original architecture, the predictions are closer to the measurements (Fig. 8). This is due to the fact that the error introduced by the assumption of independence in the predictions does not play a role here. Only the execution time of the service `DBAdapter.InsertAudioFile` is influenced by the file size of the uploaded files.

Fig. 9 depicts what is predicted if the information on the parameters is neglected and a common Markovian modelling is applied (the underlying problem is also described in [6]). Instead of executing the loop in SEFF `WebForm.UploadFiles` (Fig 4(b)) eight to twelve times as specified by the input parameter `numberOfFiles`, a loop probability p was used to determine whether the loop is (re-)entered (with probability p) or left (probability $1-p$). Thus, the loop is never iterated with probability $1-p$, once with probability $(p1-p)$, twice with probability $(p^2 1-p)$, and so on [7]. Thus, the number of loop iterations is geometrically distributed. This influence can be observed at the predicted execution time. The probability of not executing the loop is highest, after that the probability decreases and converges to zero. Obviously, the predicted curve does not match the measurements in any aspect. This shows that the Markov property for loops (the probability of re-iterating the loop does not change over time) does not hold in this case. This was to be expected and can be handled by the prediction model for loops used in our approach.

The results described above answer the questions asked in the beginning of this section. The prediction model favored the design alternative with compression, which was also the fastest during our measurements. Thus, the first question can be answered with "yes". The PMFs shown in Fig. 8 answer the second question in a non-formal way. To answer the question completely, a proper measure for the error of two PMFs describing execution times has to be found and applied to measured and predicted functions. However, a detailed analysis of the error made by the predictions is beyond the scope of this paper.

6 Related Work

The SPE methodology [16] was one of the first approaches to analyse the performance of a software system during early development stages. A survey on model-based performance prediction approaches is provided in [1]. Specifically for component-based performance predictions, there is a survey on approaches related to the one presented here in [2].

The CB-SPE approach by Bertolino et. al. [4] uses sequence diagrams and queueing networks to analyse the performance of component-based software systems. For each service, the performance is specified in dependency of so-called environment parameters like CPU time or network bandwidth. There is no characterisation of parameters passed by users to a service in this approach.

Hamlet et. al. [8] presented an approach for the performance analysis of component-based systems that relies on measurements. In this more theoretical approach, components compute single functions and their input space is divided into subdomains by profiling them. Subdomains are only created for the values of parameters, whereas in our approach we also allow to specify subdomains over the number of elements in a collection or the byte size of a parameter.

Bondarev et. al. [5] explicitly model input parameters of software components and make performance predictions. However, there is no probabilistic characterisation of parameter values in this approach, as it is assumed that a fixed parameter assignment can be identified in a certain scenario, which may be realistic for the embedded systems the approach is aiming at.

Sitaraman et. al. [14] also aim at performance predictions incorporating parameter values. In their approach, parameters are characterised using a modified form of the Big-O Notation. However, it is not shown how this characterisation can be transformed into timing values.

7   Conclusions and Future Work

An approach including the dependencies between component service parameters and performance has been presented in this paper. Service effect specifications modelling external calls of a component service were extended to include parameter dependencies using a notation based on the UML SPT profile. The case study of an component-based online shop showed that the method can support design decisions during early development stages. Parameter dependent performance specification can lead to more refined and accurate predictions. The approach is especially suited to model systems with extensive data flow, because the size of data packets transferred between components can be included into the predictions.

However, there are several pointers for future work. Modelling concurrency (e.g., multiple threads) is not supported by the method presented here and will be included in the future. Parameter dependencies can also be expressed as OCL constraints, thus existing OCL checkers could be used to validate the syntax. We will explore this direction in the future. More complex parameters like streams or pointers can not be modelled. So far, all necessary specifications have to be created by component developers manually. Thus, code analysis techniques shall be used in the future to generate parts of these specifications from source code of existing components semi-automatically.

Acknowledgements. We would like to thank Ralf Reussner and Viktoria Firus for their ideas and the fruitful discussions.

References

1. S. Balsamo, A. DiMarco, P. Inverardi, and M. Simeoni. Model-based performance prediction in software development: A survey. *IEEE Transactions on Software Engineering*, 30(5):295–310, May 2004.
2. S. Becker, L. Grunske, R. Mirandola, and S. Overhage. Performance prediction of component-based systems: A survey from an engineering perspective. In Ralf Reussner, Judith Stafford, and Clemens Szyperski, editors, *Architecting Systems with Trustworthy Components*, number To Appear in LNCS. Springer, 2005.
3. S. Becker and R. Reussner. The Impact of Software Component Adaptation on Quality of Service Properties. *L'objet*, 12(1):105–125, 2006.
4. A. Bertolino and R. Mirandola. CB-SPE Tool: Putting component-based performance engineering into practice. In I. Crnkovic, J. A. Stafford, H. W. Schmidt, and K. C. Wallnau, editors, *CBSE2004*, volume 3054 of *LNCS*, pages 233–248. Springer, 2004.
5. E. Bondarev, P. de With, M. Chaudron, and J. Musken. Modelling of input-parameter dependency for performance predictions of component-based embedded systems. In *Proceedings of the 31th EUROMICRO Conference (EUROMICRO'05)*, 2005.
6. K. Doerner and W. Gutjahr. Representation and optimization of software usage models with non-markovian state transitions. *Information & Software Technology*, 42(12):873–887, 2000.

7. V. Firus, S. Becker, and J. Happe. Parametric performance contracts for QML-specified software components. In *Proceedings of FESCA2005*, ENTCS, pages 64–79, 2005.

8. D. Hamlet, D. Mason, and D. Woit. *Properties of Software Systems Synthesized from Components*, volume 1 of *Series on Component-Based Software Development*, chapter Component-Based Software Development: Case Studies, pages 129–159. World Scientific Publishing Company, March 2004.

9. H. Koziolek and J. Happe. A quality of service driven development process model for component-based software systems. In *Proceedings of the 9th International Symposium on Component Based Software Engineering (CBSE2006)*, 2006.

10. H. Koziolek and V.Firus. Parametric performance contracts: Non-markovian loop modelling and an experimental evaluation. In *Proceedings of FESCA2006*, ENTCS, 2006.

11. M. Marzolla. *Simulation-Based Performance Modeling of UML Software Architectures*. PhD thesis, Universit'a Ca Foscari di Venezia, 2004.

12. Object Management Group OMG. UML Profile for Schedulability, Performance and Time. http://www.omg.org/cgi-bin/doc?formal/2005-01-02, 2005.

13. R. Reussner, S. Becker, and V. Firus. Component composition with parametric contracts. In *Tagungsband der Net.ObjectDays 2004*, pages 155–169, 2004.

14. M. Sitaraman, G. Kuczycki, J. Krone, W. F. Ogden, and A.L.N. Reddy. Performance specification of software components. In *Proc. of SSR '01*, 2001.

15. C. U. Smith. *Performance Solutions: A Practical Guide To Creating Responsive, Scalable Software*. Addison-Wesley, 2002.

16. C.U. Smith. *Performance Engineering of Software Systems*. Addision-Wesley, 1990.

17. X. Wu and M. Woodside. Performance modeling from software components. *SIGSOFT Softw. Eng. Notes*, 29(1):290–301, 2004.

Applying the ATAM to an Architecture for Decentralized Control of a Transportation System

Nelis Boucké, Danny Weyns, Kurt Schelfthout, and Tom Holvoet

Distrinet, KULeuven, Celestijnenlaan 200A, Leuven, Belgium
{nelis.boucke, danny.weyns, kurt.schelfthout,
tom.holvoet}@cs.kuleuven.be

Abstract. For two years, we have been involved in a challenging project to develop a new architecture for an industrial transportation system. The motivating quality attributes to develop this innovative architecture were flexibility and openness. Taking these quality attributes into account, we proposed a decentralized architecture using multiagent systems (MASs). A MAS consists of multiple autonomous entities that coordinate with each other to achieve decentralized control. The typical advantages attributed to such decentralized architecture are flexibility and openness, the motivating quality attributes to apply MAS in this case.

The Architecture Tradeoff Analysis Method (ATAM) was used to provide insights wether our architecture meets the expected flexibility and openness, and to identify tradeoffs with other quality attributes. Applying the ATAM proved to be a valuable experience. One of the main outcome of applying the ATAM was the identification of a tradeoff between flexibility and communication load that results from the use of a decentralized architecture.

This paper describes our experiences in applying the ATAM to a MAS architecture, containing both the main outcomes of the evaluation and a critical reflection on the ATAM itself.

1 Introduction

For two years, Distrinet [1] has been involved in a challenging R&D project (EMC² [2]) to develop a decentralized architecture for an industrial transportation system. Our industrial partner, Egemin N.V. [3], is a Belgian manufacturer of Automatic Guided Vehicles (AGVs) and control software for automating logistics services in warehouses and manufactories using AGVs. Traditionally, one computer system (central server) is in charge of numerous complex and time-consuming tasks such as routing, collision avoidance, or deadlock avoidance; the AGVs themselves have little autonomy. This traditional architecture has successfully been deployed in numerous practical installations, but the evolution of the market has put forward new requirements for AGV Transportation systems [4]. Especially in highly dynamic systems, where the situation changes frequently, problems are experienced. A new and innovative architecture is needed that offers additional qualities, like flexibility and openness, to cope with the highly dynamic environments.

Taking these quality attributes into account we proposed a decentralized architecture using multiagent systems (MASs). Typical advantages attributed to a MAS architecture are flexibility and openness, being the motivating quality attributes to apply MAS for the

C. Hofmeister et al. (Eds.): QoSA 2006, LNCS 4214, pp. 180–198, 2006.
© Springer-Verlag Berlin Heidelberg 2006

AGV transportation system. A second motivation, from the research perspective, was the opportunity to evaluate MASs and our reference architecture [5] in a real industrial application and asses if it really fulfilled the attributed quality attributes. The Architecture Tradeoff Analysis Method (ATAM) [6,7] was used to provide insights wether our architecture meets the expected flexibility and openness and to identify tradeoffs with other qualities. This paper describes our experiences in applying the ATAM to the MAS-based architecture, containing both the main outcomes in terms of tradeoffs and what we have learned and a critical reflection on the ATAM itself.

Overview. The remainder of this paper is structured as follows. Section 2 describes the requirements, the motivation and a short overview of the MAS architecture. Section 3 describes the outcomes of the ATAM workshop. Section 4 reflects on the ATAM workshop. Section 5 describes related work and we conclude in section 6.

2 Decentralized Architecture for Automatic Guided Vehicles

An AGV transportation system uses unmanned vehicles that are custom made to be able to transport various kinds of loads, from basic or raw materials to completed products. Typical applications are repackaging and distributing incoming goods to various branches, or distributing manufactured products to storage locations. An AGV uses a battery as its energy source. AGVs can move through a warehouse guided by a laser navigation system, or following a physical path on the factory floor that is marked by magnets or cables that are fixed in the floor. Egemin N.V., our industrial partner for the EMC^2 project, develops and delivers such AGV transportation systems tailored to the needs of the specific production-plant or warehouse. Thus AGV transportation systems is a product-line system that is used in several concrete products with different functional and (possible contradicting) quality requirements. This section describes the main functionalities, the important quality attributes, the motivation to apply a MAS architecture and a short overview of the MAS architecture for the AGV Transportation system.

2.1 Main Functionalities

The main functionality the system should perform is handling transports, i.e. moving loads from one place to another. Transports are generated by client systems. Client systems are typically warehouse management systems, but can also be particular machines, employees or service operators. In order to execute transports, the main functionalities the system has to perform are:

- Transport assignment: transports are generated by client systems and have to be assigned to AGVs that can execute them.
- Routing: AGVs must route efficiently through the layout of the warehouse when executing their transports.
- Gathering traffic information: although the layout of the system is static, the best route for the AGVs in general is dynamic, and depends on the current conditions in the system. Gathering traffic information allows the system to adapt the routing of the AGVs to these dynamic conditions.

- Collision avoidance: obviously, AGVs may not collide. AGVs can not cross the same intersection at the same moment. Similar safety measures are also necessary when AGVs pass each other on closely located paths.
- Deadlock avoidance: since AGVs are relatively constrained in their movement (they cannot divert from their path), the system must ensure that AGVs do not find themselves in a deadlock situation.

When an AGV is idle it can park at a free park location; however, when the AGV runs out of energy, it has to charge its battery at one of the charging stations.

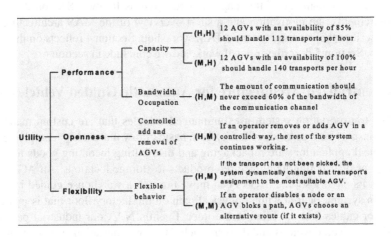

Fig. 1. Excerpt of utility tree for AGV transportation system

2.2   Quality Requirements

Fig. 1 shows an excerpt from the utility tree to illustrate important quality attributes: performance, openness and flexibility. The utility tree is an instrument to make quality attributes explicit in the form of scenarios, to structure these scenarios in a hierarchical fashion and to make the importance of each scenario explicit by putting priorities on them. Concretely, each scenario is assigned a ranking that expresses its priority relatively to the other scenarios. Prioritizing takes place in two dimensions. The first mark (High, Medium or Low) of each tuple refers to the importance of the scenario to the success of the system, the second to the difficulty to achieve the scenario. The tree serves as a guidance for design and evaluation of this architecture.

In the dictionary [8] flexibility is defined as *the quality of being adaptable, i.e. being able to change—or be changed—to fit changed circumstances.* Flexibility enables a software system to be adaptable with respect to variable circumstances during execution. For example, an AGV transportation system exposes flexibility if it is able to deal with disturbances in load supplies and exploiting opportunities. Openness is defined as *the quality of being open, i.e. characterized by an attitude of ready accessibility, affording unobstructed entrance and exit.* Openness enables a software system to cope with components that come and go during execution. For example, an AGV transport system exposes openness if this system is able to continue its work when AGVs leave or enter the system. Flexibility and openness are of importance because they were the motivating quality attributes to come up with a new architecture [4]. Finally, *performance* is of high importance because the AGV transportation system is expected to process transports as efficiently as possible: a client wants a minimal number of vehicles to handle the transportation task load.

2.3   Motivation for MAS Architecture

Taking into account the quality attributes of the previous section and our experience with MAS [5,9], we proposed to use a decentralized architecture realized by a multi-agent system (MASs).A MAS consists of a set of agents, situated in an environment, that cooperate to solve a complex problem in a decentralized way [10,11,12]. An agent is an autonomous entity that has local access to the environment. Agents can flexibly adapt their behavior according to the changing circumstances in their vicinity. The general idea of using a MAS architecture for the transportation system is to put more autonomy in the AGV vehicles itself allowing for both flexibility and openness. In the decentralized solution, the AGV vehicles and the transports become autonomous agents that make decisions based on their current situation, and that coordinate with the other agents to ensure the system as a whole processes the transports [4].

The motivations to start the project and apply a MAS architecture for the transportation system are twofold. Firstly, the evolution of the market put forward new requirements. Although the traditional centralized architecture was deployed in numerous companies, it was less suited for other companies. This was a major motivating factor for Egemin to apply a MAS architecture for a transportation system. Secondly, it provided the opportunity to evaluate MASs in a real industrial application. In this way we could obtain insights obtain insights wether our architecture meets the expected flexibility and openness quality attributes, and we could identify tradeoffs with other quality attributes.

2.4   Short Overview of the Architecture

This section provides a short overview of the architecture. The description does not cover the complete architecture but is meant for illustration purposes. For more details we refer to the architectural documentation of [13, pag 69-138].

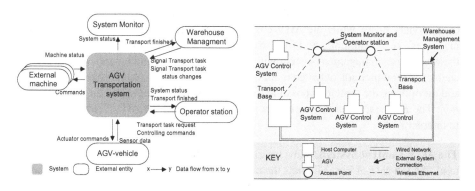

Fig. 2. Context diagram (left) and deployment view (right) of the AGV transportation system

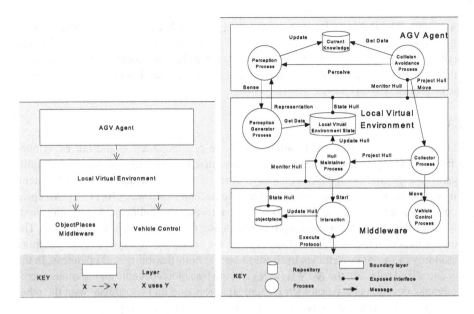

Fig. 3. Layered uses view (left) and process view (right) of AGV control system

Context Diagram and Deployment. Fig. 2 depicts the context diagram and deployment view of the *AGV Transportation System*. The AGV transportation system consists of two subsystems, *Transport Base* and *AGV Control System*. Transport bases receive transport requests from the *Warehouse Management System*, and are responsible for assigning the transports to AGVs. For each transport, a new transport agent is created. The transport agent is responsible for assigning the transport to an AGV and for reporting the status of the transport to the warehouse management system. The example contains two transport bases, each one responsible for one zone of the layout. AGV control system is responsible for ensuring that the AGV completes the assigned transport. Each AGV machine is equipped with low-level control software, called *Vehicle Control*, that takes high level commands from the AGV control system like move, pick, drop, ... The vehicle control system handles the physical interaction with the environment such as staying on track, turning, or determining the current position. The transport bases are deployed on stationary hosts, while the AGV control systems are deployed on the mobile AGV machines. The communication infrastructure provides a wired network that connects the warehouse management system with the transport bases and a wireless network that enables communication between mobile AGVs and with the transport bases. Debugging and monitoring the system is possible trough the *System Monitor* and the *Operator Station*. The *External Machines* represent possible machines the AGV Transportation has to interact with.

The AGV Control System. Now we zoom in on the internals of the AGV control system. The left side of Fig. 3 depicts the module view of AGV control system. The layers architectural pattern is used to manage complexity. The *AGV Agent* is responsible for executing transports and controlling the AGV. The *Local Virtual Environment* offers

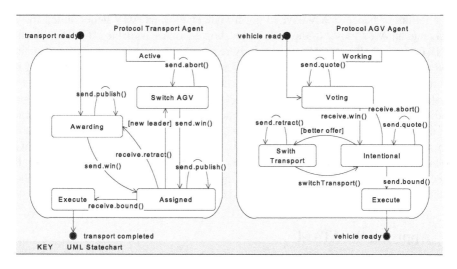

Fig. 4. Behavioral description of AGV agent (left) and transport agent (right) in the transport assignment protocol

a medium that agents can use to exchange information and coordinate their behavior. The local virtual environment handles distribution and locality, using the support offered by the ObjectPlaces middleware [9,14]. Besides a medium for coordination, the virtual environment also serves as a suitable abstraction that shields the AGV agents from low level issues, such as translating the commands for the *Vehicle Control*. The *ObjectPlaces Middleware* supports abstractions for protocol based coordination in a distributed system. The right side of Fig. 3 illustrates the processes, data repositories and interaction needed for moving around. First, the AGV agent projects a hull in the virtual environment. Such a hull demarcates the physical area the AGV will occupy during the movement. In case of conflicts, the local virtual environment executes a mutual exclusion protocol to decide which AGV can move on. The AGV agent perceives the virtual environment and only invokes the move command after it gets the permission to move on. For more information we refer to [4].

Transport Assignment. Now we zoom in on how transports are assigned to AGVs and explain the basics of the protocol. Transport assignment is done by a dynamic Contract Net (CNET) protocol [15], with multiple transport agents negotiating with multiple AGV-agents (many-to-many). A CNET protocol uses a market mechanism to assign tasks to agents. As soon as a new task enters the system, the transport agent announces that a new task is available. An available AGV-agent can bid on the task. The bid is dependent on the distance between the AGV and the task. After a fixed period of time, the transport agent chooses the best AGV-agent and the task is assigned to this agent.

The dynamic CNET protocol extends this protocol by delaying definitive assignment of the task until the AGV effectively picks up the load. Delaying definitive assignment is needed because many things can happen while the AGV moves towards the pickup location of a transport. New tasks that are better suited for this AGV can show up, e.g. being much closer or more urgent; AGVs can become unavailable, because of a failure or because they have to go in maintenance; an AGV better suited for the task, e.g. an AGV closer to the pick-up location becomes available [16]. The dynamic CNET protocol allows agents to regularly reconsider the situation in the environment and adapt the assignment if opportunities arise. Figure 4 depicts a description of the protocol behavior. As soon as a transport enters the system the transport agent will go to state Awarding and send publish messages. Free AGVs are in the Voting state and will answer with a bid. After some time, the transport agent will select a winner, send a win message and go into the Assigned state. The winning AGV will go the Intentional state and start driving to the pick location. Both the transport and AGV agent can still decide to switch the transport (the Switch state). It is only when the Execute state is reached, when the AGV picks up the load, that the protocol is ended. For more details we refer to [13, pag. 108-112].

3   Applying the ATAM

The Architectural Tradeoff Analysis Method (ATAM [6,7]) was used to evaluate if the system meets the expected performance, flexibility and openness quality attributes and to identify possible tradeoffs. The ATAM is a workshop that involves all important stakeholders. The workshop has two cornerstones: (1) make explicit and prioritize quality requirements for the system and identify tradeoffs between the quality attributes; (2) identify and make architecture approaches explicit and identify possible alternatives. Evaluating the architecture for large projects early in the development process is needed because the architecture represents an enormous risk in a development project. Making bad architectural decisions may substantially slow down the project and even lead to failure. Additionally, if some problems are identified, it is easier and cheaper to change the architecture in early stages of the development process.

In this section we describe our motivation to apply the ATAM, the context and the approach followed for the ATAM and the main outcomes from the workshop.

3.1   Motivations to Apply the ATAM

The decisions to apply the ATAM was taken in a the stage of the project where the software architecture started to take shape. There was an agreement amongst the stakeholders that a reflection about the software architecture was needed before investing much effort in the implementation. We selected the ATAM to reflect on the architecture because the method is well documented and has already proven its value in other studies [6].

The motivation for stakeholders to suggest a reflection about the architecture were threefold. Firstly, there are several quality attributes attributed to a MAS architecture, but MAS technology is relatively new and has not yet entered mainstream commercial organizations. The EMC^2 project, in which this evaluation took place, was started to test the feasibility of MAS architectures for the AGV transportation system and to evaluate if MAS effectively offers the attributed quality attributes. Reflecting early about the architecture was essential and the ATAM provided a first step of this evaluation. Secondly, the ATAM provides a way to explicitly tradeoff the new quality attributes of flexibility and openness against other (possibly better known) qualities of the AGV transportation system. In general, quality attributes can never be achieved in isolation, improving one quality attribute affects others (positively or negatively). Although tradeoffs were somewhat considered during the design of the architecture, the ATAM provides an explicit and structured approach with input from all stakeholders to investigate these tradeoffs. Finally, the ATAM provided an opportunity to finalize the architectural documentation and to wrap-up a phase of discussing the quality attributes and essential architectural choices. Because architectural approaches and quality attributes are made explicit, presented and discussed together with the important stakeholders, an agreement is reached between all stakeholders. The bundled results of the ATAM paves the way to start building the software system.

3.2   Context and Method

This was our first experience with the ATAM itself, none of us had previous hand-on experience with the method. Additionally, our industrial partner has limited experience with software architecture in general. Due to a lack of experience with ATAM we decided to operate in two phases. At first, we did an intensive preparation phase with one evaluator and four important stakeholders. Secondly, we organized a single day ATAM workshop with the complete group of stakeholders. The initiative to perform an ATAM came in a stage of the project where the basic structure of architecture became clear and an early prototype with the basic functionality was available.

We decided to evaluate the architecture for one concrete product, namely a tobacco warehouse. In this application, bins with tobacco are stored into a warehouse and 12 AGVs bring the full and empty bins from the warehouse to different tobacco-processing machines. The warehouse measuring 75 by 55 meters and has an average of 112 transports per hour. An 11 Mbits wireless Ethernet is available for communication with the mobile vehicles, but the network is also used by the warehouse management system. The warehouse itself is split into different zones according to the type of tobacco-processing machines. The machines can be put in normal-capacity mode or high-capacity mode. When the machines are in normal-capacity mode the AGVs should be spread evenly over the different zones and they should stay in that particular zone. When the machines in a zone are put in high-capacity mode, the supply of tobacco to these machines gets absolute priority and AGVs can leave a normal capacity-zone to maximize the speed of provisioning in the high-capacity zone. Additionally, there arise lots of opportunities. Examples are better suited AGVs becoming available or new task who are on the way of available AGVs (as explained in the section on the dynamic CNET protocol 2.4). Due to the flexibility in behavior needed with these mode switches, the tobacco warehouse lends itself perfectly for the ATAM workshop.

Specification of Requirements Before the ATAM. The functional requirements were discussed and made explicit using scenario's during several kick-off meetings of the project. Obviously, the exact functional requirements and the scenario's evolved over time as our understanding of the system increased.

On the contrary, the quality attributes were handled in a less structured fashion. It was clear from the start that flexibility and openness were the motivating factors to

Step	Start	Activity
1	9:00	Introduction on ATAM and program
2	10:00	Present business driver
	10:45	Break
3	11:00	Present architecture
4	12:00	Identify architectural approaches
	12:30	Lunch
5	13:45	Generate Utility tree
6	14:45	Generate Utility tree
	15:45	Break
7	16:00	Analysis of architectural approaches
8	17:00	Closing

Fig. 5. Program of ATAM workshop

come up with a new and innovative architecture, but these qualities were only specified at a high level. Additionally, various architectural decisions that involved a tradeoff between quality attributes were made on an ad-hoc basis.

Preparation. According to the template in [6, pag 71], the first steps during the preparation are establishing the partnership and preparing the necessary material for holding the ATAM workshop itself. Next to the usual preparation we performed two main activities. Firstly, as our understanding of software architecture and quality attributes increased, we realized that structuring and concretizing the quality attributes is essential. It was only then that we produced a first version of the concrete quality attribute scenario's and the utility tree (as described in 2.2). Apart from learning and reading about the utility tree, it took at least four full days of discussion with four stakeholders and one evaluator to build up a decent utility tree. This tree was used as input for the discussion about quality attributes on the ATAM workshop itself. The end result can be found in [13, pag 140-143]. Secondly, the architectural documentation of the system was not well structured and some views were only documented partially or were lacking. This was the case for the process view where several documents were missing and the deployment view that was lacking. During the preparation of the ATAM the architectural team worked hard to complete the architectural documentation following the guidelines and examples of Clements et al. [17].

The ATAM Workshop. The ATAM itself was conducted by a team of three evaluators and nine stakeholders. Fig. 5 describes the program of our ATAM workshop. Originally, we planned to start the discussions on analysis of scenarios at 14:45 (based on the schedule of [6, pag 79]), but the discussion on the utility tree brought up important issues that required additional discussion. The main artifacts produced on the workshop are the utility tree, the architectural approaches and an analysis of the architectural approaches with respect to the quality attributes. All presentations and artifacts produced in the context of the ATAM are bundled in a technical report [13].

Afterwards. Next to the typical activities of finishing up documents and updating documentation we performed two main activities. Firstly, we performed a second round of analysis of the architectural approaches with a team of four main stakeholders and one evaluator to structure the results and to ensure that all risk and sensitivity points were covered. Secondly, we performed a detailed analysis of several risks by consulting experts, running tests and we developed an additional prototype to perform a number of tests. The tests are described in the next section.

3.3   Main Outcomes

Applying the ATAM proved to be a valuable experience since it exposed several tradeoffs and points of improvement. In this section we provide several examples of problems that have been identified and how we have dealt with them.

Tradeoff Flexibility Against Communication Load. One of the main outcomes of applying the ATAM was the identification of the tradeoff between flexibility and the communication load, inherent in using decentralized control. In the AGV transportation system, there are several functional requirements that require more communication in a decentralized architecture (compared with the centralized architecture). Examples are transport assignment, deadlock avoidance, flexible routing and collision avoidance. In this section we focus on the tradeoff between flexible transport assignment (quality attribute scenario 3) and communication load (quality attribute scenario 5) as an example.

Fig. 6 contains an overview of our analysis of architectural decisions, both from the perspective of flexible transport assignment (left table) and the perspective of communication load (right table). We only included the architectural decisions relevant for the tradeoff between flexibility and communication load. As can be seen, the tradeoff is identified in several design decisions. The tradeoffs T1, T2, T3 represent manifestations of flexibility versus required bandwidth in different circumstances. The nonrisk NR2 is about limiting the communication load and the risk R2 is about the risk involved in having to much communication. The sensitivity point S3 is about using .NET remoting with unicast communication or using multicast as underlying implementation framework.

The tradeoff between flexibility and communication was not completely new for the architectural team, they had always realized that the decentralized approach needed more communication. However, on the ATAM workshop the assembled stakeholders (including several experienced developers of previous AGV transportation systems) put this tradeoff forward as a crucial factor for the applicability –and the success– of the decentralized approach. The ATAM provided the perfect opportunity to unravel the tradeoff in a structured way and to uncover the essential architectural decisions. The analysis of architectural approaches (step 7) revealed several architectural decisions that never really had been made. For example, the discussions revealed the choice for unicast in the middleware (AD8) producing some overhead. The influence of unicast, multicast and broadcast on the communication bandwidth is currently being investigated. As a second example, the discussion about AD7 revealed that the choice for a dynamic Contract Net (based on [15,10], described in section 2.4) protocol has a significant impact on the amount of communication in the system. Especially, how fast the protocol needs to reconsider the situation in the environment was an important choice that had not been made. The result of the ATAM regarding the tradeoff was that we gained better insight

Scenario: As long as a transport has not been picked, the system dynamically changes that transports assignment to the most suitable AGV			
Decisions	Sensitivity Tradeoff	Risk	Nonrisk
AD1 Negotiating agents	T1		NR1
AD2 Locality	S1		NR2
AD3 Separation of coordination and decisions making			NR3
AD4 Dynamic Transport Assignment		R1	

Scenario: The amount of communication, with maximal 12 AGVs and a maximal load of 140 transports per hour, does not exceed 60% of the bandwidth of the 11Mbps communication channel.			
Decisions	Sensitivity Tradeoff	Risk	Nonrisk
AD5 Use .Net remoting	S2		NR4
AD6 Agents located on AGVs		T2 R2	
AD7 Dynamic transport assignment		T3	
AD8 Unicast communication in Middleware	S3		

AD1	An agent is associated with each AGV and each transport in the system. To assign transports, multiple AGV agents negotiate with multiple transport agents (many-to-many protocol). Agent continuously reconsider the (possible changing) situation to improve transport assignment, until the load is picked. The negotiating agents approach for transport assignment was noted as non-risk NR1 from the perspective of flexibility. The continuous reconsideration of transport assignments implies a significant cost of communication. Flexibility versus required bandwidth was registered as tradeoff T1.
AD2	For their decision making, agents only take local information (from themselves and other agents in the neighborhood) into account. Using only local information and only exchange information with other local agents limits the amount of communication needed and was registered as non-risk NR2. The most suitable range varies per type and information and may even vary over time e.g. the number of candidate transports, vehicles to avoid collisions. The determination of this range for various functionalities is a sensitivity point, denoted as S1.
AD6	Each AGV machine is controlled by an agent that is physically deployed on the machine. This decentralized approach induces a risk with respect to the required bandwidth for inter-agent communication, recorded as risk R2. Decentralization of control implies a tradeoff between communication cost on the one hand, and flexibility and openness on the other hand, noted as T2.
AD7	The dynamic CNET protocol for transport assignment (as described in 2.4) enables flexible assignment of transports among AGVs. Yet, the continuous reconsideration of the transport assignment implies an additional communication cost. This tradeoff was denoted as T3 (see also T1).
AD8	The middleware uses unicast communication because this is supported by .NET remoting. However, some messages have to be transmitted to several agents, causing overhead. This potential problem was registered as sensitivity point S3.

Fig. 6. Analysis of architectural decisions from perspective of flexibility (left) and communication load (right)

in the main difficulties, agreed to further investigate the communication load and put forward a concrete testing plan.

Post ATAM Tests on Communication Load. The test on the communication load were performed in two ways. Firstly, we investigated to vary the period between reconsiderations for the transport assignment protocol. Obviously, this period strongly affects

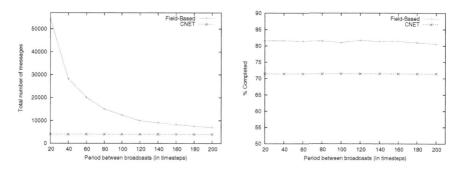

Fig. 7. Test results of varying the reconsideration period (Field-based is with reconsideration, CNET is without reconsideration)

the amount of messages being sent. Making the period too short produces a huge number of useless messages, but each agent in the system has up-to-date information. On the other hand, if the period is too long, AGVs may have outdated information and probably miss some opportunities. The tests are performed in an in-house developed simulator and are published in [18].

Figure 7 summarizes the most important results. The left figure shows the expected decrease in number of messages sent if the period between two broadcasts increases. BR20 corresponds to reconsidering the situation each 20 time steps. With a reconsideration rate of each 200 time steps (BP200, i.e. every 10 s) the number of messages sent with the dynamic protocol is 1.7 times higher then a protocol without reconsideration. The right-hand side of fig. 7 depicts the percentage of transports handled as a function of the reconsideration rate. It can be seen that the percentage of completed tasks fluctuates around 81,5% and slowly decreases, the difference between BR20 and BR200 is only 1% but still significantly better then the protocol without reconsideration. The results show that the communication load of a dynamic protocol can drastically be reduced by lengthening the period between reconsiderations without losing the advantages of a flexible protocol.

Secondly, we performed a stress test to measure the bandwidth usage of a the prototype implementation of the AGV transportation system on a real factory layout using a 11Mbps IEEE 802.11 wireless network. Fig. 6 shows the bandwidth usage relative to the bandwidth, divided into four tests. The first test has three AGVs, of which two were artificially put in deadlock (a situation which is avoided under normal operation, this situation is created by manually positioning the AGVs), because then the collision avoidance protocol is continually restarted, and never succeeds. The second test has 3 AGVs driving around freely. The third test has five AGVs driving around freely. The fourth tests has five AGVs, all artificially in deadlock. During the time in between test runs, AGVs were repositioned manually (thus the system is suspended in the time in between the tests). All the tests are worst case tests (with deadlock) that we artificially created but that are prevented during normal operation.

The general conclusions after the tests was that the decentralized approach seemed feasible for 12 AGV with a 11Mbps IEEE 802.11 wireless network. The tests showed that the communication load for five AGVs under normal operation (e.g. the time between

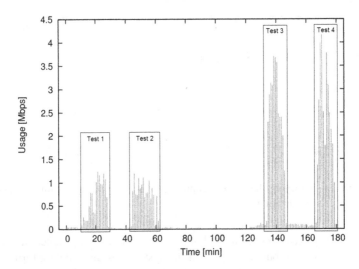

Fig. 8. Results of stress tests on bandwidth usage (in %)

154 and 168 min) is very low and obviously within the bounds of the available bandwidth. Looking to the stress tests, the communication load is a factor higher but still within the bounds. But there is a significant increase in communication load between the tests with three and five AGVs.

Architecture Constraints the Implementation. A second interesting issue that came up during the ATAM was that the implementation was not always conform with the architecture. Non conformance was identified in two phases of the evaluation. Firstly, while building up the architectural documentation in preparation of the ATAM and while discussing this with the developers of the prototype system. Secondly, during the discussion after the architect presented the architectural approaches on the ATAM workshop itself.

For example, consider Fig. 3 containing a view describing the layers and the usage relations between layers of the internal AGV control system (left) and a view describing the processes (mapped on the layers) and the interaction between these processes. During the discussion the issue came up that the developers accessed a repository in AGV agent layer from a process that was in the Local Virtual Environment layer, instead of using the appropriate interface. This breaks the encapsulation of layers and the implementation had to be changed. The reverse also happened. During an early prototype, the developers proposed a simplification of the architecture, making some processes and repositories obsolete. In this case the architectural documentation was adapted to reflect this change. From this and other discussions we learned that the *architecture constraints the implementation* and that it is very important to closely work together with the development team.

Improving the Architecture. Finally, the ATAM exposed several opportunities to improve the architecture. Two examples are provided.

A first example is an issue raised by a developer of the original centralized system. The AGV transportation system is built on top of a library that supports logging, persistence, security, etc. This library is also used in other projects and evolved since the start of the project (which still used an old version of the library). The architecture had to be adapted to better align with the library, so that the library can evolve without changing the AGV transportation system.

A second example is the use of a Free-flow tree [19,20,21] as decisions infrastructure inside the AGV agent. Free-flow trees are a proven technique to control mobile robots in highly dynamic circumstances where the robot must perform several activities in parallel. But the activities in the AGV transportation system are rather sequential (look for a task → drive to the task → perform the task → ...). Additionally, a free-flow tree is not so easy to extend or change which is essential in the AGV transportation system with often changing requirements.

4   Reflection on the ATAM Workshop

Although the ATAM itself was not worked out in full detail, the ATAM workshop was a valuable experience. It was the first time that there was such an in-depth discussion with a complete group of stakeholders. Everybody agreed that their insight had improved on: (1) the importance of software architecture in software engineering; (2) the importance of business drivers for architectural design; (3) the importance of making explicit and prioritize quality attributes with the stakeholders; (4) the strengths and weaknesses of the architecture and architectural approaches. Especially, we improved our understanding of the quality attributes and the other stakeholders improved their understanding of the fundamental architecture of the system and the important design decisions. Finally, we gained better insight into the tradeoffs associated with the flexibility and openness quality attributes, which is the most valuable outcome of this ATAM-workshop.

Some critical notes are:

- A thorough and complete evaluation with the ATAM of a realistic industrial application is not manageable in a single day. It would indeed be better, as suggested in the ATAM documentation, to organize a three day workshop.
- The utility tree proved to be the most important instrument in the ATAM. Several in-depth discussions have contributed to a better understanding of the required qualities and the importance of tradeoff between different quality attributes. But coming up with a utility tree proved to be difficult, time consuming, and at times tedious. A lack of experience and clear guidelines of how to build up such a tree hindered and slowed down the discussion. Good preparation of the tree and a good chairman to manage the discussion are essential. A suggestion, brought to us on the latest SATURN workshop[1], was to prevent brainstorming to come up with appropriate scenario's. Instead, every stakeholder should prepare two or three scenarios in advance. These scenarios serve as a good starting point for building up the utility tree, and speed up and improve the discussions.
- During discussions on the utility tree, there was a tendency by the architects to introduce quality attributes to motivate certain architectural decisions. This is of

---

[1] http://www.sei.cmu.edu/architecture/saturn/

course the reverse of what should happen: quality attributes influence the architecture and not the other way around. Similar problems were identified for the ALMA [22] evaluation method. The ATAM partially supports resolving such issues by obligating the stakeholders to prioritize the scenarios, thus filtering out less important scenarios. Still, the evaluation team must be watchful for artificially introduced scenarios and encourage everyone to think what the client really needs.

– During the discussions there was a tension between the AGV transport system architecture developed for several automation projects (the product-line architecture) and the fact we evaluated it within a single project (the product architecture). We decided to evaluate the architecture for a concrete product for three reasons. Firstly, Egemin installed dozens of systems, each of them tailored to the specific needs of the client. The installed products both differ in functionality, required quality attributes and can largely differ in size and complexity. Early in the preparation phase it became clear that the differences in requirements largely hindered the discussions. Often, stakeholders came up with contradicting requirements of different clients. Especially the variation in relative importance of qualities with respect to each other posed a problem. Secondly, the evolution of the market has put forward new requirements for AGV Transportation systems. Especially in highly dynamic systems, where the situation changes frequently, problems are experienced. This are the target systems for our architecture and we only wanted to focus on these type of requirements. Finally, the fact that the AGV Transportation system is a product-line system introduces specific qualities by itself. For example, the product-line architecture must be tailorable to specific needs of clients in different products. But the ATAM is made to evaluate a single architecture and not a product-line architecture.

To improve the discussions, the main stakeholders selected a single product (a tobacco warehouse). The tobacco warehouse was the best fit to the criteria that the product needed to be a highly dynamic system (the main reason to introduce the decentralized architecture) and represents the typical size and complexity of systems installed by Egemin. The choice for the single product and the reason to work with this single product where clearly communicated to all stakeholders of the ATAM. After this choice the discussions improved and became more focussed. Still, the tensions between product-line architecture and the concrete product architecture sometimes hindered the discussions. At the time of finishing this paper an extension of the ATAM to handle such a product line architecture has been published [23].

– A final remark is that there is a lack of good tool support to document software architectures. Currently, drawing architectural diagrams and building up the architectural documentation incurs much overhead. Especially changing the documentation and keeping everything up-to-date (e.g. cross references and relations between different parts of the documentation) turned out to be hard and time consuming. Good tool support would be helpful.

5 Related Work

Architecture in MAS. Initially, architecture in MAS was associated with the internal agent architecture. There exist large number of internal architectures, some examples are Belief Desire Intention (BDI), the subsumption architecture [24] and the free-flow tree [20]. Later on, the focus of architectural development shifted to social structures in MAS. Several methodologies specifically tailored to develop software offer support for such social structures, e.g. the organizational metaphor of Gaia methodology [25] and the society and environment model of the SODA methodology [26]. Finally, there are some approaches that take an architectural-centric approach to software development, using the classical notion of software architecture. PROSA [27] offers a reference architecture for coordination in manufacturing control. [28] proposes an aspect-oriented approach to develop MAS architectures, stressing the importance of separation of concerns. Our work differs from previous work on software architecture because it is quality attribute driven. The existing architectural approaches mainly focus on the system functionality but do not reason explicitly about qualities.

Shehory [29] considers MAS from the perspective of architectural styles and reasons about the qualities that are typically attributed to the MAS styles. The author explicitly recognizes flexibility and openness as important qualities for MAS architectural styles. Our work in this paper extends this with architectural evaluation to asses wether the architecture effectively fulfills the expected qualities.

Decentralization. Decentralized control of automated warehouse transportation systems is an active area of research [4]. [30] also discusses a behavior based architecture for decentralized control of AGV vehicles and [31] discusses a decentralized cognitive planning approach for collision-free movement of vehicles. Ong [32] gives an extensive overview of decentralized agent based manufacturing control and compares the pros and cons of centralized versus decentralized control. According to Ong, the advantages of decentralized control are that processing power is used more economically and that it is more reliable. The disadvantages are that performance may be affected by the speed of communication links, that there is a tradeoff between reactivity of the system to disturbances and performance and that suboptimal decisions may be made due to the lack of global information.

Experiences with Architectural Evaluation for MAS. Woods et al. [33] specifically describes experiences with an ATAM for collaborative agent-based systems. The quality attributes identified in the report are performance predictability, security against data corruption and spoofing, adaptability to changes in the environment (protocols, message formats, new types of agents) and availability and fault tolerance and are specifically aimed at applications of MAS technology for the internet or network infrastructures.

Architectural Evaluation. A good overview of other architectural evaluation methods can be found in [34,35]. Several of these architectural methods are aimed at a specific quality attributes (e.g. SAAM, ALMA, ...) and do not support evaluation with new type of quality attributes. Other architectural evaluation methods are primarily performed by the design team only, e.g. ARID, SBAR, ... For us, the ATAM workshop provided a good opportunity because of the explicit treatment of tradeoffs between different qualities and architectural approaches and the involvement of all stakeholders. Additionally, it aligned perfectly with our architectural documentation who was based on [36,17].

6 Conclusions

In this paper, we reported our experiences with applying the ATAM to a MAS architecture for an AGV transportation system. The main quality requirements in this application are flexibility, openness and performance. The report contains both the main outcomes of the architecture evaluation and a critical reflection on our experiences with the ATAM itself. One important insight we derived from evaluating the architecture is the tradeoff between flexibility and communication load in the decentralized architecture.

The ATAM workshop was a very valuable experience. We summarize three important lessons learned. First, we learned that assessing the qualities of the system can be done directly on the software architecture, early in the development process without the need for a complete implementation. A second important lesson we learned is that structuring and concretizing the quality attributes is essential when building complex large scale systems. Third, we learned that there is a strong connection between MAS and software architecture. Applying the ATAM deepened our understanding of this relationship.

Egemin plans to apply the first results of the project in one of the systems that is currently in the startup phase. In particular, Egemin experiences the need for improved flexibility in this application and plans to apply the order assignment approach applied in the MAS architecture. The highly dynamic nature of this application urges for improved flexibility and that is one of the qualities where the MAS architecture can make the difference.

Acknowledgement

The EMC^2 project and Nelis Boucké are supported by the Institute for the Promotion of Innovation through Science and Technology in Flanders (IWT-Vlaanderen).

References

1. Distrinet: Distrinet research group website. (www.cs.kuleuven.ac.be/cwis/research/distrinet/)
2. Egemin, DistriNet: Emc^2: Egemin modular controls concept. (IWT-funded project with Distrinet and Egemin. http://emc2.egemin.com)
3. Egemin: Egemin website. (www.egemin.com)
4. Weyns, D., Schelfthout, K., Holvoet, T., Lefever, T.: Decentralized control of E'GV transportation systems. In: International Conference on Autonomous Agents and Multi-Agent Systems, Industry Track. (2005) 25–29
5. Weyns, D., Holvoet, T.: A reference architecture for situated multiagent systems. In: 3rd International Workshop on Environments for Multiagent Systems, E4MAS06. (2006)
6. Clements, P., Kazman, R., Klein, M.: Evaluating Software Architectures: Methods and Case Studies. Addison Wesley Publishing Comp. (2002)
7. Kazman, R., Klein, M., Clements, P.: Atam: Method for architecture evaluation. Technical Report CMU/SEI-2000-TR-004, SEI, Carnegie Mellon University (2000)
8. WordNet 2.1., Princeton University Cognitive Science Library. (http://wordnet.princeton.edu/)

9. Schelfthout, K., Weyns, D., Holvoet, T.: Middleware for protocol-based coordination in dynamic networks. In: MPAC '05: Proceedings of the 3rd international workshop on Middleware for pervasive and ad-hoc computing, New York, NY, USA, ACM Press (2005) 1–8
10. Wooldridge, M.: An introduction to Multiagent Systems. John Wiley & Sons, LTD (2002)
11. Ferber, J.: Multi-agent Systems, An Introduction to Distributed AI. Addison-Wesley (1999)
12. Weyns, D., Parunak, H.V.D., Michel, F., Holvoet, T., Ferber, J.: Environments for multiagent systems: State-of-the-art and research challenges. In: Revised papers of the E4MAS workshop at AAMAS'04. Volume LNCS 3374. (2005)
13. Boucké, N., Holvoet, T., Lefever, T., Sempels, R., Schelfthout, K., Weyns, D., Wielemans, J.: Applying the Architecture Tradeoff Analysis Method (ATAM) to an industrial multi-agent system application. Technical Report CW431, Departement of Computer Sience, KULeuven (2005)
14. Schelfthout, K., Holvoet, T.: Coordination middleware for decentralized applications in dynamic networks. In: DSM '05: Proceedings of the 2nd international doctoral symposium on Middleware, New York, NY, USA, ACM Press (2005) 1–5
15. Smith, R.G.: The contract net protocol: high-level communication and control in a distributed problem solver. Distributed Artificial Intelligence (1988) 357–366
16. Boucké, N., Weyns, D., Holvoet, T., Mertens, K.: Decentralized allocation of tasks with delayed commencement. In Chiara, G., Ciorgini, P., van der Hoek, W., eds.: EUMAS04 Proceedings. (2004) 57–68
17. Clements, P., Bachman, F., Bass, L., Garlan, D., Ivers, J., Little, R., Nord, R., Stafford, J.: Documenting Software Architectures, Views and Beyond. Addison Wesley (2003)
18. Weyns, D., Boucké, N., Holvoet, T.: Gradient field based task assignment in an agv transportation system. In: International Conference on Autonomous Agents and Multiagent Systems (AAMAS). (2006)
19. Rosenblatt, J.K., Payton, D.W.: A fine-grained alternative to the subsumption architecture for mobile robot control. In: In Proceedings of the IEEE International Conference on Neural Networks. Volume 2. (1989) 317–324
20. Tyrrell, T.: Computational Mechanisms for Action Selection. PhD thesis, University of Edinburgh. Centre for Cognitive Science (1993)
21. Weyns, D., Steegmans, E., Holvoet, T.: Protocol based communication for situated multiagent systems. In: In Proceeding of the Third International Joint Conference on Autonomous Agents and Multi-Agent Systems, AAMAS'04, ACM Press, New York (2004) 118–126
22. Lassing, N., Bengtsson, P., van Vliet, H., Bosch, J.: Experiences with ALMA: Architecture-level modifiability analysis. Journal of Systems and Software 61(1) (2002) 47–57
23. Olumofin, F.G., Misic, V.B.: Extending the ATAM architecture evaluation to product line architectures. In: IEEE/IFIP Working Conference on Software Architecture, WICSA. (2005)
24. Brooks, R.: Intelligence without representation. Artificial Intelligence 47 (1991) 139–159
25. Zambonelli, F., Jennings, N., Wooldridge, M.: Developing multiagent systems: the gaia methodology. ACM Transactions on Software Engineering and Methodology 12(3) (2003)
26. Omicini, A.: Soda: Societies and infrastructures in the analysis and design of agent-based systems. Lecture Notes in Computer Science 1957 (2001)
27. Brussel, H.V., Wyns, J., Valckenaers, P., Bongaerts, L., Peeters, P.: Reference architecture for holonic manufacturing systems: Prosa. Computers in Industry 37 (1998)
28. Garcia, A., Kulesza, U., Lucena, C.: Aspectizing multi-agent systems: From architecture to implementation. Software Engineering for Multi-Agent Systems III LNCS 3390 (2004) 121–143
29. Shehory, O.: Architectural properties of multiagent systems. Technical Report CMU-RI-TR-98-28, Robotics Institute, Carnegie Mellon University, Pittsburgh, PA (1998)
30. Berman, S., Edan, Y., Jamshidi, M.: Decentralized autonomous agvs in material handling. Transactions on Robotics and Automation 19(4) (2003)

31. Pallottino, L., Scordio, V.G., Frazzoli, E., Bicchi, A.: Decentralized cooperative con ict resolution for multiple nonholonomic vehicles. In: AIAA Conference on Guidance, Navigation and Control. (2005)
32. Ong, L.: An investigation of an agent-based scheduling in decentralised manufacturing control. PhD thesis, University of Cambridge (2003)
33. Woods, S.G., Barbacci, M.: Architectural evaluation of collaborative agent-based systems. Technical Report CMU/SEI-99-TR-025, CMU/SEI (1999)
34. Dobrica, L., Niemela, E.: A survey on software architecture analysis methods. IEEE Transactions on Software Engineering **28**(7) (2002)
35. Babar, M.A., Zhu, L., Jeffery, R.: A framework for classifying and comparing software architecture evaluation methods. In: Proceedings Australian Software Engineering Conference (ASWEC). (2004)
36. Bass, L., Clements, P., Kazman, R.: Software Architectures in Practice (Second Edition). Addison-Wesley (2003)

Towards an Integration of Standard Component-Based Safety Evaluation Techniques with SaveCCM

Lars Grunske

School of Information Technology and Electrical Engineering
ARC Centre for Complex Systems,
University of Queensland,
4072 Brisbane (St.Lucia), Australia
grunske@itee.uq.edu.au

Abstract. To deliver complex functionalities in a cost effective manner, embedded software should ideally be developed with standardized interoperable components. At the same time, most of these embedded systems must be demonstrably safe and reliable. This paper aims to extend SaveCCM, a modelling language for component-based embedded systems, with standard safety evaluation models. Based on this extension, failure and hazard probabilities can be estimated early in the development process and can be used to check if a system can fulfil its safety requirements. The procedure of the safety evaluation is demonstrated with the case study of a computer assisted braking system.

1 Introduction

Modern safety-critical real-time systems in various application domains, such as automotive, avionic, defence and medical systems, are becoming increasingly complex ensembles of hardware and software components. Design and development of these complex component-based systems including their architectures is challenging, because systems and software engineers need to deal with strict non-functional requirements, such as safety, availability, reliability, performance, memory consumption and real-time requirements [1,2], while keeping development and life-cycle costs low and practicable. Therefore, component-based software engineering technologies in these domains must be capable of predicting dependability attributes of a system assembled from components. Currently, several component-based modelling languages and component frameworks aim to solve this problem. Examples are the PECT (Prediction-enabled Component Technology) [3] initiative of the Software Engineering Institute at the Carnegie Mellon University, the Ptolemy II project [4] of the University of California at Berkeley and the KOALA component model [5], which is used at Philips for embedded software in consumer electronic devices.

This paper focuses on SaveComp [6]; a recent component-based development framework for embedded control applications in automotive (vehicular) systems. This framework is based on a control flow paradigm and its basic aim is to create predictable component-based systems. The underlying formalism for the construction of SaveComp systems is the architecture description language SaveCCM (SaveComp Component Model). This language has a simple graphical syntax [6] and a formal semantics [7],

C. Hofmeister et al. (Eds.): QoSA 2006, LNCS 4214, pp. 199–213, 2006.
© Springer-Verlag Berlin Heidelberg 2006

which uses the theory of timed automata [8]. Based on this semantics, system properties can be checked with the UPPAAL [9] model checker. Other prediction techniques [6,10] provide the ability to predict Worst-Case Execution Time (WCET) of components, Worst Case Response Time (WCRT) of an assembled system or resource utilization of a set of components. The early prediction of these correctness and real-time properties allows reducing the number of design failures in the software system. These design failures are also known as systematic failures, because they systematically occur during runtime, if the system is operated with a certain sequence of input requests. However, for a complete safety analysis, additionally random and wear-out failures of the hardware elements have to be considered. These failures occur stochastically distributed over the mission time of the system and they are generally quantified with probabilistic metrics [11], such as failure rates (λ), Mean Time To Failure ($MTTF$) or Mean Time Between Failures ($MTBF$).

To facilitate a quantitative safety analysis of component-based systems, encapsulated evaluation models, such as Component Fault Trees (CFT) [12] or State-Event Fault Trees (SEFT) [13] have been developed. Generally, an encapsulated evaluation model specifies all necessary information to reason about quality attributes independently from the deployment context and the environment of an architectural entity. In the case of safety evaluation, these encapsulated evaluation models describe possible failures of component services and enable the estimation of their failure probabilities. The overall goal of this paper is to identify if these models can be integrated within the SaveComp modelling framework. In detail, the contributions of this paper are as follows:

- Identify a suitable formalism for safety evaluation (failure specification and analysis) within SaveCCM
- Create a methodology to systematically generate safety evaluation models
- Validate the methodology with a complex case study
- Identify the limitation of this approach and proposed future research directions to overcome these limitations

This rest of this paper is structured as follows. Section 2 reviews related work and describes state-of-the-art techniques in the area of safety evaluation for component-based systems. The basic concepts of SaveCCM are introduced in Section 3. An integration of the standard safety evaluation techniques and SaveCCM is presented in Sections 4 and 5. The general aim of these sections is to describe how probabilistic failures can be specified and how failure propagation models can be generated. The presented approach will be validated in Section 6 with the case study of a computer assisted braking system. Finally, conclusions as well as relevant directions for future work are given in Section 7.

2   Related Work

The related work can be distinguished into two categories. The first category contains analysis techniques for quality attributes, which are preliminaries for safety evaluation and which have been already integrated with SaveCCM. The second category contains detailed approaches for safety evaluation for other component-based specification languages.

Within SaveCCM, as already mentioned in the introduction, prediction techniques for real-time and resource consumption properties [6,10] have been integrated. The prediction of both properties is needed as a prerequisite for a complete safety evaluation. An approach that focuses on correctness and robustness of component-based specifications (with a focus on SaveCCM) is described by Elmqvist, Nadjm-Tehrani and Minea [14]. This approach reasons about these two safety-relevant properties with a formalism called safety interfaces. A safety interface describes the capability of components to provide correct behavior in an environment in the presence of single or multiple faults. The interesting innovation of this work is that these safety interfaces can be automatically generated for a specific safety property. The generation algorithm uses component behavior specification based on reactive modules [15] and a model checking technique that is similar to the counter example driven abstraction-refinement (CEDAR) principle [16]. More specifically in this approach, the ideal environment is weakened until the most restrictive environment in terms of environment failures is found, under which the component still fulfils the system level safety property. If this technique can be extended to allow the automatic generation of probabilistic safety interfaces, an integration into the approach presented in this paper seems to be very promising and could be beneficial for both approaches.

A major research stream on safety evaluation of general component-based software architectures is nowadays directed towards creating encapsulated failure propagation models [12,13,17,18,19]. These failure propagation models describe how failure modes of incoming messages (input failure) together with internal component faults propagate to failure modes of outgoing messages (output failure). The first notation that promotes these failure propagation models is the Failure Propagation Transformation Notation (FPTN) [17]. Other relevant notations are the Tabular Failure Annotations (TFA) in the context of the Hierarchically Performed Hazard Origin and Propagation Studies (HiP-HOPS) methodology [19] and Component Fault Trees (CFT) [18]. For specific component-based specification languages, these two newer models allow a tool-supported and automated generation of the safety evaluation model. This automation is needed for a successful technology transfer to industrial practise, since manually performed safety analysis techniques are error-prone or even infeasible for complex component-based systems. Examples for supported component-based specification languages are Matlab-Simulink models in the case of HiPHOPS [20] and ROOM models annotated with Interface Automata in the case of CFTs [21]. A limitation of each of the current failure propagation models is their inability to handle cyclic data- and control-flow structures in the system architecture. This is a major drawback of these techniques as many real-world control systems contain closed feedback loops. To overcome this problem, Wallace introduces in [22] his Fault Propagation and Transformation Calculus (FPTC). This calculus solves the problem of cyclic dependencies in the failure propagation model by using fixed-point evaluation techniques. However, the practicability of this calculus in industrial case studies remains to be proven.

From a high-level viewpoint, all four encapsulated failure propagation models (TFA, FPTN, CFT and FPTC) have a similar expressiveness and an identical conceptual foundation [12]. The only differences can be identified in the tool support, representation (graphical vs. textual) and methodological support. Consequently, for this research it does not matter which of these failure propagation models is used, as the result of this research can also be transferred to another model.

3   Description of SaveCCM

SaveCCM describes the architecture of a system with three basic syntactical elements [6]: *Components*, *Switches* and *Assemblies*. *Components* are the basic elementary units. They cannot be decomposed any further and contain a behavior specification that describes the functionality of a component in the SaveComp execution framework [6,7]. *Switches* provide facilities to dynamically change component interconnection structures between the *Components*. Consequently, they allow a reconfiguration of the system at runtime. Finally, *Assemblies* are used as building blocks for complex systems. They can contain *Components* and *Switches* as well as other *Assemblies* and specify how these elements must be connected. Each of the three syntactical elements are graphically represented by a box which contains the name of the component and a stereo type which specifies the element type ($\langle\langle$SaveComp$\rangle\rangle$, $\langle\langle$Switch$\rangle\rangle$ or $\langle\langle$Assembly$\rangle\rangle$).

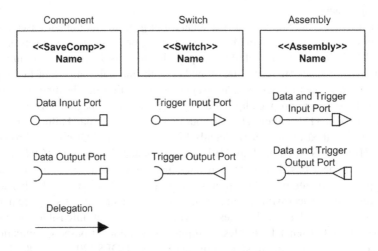

Fig. 1. Syntax Elements of SaveCCM

The interaction of SaveCCM elements with their environment is only allowed via well-defined interface elements called ports. Two basic types of ports are distinguished in SaveCCM: *Input Ports* and *Output Ports*. Ports are further distinguished by the information they allow to send or receive. More specifically in SaveCCM the following port subtypes can be specified: (a) *Data Ports*, (b) *Trigger Ports* and (c) *Data and Trigger Ports*. Data Ports, which are also named as *Data Only Ports* in [6], are one-element buffers of a pre-specified datatype (e.g. Boolean, Integer, Real, String etc.). This therefore enables a *Data Output Port* to write an element of the specified type to the buffer whilst a *Data Input Port* is able to read and consume this particular data element. Since the buffer can contain only one element, each additional write operation of the *Data Ouput Port* will overwrite its last value. *Trigger Ports*, or *Trigger Only Ports* [6], are used for controlling the activation of a *Component*. Semantically, *Trigger Ports* are described by a Boolean variable, which is set to TRUE in order to activate a component. If a component contains more than one *Input Trigger Ports* each of these *Input Trigger Ports* mmust be activated in order to activate the component. *Data and Trigger Ports* combine the features of both previously described port types.

Finally, to connect external ports of assemblies with corresponding ports of internal elements another syntax element is required. This syntax element is called *Delegation* and can only be used to connect input or output ports of an assembly with input or output ports of the same type of internal elements. Each of the syntax elements is represented in a UML 2.0 like graphical notation. The graphical symbols of this notation are given in Figure 1.

4   Specification of Encapsulated Failure Propagation Model Within SaveComp

To integrate encapsulated failure propagation models [12,13,17,18,19] with the Save-Comp development framework, SaveCCM elements (*Switches* and *Components*) have to be annotated with failure propagation specifications. An annotation of SaveCCM *Assemblies* is not necessary, because they are just a purely syntactic concept that provides a name for a collection of components, and restricts the way in which they can be connected to components outside the assembly. Consequently, they do not influence the semantic and emergence of failures at all.

Within the SaveComp development framework, failure propagation specifications should describe the emergence of incorrect behavior (failures) and the propagation and transformation of failures. For safety evaluation, specifically output failures have to be analyzed. These output failures logically depend on either internal faults or input failures that are caused by the environment of a SaveCCM element. Since SaveCCM components, switches and assemblies have well-defined interfaces and are strongly encapsulated, we assume that output failures can only be observed at the output ports. Similarly, input failures can only occur at input ports. This restricts the complexity of the failure propagation specification. However, the number of failures, which can occur at an input port or can be observed at an output port, are either very large or even infinite. To reduce the number failure propagation models, an accepted categorization is used [23] to classify each failure into one of the following failure types:

- **v:** value failure (wrong data or service result)
- **te:** timing failure - too early (event or service is delivered before it was expected)
- **tl:** timing failure - too late (expected event or service is delivered after the defined deadline has expired)
- **o:** omission (no event or service is delivered when it is expected)
- **c:** commission (unexpected event or service)

Within the SaveCCM modelling framework, value failures can only occur at *Data Ports* and *Trigger and Data Ports*. Timing failures as well as omission and commission failures can only be associated to *Trigger Ports* and *Trigger and Data Ports*.

To explain the specification of failure propagation models a triggered 2-bit full adder component specified as a SaveCCM component (Figure 2) will be used in the following as an example. This component provides an incorrect value at the Output Data Port O if one of the two Input Data Ports I_1, I_2 or the "carry in" port C_{in} receives a wrong value ($I_1.v$, $I_2.v$ or $C_{in}.v$) or if this component has an internal design fault $InternalFault$. Furthermore, timing, omission or commission failures of the Trigger Port T may lead also to a failure. For example they result in a wrong value at the output of the adder, in cases of an early trigger ($T_{in}.te$), because the correct values of the Input Ports has not been written to

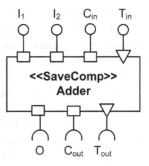

Fig. 2. SaveCCM Component: 2 Bit Full Adder

the buffer or if there is a delay in the trigger ($T_{in}.tl$) the values of the Input Ports may have be overwritten by newer values. In case of a trigger omission ($T_{in}.o$) the value at the output buffer is still the value of the last calculation and if the trigger occurs unexpectedly ($T_{in}.c$), then the correct value of the Output Buffer may become overwritten by newer results. As a result, a value failure of the Data Output Port O must be described by the following failure propagation model which contains only disjunctions:

$O.v = I_1.v \lor I_2.v \lor C_{in}.v \lor InternalFault \lor T_{in}.te \lor T_{in}.tl \lor T_{in}.o \lor T_{in}.c$

For a complete specification of the failure propagation model for the 2-bit adder a similar logical formula has to be created for possible failures of the Output Ports C_{out} and T_{out}. If for all internal faults and input failures probabilistic measures, like failure rates or failure probabilities, are available then the probability of an output failure can be determined by a basic fault tree analysis. However, the assumption must hold that all the input failures and internal faults are stochastically independent.

5 Safety Analysis Within SaveCCM

In the previous section, basic concepts to allow the specification of failure propagation models within the SaveComp development framework where given. To be applicable to complex specifications methodological support is needed that guides safety analysts (a) to create an encapsulated failure propagation model for each elementary component in the system and (b) to use these encapsulated evaluation models to check if a system built with these components could fulfil its safety requirements. To provide this methodological support, first, a basic process model is introduced, which explains the basic tasks that are needed to perform a structured hazard analysis within the SaveComp framework. Secondly, each of the required steps of this process are explained and techniques and tools are presented that can be used to guide these tasks.

5.1 Basic Process Model

A safety analysis process with failure propagation models can be generally structured into three phases [13,24]. For the safety evaluation of SaveCCM architectures, in the first phase an encapsulated failure propagation model has to be constructed for each

SaveCCM *Component* and *Switch*. This task must be performed by the component developer or by the component supplier. To generate an encapsulated failure propagation model for a SaveCCM *Component* or *Switch* a HAZOPS (HAZard and OPerability Studies)-based technique called SHARD (Software Hazard Analysis and Resolution in Design) [25] can be used. SHARD has been especially designed to handle software and hardware components and its procedure is described in section 5.2.

In the second phase, a fault propagation model must be constructed for the entire architecture. To perform this task SaveCCM *Assemblies* are investigated and a failure propagation model needs to be constructed recursively according to the hierarchical structure of these *Assemblies*.

In the final phase, the fulfilment of the safety requirements needs to be verified based on the complete failure propagation model of the system. A safety requirement is a (more or less formal) description of a hazard combined with the tolerable probability of this hazard [12]. In control systems, a hazard can be caused by single or multiple failures. Consequently, the first task is to identify which output failures of the failure propagation model lead to which hazards and what is the logical relation between output failures and hazards. As a technique to perform this task, again SHARD can be used. The next task is to calculate probabilities of output failures by analyzing the system-level failure propagation model. Then, based on the logical relations between output failures and hazards, hazard probabilities can be calculated. Both tasks are computationally expensive and should be performed by a suitable tool (e.g. HiPHOPS [19] or ESSaReL [26]). Finally, the safety engineer must check if the probability of a hazard is lower than its tolerable hazard probability. If the probability is lower than the tolerable hazard probability, then the architecture specification fulfils its safety requirements. If not, the architecture must be revised and additional safety mechanisms (e.g. watchdogs or redundancy) should be included.

To summarize, the inputs for a safety evaluation are: (a) the SaveCCM specification, which describes the architecture of the system, (b) a failure propagation model for each element of the SaveCCM specification and (c) a list of relevant hazards and its tolerable hazards probabilities. The necessary steps are:

1. Generate an encapsulated failure propagation model for each SaveCCM *Component* and *Switch*.
2. Identify the relations between system output failures and hazards.
3. Construct an encapsulated failure propagation model for each SaveCCM *Assembly*.
4. Calculate the output failure probabilities of the system-level *Assembly* and accordingly the hazard probabilities of the system.
5. Compare the calculated hazard probabilities with the tolerable hazard probabilities.

5.2 Applying SHARD for Identifying Fault Propagation Models of SaveCCM Components and Switches

SHARD, as proposed in [25], is a structured design assessment to identify potentially hazardous behavior in software systems. SHARD is a team-based approach that focuses on the information flows between software components in a system. Each information flow is sequentially investigated with the set of guidewords for failure propagation models to prompt consideration of possible deviations from the intended behavior. For each deviation considered, the team must determine all plausible causes in terms of input failures and internal faults. Additionally, in a complete SHARD analysis safety engineers need to determine whether a deviation can contribute to system-level hazards and they must propose resolutions.

For the generation of failure propagation models of SaveCCM *Components* and *Switches*, the last two tasks are not required and furthermore these activities cannot be performed for a single component without considering the system context. Due to this, the main activity for the generation of fault propagation models is to sequentially investigate each outgoing information flow

Table 1. SHARD table for 2-bit full adder

	$O.v$	$C_{out}.v$	$T_{out}.tl$	$T_{out}.te$	$T_{out}.o$	$T_{out}.c$
$I_1.v$	✗	✗				
$I_2.v$	✗	✗				
$C_{in}.v$	✗	✗				
$T_{in}.tl$	✗	✗	✗		✗	
$T_{in}.te$	✗	✗		✗		
$T_{in}.o$	✗	✗	✗		✗	
$T_{in}.c$	✗	✗				✗

and to identify possible causes in terms of input failures and internal faults. Note that the possible deviations (*te*, *tl*, *v*, *o* and *c*) of an information flow within the SaveComp framework are restricted by the type of the SaveCCM port (Data vs Trigger ports), which simplifies the analysis. The results of the investigation should be documented in a table, where the columns show possible deviations of outgoing information flows (*consequences*) and the rows represent deviations of the input information flows or internal faults (*causes*). A ✗ in a cell (*x,y*) of this table means that if *cause y* occurs then a possible result could be *consequence x*. An example of such a table is presented in Table 1 for the 2-bit full adder component introduced in Section 4.

To improve the results, the investigation should also be performed in the opposite direction, from causes to consequences [27]. This will result in a deeper understanding of the SaveCCM *Components* and *Switches* and completes the cause-consequence matrix.

The final task is to create a failure propagation model based on the SHARD table. In this task, basically, a logical formula must be identified that represents the relations between an outgoing failure of a component and its causes. To do so, each column in the SHARD table has to be investigated and each cause marked with a ✗ must be logically related to the outgoing failure. The most common logical relations are *AND* and *OR* relations. An *OR* relation means that each one of the causes can lead to the output failure. In case of an *AND* relation, all causes must occur to cause the consequence. The overall semantics is identical to the fault tree logic [28].

5.3 SHARD to Identify Relevant System Level Failures That Can Cause a Hazard

Similar to the procedure of SHARD at the component level (SaveCCM *Components* and *Switches*), SHARD could be also applied at the system level. The goal of this application is to investigate the relationships between system level failures (deviation of the outgoing failure flows) and hazards that can cause harm to the environment [29]. The results of the system-level SHARD should also be documented in a table. In this

table columns represent hazard conditions, rows represent deviations of outgoing information flows and a ✗ indicates a possible relationship. An example of such a table is
given in Section 6 in Table 2 for relations between hazards and system level failures for
the case study of a computer assisted braking system.

Based on the SHARD table the logical relationships between the hazards and the
system level failures must be identified. These logical relationships become the top-
level formulas for the safety evaluation model that must be entered in the evaluation
tool as described in [12].

5.4   Constructing Fault Propagation Models for SaveCCM Assemblies

To construct failure propagation models for SaveCCM *Assemblies* all embedded Save-
CCM elements must be first annotated with a failure propagation model. Then each possible failure propagation between these embedded elements must be identified. Since
SaveCCM elements are strongly encapsulated, we assume that these failure propaga-
tions can only occur via connections of output and input ports. As a result of this assumption, the following two cases need to be distinguished: (a) the failure propagation
within the assembly between two embedded SaveCCM elements and (b) the failure
propagation between the environment (input and output ports of the assembly) and an
internal component/switch/assembly. To resolve the failure propagation between two
embedded SaveCCM elements the associated failure types of the input port need to be
substituted with corresponding failure propagation formulae of the output port. This
substitution is also the reason why fault propagation models and the corresponding data
and control flow architecture must be acyclic, because in case of a cycle this substitution will not terminate. To resolve the failure propagation between the environment and
internal components a renaming is needed that renames failure flows according to the
input and output port of the assembly.

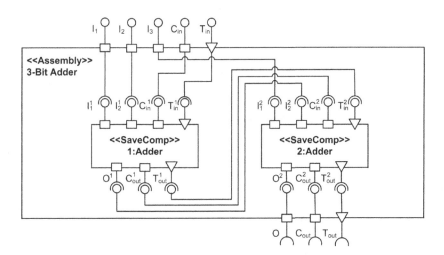

Fig. 3. 3-Bit-Adder SaveCCM-Assembly

To explain this procedure, we will assume a 3-bit adder *Assembly*, which uses a series connection of two 2-bit adder (Figure 2). In this assembly, the output ports O^1, C^1_{out} and T^1_{out} of the first 2-bit adder are connected to the input ports I^2_2, C^2_{in} and T^2_{in} of the second 2-bit adder. Note, the superscripts denote the instance of the 2-bit adder (first vs. second). All other ports are delegated to external ports of the 3-bit adder (I_1, I_2, I_3, O, T_{in} and T_{out}). In this example, we will focus on the value failure of the data output port O of the 3-bit adder which depends on the output of the second 2-bit adder. Consequently, the failure propagation formula $O^2.v$ for the 2-bit adder as described in section 4 must be used as a starting point. Then each failure that is related to an output of the first 2-bit adder needs to be substituted by the corresponding failure propagation formulae. The failure propagation model after the substitution of the value failure of the input port I^2_2 are as follows:

$$O.v = I^2_1.v \lor \left(I^1_1.v \lor I^1_2.v \lor C^1_{in}.v \lor InternalFault^1 \lor T^1_{in}.te \lor T^1_{in}.tl \lor T^1_{in}.o \lor T^1_{in}.c\right)$$
$$\lor C^2_{in}.v \lor InternalFault^2 \lor T^2_{in}.te \lor T^2_{in}.tl \lor T^2_{in}.o \lor T^2_{in}.c.$$

Similar to the substitution of the failure flows of the input port I^2_2, the failure flows of the input ports C^2 and T^2_{in} need to be substituted. Finally, the internal input port names need to be substituted with the input port names of the assembly, to describe the failure propagation between the environment and internal components. Consequently, based on the SaveCCM *Delegations* in the model of the 3-bit adder the following renaming should be applied: $I^1_1 \rightarrow I_1$, $I^1_2 \rightarrow I_2$, $I^2_1 \rightarrow I_3$, $C^1 \rightarrow C$ and $T^1_{in} \rightarrow T_{in}$.

6   Case Study

To explain the presented approach in more detail a computer assisted braking system is chosen as an example case study [30]. Variations of this system are currently used in most modern cars to enhance their braking performance. A complete description of the system including its components can be found in [29,31,30]. In addition to traditional hydraulic brakes the computer assisted braking system adds the following new functions: anti (b)lock braking, emergency stop detection and enhancement and load balancing of the four brakes corresponding to the road and driving condition. The anti (b)lock braking function (ABS) is used to prevent skidding and help drivers maintain steering control on wet and slippery roads. The Emergency Stop Detection function automatically maximizes the brake pressure if it detects any sudden pedal movement associated with an emergency stop. The load balancing function aims to improve the braking

Hazard ID	Effect Description	Risk Class	Tolerable Hazard Rate (THR) (per hour)
H1	Complete lack of braking	Catastrophic	10^{-8}
H2	Lock up (1–4 wheels)	Catastrophic	10^{-8}
H3	Unexpected application/release of the brakes	Catastrophic	10^{-8}
H4	Braking response not proportional to demand	Catastrophic	10^{-8}
H5	Tardy/slow response	Major	10^{-7}
H6	Uneven braking (pressures vary "wildly" in response to constant demand)	Major	10^{-7}
H7	Unequal braking (1-3 wheels brake less or more than required)	Major	10^{-7}

Fig. 4. Results of the PHA for the computer assisted braking system [30]

performance by compensating uneven braking due to heavy or unbalanced loading of the vehicle. A failure in any of the three functions could lead to serious accidents. Consequently, there is a need to prove that the system fulfils the safety requirements that have been identified in a preliminary hazard analysis [30]. These safety requirements are summarized in Figure 4.

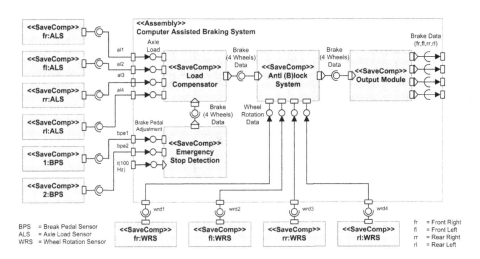

Fig. 5. SaveCCM architecture of the computer assisted braking system

The SaveCCM architecture for the system is given in Figure 5. To meet the timing requirements of a 20 ms latency from brake pedal movement to brake effect, a 10 ms period (100Hz) has been selected for the main tasks [30]. Please note that the sensors (*ALS*,*BPS* and *WRS*) in the architecture have no trigger input ports, consequently they do not get activated and hence they are not complete SaveCCM *Components*. However, in this case study, we assume that these sensors are electronic units that continuously provide the required information. To perform the safety evaluation a SHARD has been performed for each component in the system. An example of a resulting SHARD table is presented in Table 3. Additionally, in [29], SHARD has also been applied to identify the relationships between system hazards and system-level failures (cp. Table 2).

Table 2. Effect of failures of the Brake Data Output on Hazardous Failure Modes H1-H7 [29]

System	Hazardous Failure Modes						
Output	H1	H2	H3	H4	H5	H6	H7
BrakeData.o	✗	✗		✗	✗		
BrakeData.c		✗	✗	✗		✗	
BrakeData.te							
BrakeData.tl		✗			✗		
BrakeData.v	✗	✗	✗	✗		✗	✗

Based on the SHARD tables, in the next step a fault propagation model has been generated for each component. As an example, the fault propagation model for the Emergency Stop Detection component looks as follows:

Table 3. SHARD Table for the SaveCCM Component - Emergency Stop Detection [29]

SaveCCM Component Emergency Stop Detection	Output Failure Flow				
	Brake (4 Wheels) Data (B4WD)				
	B4WD.v	B4WD.te	B4WD.tl	B4WD.o	B4WD.c
bpa1.v	✗				
bpa2.v	✗				
t(100Hz).te		✗			
t(100Hz).tl			✗		
t(100Hz).o			✗	✗	
t(100Hz).c		✗			✗
Internal timing problem (Int1)		✗	✗	✗	✗
Wrong interpretation of the input data(Int2)	✗				
Hardware failure of the underlying control unit(Int3)		✗	✗	✗	✗
Memory problem in the data segment of the underlying control unit(Int4)	✗				

- $B4WD.v = (bpa1.v \land bpa1.v) \lor Int2 \lor Int4$
- $B4WD.te = t(100Hz).te \lor t(100Hz).c \lor Int1 \lor Int3$
- $B4WD.tl = t(100Hz).tl \lor t(100Hz).o \lor Int1 \lor Int3$
- $B4WD.o = t(100Hz).o \lor Int1 \lor Int3$
- $B4WD.c = t(100Hz).c \lor Int1 \lor Int3$

All fault propagation models have been translated to component fault trees (CFTs) and have been modelled with the tool UWG, which was developed in the ESSaRel project [26]. UWG is an academic prototype for the specification and evaluation of CFTs which is currently also used in industrial projects. However, beside this tool support, one general problem in the construction of analyzable fault propagation models such as CFTs is to identify the failure probabilities of the internal faults [32]. In this case study, a failure rate of 10^{-8} per hour has been assumed for all software-base failures. This assumption is based on the fact that the software must be developed with rigorous software development methods to comply with safety integrity level (SIL) four [33]. The failure rates of hardware-based failures have been taken from the specifications published in [29]. Based on the component fault trees and the internal fault probabilities the probabilities of safety critical failures of the system has been determined. To repeat this evaluation, the complete model can be downloaded from the author's web-page (http://www.itee.uq.edu.au/ grunske/ QOSA2006/cabs.uw3). The results of this evaluation clearly indicate that the initial design does not fulfill the safety requirements. This result is not unexpected since the initial design does not include any safety or reliability improving concepts (e.g. redundancy or watchdogs). Better designs for this case study are described in [29,31].

7   Conclusion and Future Work

To evaluate safety characteristics of SaveCCM specifications, this paper proposes an integration of failure propagation models with the SaveComp modelling framework. For this purpose each SaveCCM element has to be annotated with a failure propagation model that describes how failure modes of incoming messages (input failure) together with internal faults of the components propagate to failure modes of outgoing messages (output failure). Consequently, these failure propagation models describe the emergence of incorrect behavior independent from the component's environment. If each SaveCCM element is annotated with a fault propagation model, a fault propagation model can be constructed for a complete SaveCCM specification. Based on this system-level failure propagation model and an operational profile, that quantifies call and failure probabilities of the system's environment, probabilities of system output failures can be calculated. These system output failures can be related to system hazards and their probabilities can be calculated too. If all hazard probabilities are lower than their tolerable hazard probabilities then the SaveCCM specification fulfils its safety requirements. If not, quality improving transformations need to be performed [34].

The described method is still an early attempt for safety evaluation of SaveCCM specification and it has some major limitations and drawbacks. First, as mentioned in the related work section the fault propagation models must be acyclic. Consequently, the approach isn't applicable to systems with cyclic data and control flow dependencies (e.g. control systems with closed feedback loops). Second, to obtain correct results the internal failure modes must be stochastically independent. To assure this a common cause failure analysis should be performed based on system-level fault propagation model. Third, the generation of fault propagation models for SaveCCM *Components* and *Switches* is currently based on expert knowledge and a team-based assessment with SHARD. An automated approach to generate these fault propagation models seems currently hard to achieve, but could increase the acceptance of the method significantly. Fourth and finally, the estimation of failure probabilities for systematic faults (e.g. design faults) is generally a hard task for software-based systems [11,32].

To conclude this paper, there are some general problems that should be solved for a successful technology transfer to industrial practice. However, these problems are not specifically related to SaveCCM. Moreover, the results presented in this paper are very promising and have shown that a safety evaluation of SaveCCM models is possible and benefits from the clear and elegant syntax of the specification language.

References

1. Laprie(ed), J.C.: Dependability: basic concepts and terminology. Springer Verlag (1992)
2. Lee, E.A.: 2. In: Embedded Software. Volume 56. Advances in Computers, Academic Press, London (2002) 56–97
3. Hissam, S.A., Moreno, G.A., Stafford, J.A., Wallnau, K.C.: Packaging Predictable Assembly. In Bishop, J.M., ed.: Component Deployment, IFIP/ACM Working Conference, CD 2002, Berlin, Germany, June 20-21, 2002, Proceedings. Volume 2370 of Lecture Notes in Computer Science., Springer (2002) 108–124

4. PtolemyII : PtolemyII project website: http:// ptolemy.eecs.berkeley.edu/ ptolemyII/ (2006)
5. van Ommering, R., van der Linden, F., Jeff, K., Magee, J.: The Koala component model for consumer electronics software. Computer **33** (2000) 78–85
6. Hansson, H., Åkerholm, M., Crnkovic, I., Törngren, M.: SaveCCM - A component model for safety-critical real-time systems. In: 30th EUROMICRO Conference 2004, 31 August - 3 September 2004, Rennes, France, IEEE Computer Society (2004) 627–635
7. Carlson, J., Håkansson, J., Pettersson, P.: SaveCCM: An analysable component model for real-time systems. In: International Workshop on Formal Aspects of Component Software, Macao, Elsevier (2005)
8. Alur, R.: A theory of timed automata. Theoretical Computer Science **126** (1994) 183–235
9. Larsen, K.G., Pettersson, P., Yi, W.: UPPAAL in a nutshell. International Journal on Software Tools for Technology Transfer **1** (1997) 134–152
10. Möller, A., Peake, I., Nolin, M., Fredriksson, J., Schmidt, H.: Component-based context-dependent hybrid property prediction. In: ERCIM - Workshop on Dependable Software Intensive Embedded systems, Porto, Portugal, ERCIM (2005)
11. Birolini, A.: Reliability Engineering: Theory and Practice. Third edn. Springer (1999)
12. Grunske, L., Kaiser, B., Reussner, R.H.: Specification and evaluation of safety properties in a component-based software engineering process. In: Embedded Software Development with Components -An Overview on Current Research Trends, Springer-Verlag (2005) 737–738
13. Grunske, L., Kaiser, B., Papadopoulos, Y.: Model-driven safety evaluation with state-event-based component failure annotations. In Heineman, G.T., Crnkovic, I., Schmidt, H.W., Stafford, J.A., Szyperski, C.A., Wallnau, K.C., eds.: Component-Based Software Engineering, 8th International Symposium, CBSE 2005, St. Louis, MO, USA, May 14-15, 2005, Proceedings. (2005) 33–48
14. Elmqvist, J., Nadjm-Tehrani, S., Minea, M.: Safety interfaces for component-based systems. In Winther, R., Gran, B.A., Dahll, G., eds.: Computer Safety, Reliability, and Security, 24th International Conference, SAFECOMP 2005, Fredrikstad, Norway, September 28-30, 2005, Proceedings. Volume 3688 of Lecture Notes in Computer Science., Springer (2005) 246–260
15. Alur, R., Henzinger, T.A.: Reactive modules. Formal Methods in System Design: An International Journal **15** (1999) 7–48
16. Clarke, E.M., Grumberg, O., Jha, S., Lu, Y., Veith, H.: Counterexample-guided abstraction refinement. In: Computer Aided Verification. (2000) 154–169
17. Fenelon, P., McDermid, J., Nicholson, M., Pumfrey., D.J.: Towards integrated safety analysis and design. ACM Computing Reviews, **2** (1994) 21–32
18. Kaiser, B., Liggesmeyer, P., Mäckel, O.: A new component concept for fault trees. In: Proceedings of the 8th Australian Workshop on Safety Critical Systems and Software (SCS'03), Adelaide (2003) 37–46
19. Papadopoulos, Y., McDermid, J.A., Sasse, R., Heiner, G.: Analysis and synthesis of the behaviour of complex programmable electronic systems in conditions of failure. Int. Journal of Reliability Engineering and System Safety **71** (2001) 229–247
20. Papadopoulos, Y., Maruhn, M.: Model-based synthesis of fault trees from matlab-simulink models. In: 2001 International Conference on Dependable Systems and Networks (DSN 2001) (formerly: FTCS), 1-4 July 2001, Göteborg, Sweden, Proceedings, IEEE Computer Society (2001) 77–82
21. Grunske, L.: Annotation of component specifications with modular analysis models for safety properties. In: Proceedings of the 1st International Workshop on Component Engineering Methodology (WCEM), Erfurt (2003) 737–738
22. Wallace, M.: Modular architectural representation and analysis of fault propagation and transformation. Electr. Notes Theor. Comput. Sci. **141** (2005) 53–71

23. Bondavalli, A., Simoncini, L.: Failure Classification with respect to Detection. Esprit Project Nr 3092 (PDCS: Predictably Dependable Computing Systems) (1990)
24. Grunske, L., Kaiser, B.: Automatic generation of analyzable failure propagation models from component-level failure annotations. In: Fifth International Conference on Quality Software (QSIC 2005), 19-20 September 2005, Melbourne, IEEE Computer Society (2005) 117–123
25. Pumfrey, D.J.: The Principled Design of Computer System Safety Analyses. PhD thesis, Department of Computer Science, University of York (1999)
26. ESSaRel: Embedded Systems Safety and Reliability Analyser, The ESSaRel Research Project,Homepage: http://www.essarel.de/index.html (2005)
27. Lutz, R.R.: Software engineering for safety: a roadmap. In: ICSE - Future of SE Track. (2000) 213–226
28. IEC 61025(International Electrotechnical Commission): Fault-Tree-Analysis (FTA) (1990)
29. Prasad, D.K.: Dependable Systems Intergration using Measurement Theory and Decision Analysis. PhD thesis, Department of Computer Science, University of York (1998)
30. David Pumfrey and Marc Nicholson: Hazard Analysis of a Computer Assisted Braking System, In Hazard Analysis Course for MSc in Safety Critical Systems (1996)
31. Nicholson, M.: Selecting a Topology for Safety-Critical Real-Time Control Systems. PhD thesis, Department of Computer Science, University of York (1998)
32. Musa, J.D., Iannino, A., Okumoto, K.: Software Reliability: Measurement, Prediction, Application. MacGraw-Hill (New York NY), ; ACM CR 8712-0965 (1987)
33. CENELEC (European Committee for Electro-technical Standardisation): CENELEC EN 50126: Railway Applications – the specification and demonstration of Reliability, Availability, Maintainability and Safety. CENELEC EN 50128: Railway Applications: Software for Railway Control and Protection Systems CENELEC, Brussels (2000)
34. Grunske, L.: Identifying "good" architectural design alternatives with multi-objective optimization strategies. In Osterweil, L.J., Rombach, H.D., Soffa, M.L., eds.: 28th International Conference on Software Engineering (ICSE 2006), Shanghai, China, May 20-28, 2006, ACM (2006) 849–852

Author Index

Lecture Notes in Computer Science

For information about Vols. 1–4233

please contact your bookseller or Springer

Vol. 4274: Q. Huo, B. Ma, E.-S. Chng, H. Li (Eds.), Chinese Spoken Language Processing. XXIV, 805 pages. 2006. (Sublibrary LNAI).

Vol. 4273: I. Cruz, S. Decker, D. Allemang, C. Preist, D. Schwabe, P. Mika, M. Uschold, L. Aroyo (Eds.), The Semantic Web - ISWC 2006. XXIV, 1001 pages. 2006.

Vol. 4272: P. Havinga, M. Lijding, N. Meratnia, M. Wegdam (Eds.), Smart Sensing and Context. XI, 267 pages. 2006.

Vol. 4271: F.V. Fomin (Ed.), Graph-Theoretic Concepts in Computer Science. XIII, 358 pages. 2006.

Vol. 4270: H. Zha, Z. Pan, H. Thwaites, A.C. Addison, M. Forte (Eds.), Interactive Technologies and Sociotechnical Systems. XVI, 547 pages. 2006.

Vol. 4269: R. State, S. van der Meer, D. O'Sullivan, T. Pfeifer (Eds.), Large Scale Management of Distributed Systems. XIII, 282 pages. 2006.

Vol. 4268: G. Parr, D. Malone, M. Ó Foghlú (Eds.), Autonomic Principles of IP Operations and Management. XIII, 237 pages. 2006.

Vol. 4267: A. Helmy, B. Jennings, L. Murphy, T. Pfeifer (Eds.), Autonomic Management of Mobile Multimedia Services. XIII, 257 pages. 2006.

Vol. 4266: H. Yoshiura, K. Sakurai, K. Rannenberg, Y. Murayama, S. Kawamura (Eds.), Advances in Information and Computer Security. XIII, 438 pages. 2006.

Vol. 4265: L. Todorovski, N. Lavrač, K.P. Jantke (Eds.), Discovery Science. XIV, 384 pages. 2006. (Sublibrary LNAI).

Vol. 4264: J.L. Balcázar, P.M. Long, F. Stephan (Eds.), Algorithmic Learning Theory. XIII, 393 pages. 2006. (Sublibrary LNAI).

Vol. 4263: A. Levi, E. Savaş, H. Yenigün, S. Balcısoy, Y. Saygın (Eds.), Computer and Information Sciences - ISCIS 2006. XXIII, 1084 pages. 2006.

Vol. 4262: K. Havelund, M. Núñez, B. Wolff, G. Roşu (Eds.), Formal Approaches to Software Testing and Runtime Verification. VIII, 255 pages. 2006.

Vol. 4261: Y. Zhuang, S. Yang, Y. Rui, Q. He (Eds.), Advances in Multimedia Information Processing - PCM 2006. XXII, 1040 pages. 2006.

Vol. 4260: Z. Liu, J. He (Eds.), Formal Methods and Software Engineering. XII, 778 pages. 2006.

Vol. 4259: S. Greco, Y. Hata, S. Hirano, M. Inuiguchi, S. Miyamoto, H.S. Nguyen, R. Słowiński (Eds.), Rough Sets and Current Trends in Computing. XXII, 951 pages. 2006. (Sublibrary LNAI).

Vol. 4257: I. Richardson, P. Runeson, R. Messnarz (Eds.), Software Process Improvement. XI, 219 pages. 2006.

Vol. 4256: L. Feng, G. Wang, C. Zeng, R. Huang (Eds.), Web Information Systems - WISE 2006 Workshops. XIV, 320 pages. 2006.

Vol. 4255: K. Aberer, Z. Peng, E.A. Rundensteiner, Y. Zhang, X. Li (Eds.), Web Information Systems - WISE 2006. XIV, 563 pages. 2006.

Vol. 4254: T. Grust, H. Höpfner, A. Illarramendi, S. Jablonski, M. Mesiti, S. Müller, P.-L. Patranjan, K.-U. Sattler, M. Spiliopoulou, J. Wijsen (Eds.), Current Trends in Database Technology – EDBT 2006. XXXI, 932 pages. 2006.

Vol. 4253: B. Gabrys, R.J. Howlett, L.C. Jain (Eds.), Knowledge-Based Intelligent Information and Engineering Systems, Part III. XXXII, 1301 pages. 2006. (Sublibrary LNAI).

Vol. 4252: B. Gabrys, R.J. Howlett, L.C. Jain (Eds.), Knowledge-Based Intelligent Information and Engineering Systems, Part II. XXXIII, 1335 pages. 2006. (Sublibrary LNAI).

Vol. 4251: B. Gabrys, R.J. Howlett, L.C. Jain (Eds.), Knowledge-Based Intelligent Information and Engineering Systems, Part I. LXVI, 1297 pages. 2006. (Sublibrary LNAI).

Vol. 4250: H.J. van den Herik, S.-C. Hsu, T.-s. Hsu, H.H.L.M. Donkers (Eds.), Advances in Computer Games. XIV, 273 pages. 2006.

Vol. 4249: L. Goubin, M. Matsui (Eds.), Cryptographic Hardware and Embedded Systems - CHES 2006. XII, 462 pages. 2006.

Vol. 4248: S. Staab, V. Svátek (Eds.), Managing Knowledge in a World of Networks. XIV, 400 pages. 2006. (Sublibrary LNAI).

Vol. 4247: T.-D. Wang, X. Li, S.-H. Chen, X. Wang, H. Abbass, H. Iba, G. Chen, X. Yao (Eds.), Simulated Evolution and Learning. XXI, 940 pages. 2006.

Vol. 4246: M. Hermann, A. Voronkov (Eds.), Logic for Programming, Artificial Intelligence, and Reasoning. XIII, 588 pages. 2006. (Sublibrary LNAI).

Vol. 4245: A. Kuba, L.G. Nyúl, K. Palágyi (Eds.), Discrete Geometry for Computer Imagery. XIII, 688 pages. 2006.

Vol. 4244: S. Spaccapietra (Ed.), Journal on Data Semantics VII. XI, 267 pages. 2006.

Vol. 4243: T. Yakhno, E.J. Neuhold (Eds.), Advances in Information Systems. XIII, 420 pages. 2006.

Vol. 4242: A. Rashid, M. Aksit (Eds.), Transactions on Aspect-Oriented Software Development II. IX, 289 pages. 2006.

Vol. 4241: R.R. Beichel, M. Sonka (Eds.), Computer Vision Approaches to Medical Image Analysis. XI, 262 pages. 2006.

Vol. 4239: H.Y. Youn, M. Kim, H. Morikawa (Eds.), Ubiquitous Computing Systems. XVI, 548 pages. 2006.

Vol. 4238: Y.-T. Kim, M. Takano (Eds.), Management of Convergence Networks and Services. XVIII, 605 pages. 2006.

Vol. 4237: H. Leitold, E. Markatos (Eds.), Communications and Multimedia Security. XII, 253 pages. 2006.

Vol. 4236: L. Breveglieri, I. Koren, D. Naccache, J.-P. Seifert (Eds.), Fault Diagnosis and Tolerance in Cryptography. XIII, 253 pages. 2006.

Vol. 4234: I. King, J. Wang, L. Chan, D. Wang (Eds.), Neural Information Processing, Part III. XXII, 1227 pages. 2006.